Lecture Notes in Artificial Intell

Edited by J. G. Carbonell and J. Siekmann

Subseries of Lecture Notes in Computer Science

Brahim Hnich Mats Carlsson
François Fages Francesca Rossi (Eds.)

Recent Advances in Constraints

Joint ERCIM/CoLogNET International Workshop
on Constraint Solving and Constraint Logic Programming
CSCLP 2005
Uppsala, Sweden, June 20-22, 2005
Revised Selected and Invited Papers

Springer

Volume Editors

Brahim Hnich
Izmir University of Economics
Faculty of Computer Science
Sakarya Caddesi No.156, 35330 Balcova, Izmir, Turkey
E-mail: brahim.hnich@ieu.edu.tr

Mats Carlsson
Swedish Institute of Computer Science, SICS
Uppsala Science Park, 75183 Uppsala, Sweden
E-mail: Mats.Carlsson@sics.se

François Fages
Institut National de Recherche en Informatique et en Automatique, INRIA
Domaine de Voluceau, Rocquencourt, 78153 Le Chesnay Cedex, France
E-mail: francois.fages@inria.fr

Francesca Rossi
University of Padova
Department of Pure and Applied Mathematics
Via G.B. Belzoni 7, 35131 Padova, Italy
E-mail: frossi@math.unipd.it

Library of Congress Control Number: 2006925094

CR Subject Classification (1998): I.2.3, F.3.1-2, F.4.1, D.3.3, F.2.2, G.1.6, I.2.8

LNCS Sublibrary: SL 7 – Artificial Intelligence

ISSN 0302-9743
ISBN-10 3-540-34215-X Springer Berlin Heidelberg New York
ISBN-13 978-3-540-34215-1 Springer Berlin Heidelberg New York

Springer is a part of Springer Science+Business Media

springer.com

Printed in Germany

Typesetting: Camera-ready by author, data conversion by Scientific Publishing Services, Chennai, India
Printed on acid-free paper SPIN: 11754602 06/3142 5 4 3 2 1 0

Preface

Constraints are a natural means of knowledge representation. This generality underpins the success with which constraint programming has been applied to a wide variety of disciplines in academia and industry such as production planning, communication networks, robotics, and bioinformatics.

This volume contains the extended and reviewed version of a selection of papers presented at the Joint ERCIM/CoLogNET International Workshop on Constraint Solving and Constraint Logic Programming (CSCLP 2005), which was held during June 20–22, 2005 in Uppsala, Sweden.

It also contains papers that were submitted in response to the open call that followed the workshop. The papers in this volume present research results regarding many aspects of constraint solving and constraint logic programming. This includes global constraints, search and heuristics, implementations of constraint systems, and a number of applications.

The editors would like to take the opportunity and thank all the authors who submitted a paper to this volume, as well as the reviewers for their helpful work.

This volume has been made possible thanks to the support of the European Research Consortium for Informatics and Mathematics (ERCIM), the European Network on Computational Logic (CoLogNET), the Swedish Institute of Computer Science (SICS), Science Foundation Ireland (Grant No. 00/PI.1/C075), and the Department of Information Science (DIS) at Uppsala University in Sweden.

We hope that the present volume is useful for anyone interested in the recent advances and new trends in constraint programming, constraint solving, problem modelling, and applications.

March 2006

B. Hnich, M. Carlsson, F. Fages, and F. Rossi
Organizers
CSCLP 2005

Organization

CSCLP 2005 was organized by the ERCIM Working Group on Constraints and the CoLogNET area on Logic and Constraint Logic Programming.

Organizing and Program Committee

Brahim Hnich	Izmir University of Economics, Turkey
Mats Carlsson	Swedish Institute of Computer Science, Sweden
François Fages	INRIA Rocquencourt, France
Francesca Rossi	University of Padova, Italy

Referees

O. Angelsmark
R. Barták
N. Beldiceanu
C. Bessiere
M.A. Carravilla
E. Coquery
T. Frühwirth
R. Haemmerlé
R. Hatamloo
E. Hebrard
Z. Kiziltan
A. Lodi
A. Meisels
I. Miguel
R. Martin
P. Moura
M.S. Pini
C-G. Quimper
I. Razgon
C. Ribeiro
C. Schulte
G. Schrader
T. Schrijvers
F. Spoto
G. Tack
S.A. Tarim
J. Thapper
W-J. van Hoeve
R.J. Wallace
T. Walsh
A. Wolf

Sponsoring Institutions

ERCIM Working Group on Constraints
European Network of Excellence CoLogNET
Science Foundation Ireland
Swedish Institute of Computer Science
Uppsala University (Department of Information Science)

Table of Contents

Modeling

The All Different and Global Cardinality Constraints on Set, Multiset and Tuple Variables

Claude-Guy Quimper[1] and Toby Walsh[2]

[1] School of Computer Science, University of Waterloo, Canada
cquimper@math.uwaterloo.ca
[2] NICTA and UNSW, Sydney, Australia
tw@cse.unsw.edu.au

Abstract. We describe how the propagator for the ALL-DIFFERENT constraint can be generalized to prune variables whose domains are not just simple finite domains. We show, for example, how it can be used to propagate set variables, multiset variables and variables which represent tuples of values. We also describe how the propagator for the global cardinality constraint (which is a generalization of the ALL-DIFFERENT constraint) can be generalized in a similar way. Experiments show that such propagators can be beneficial in practice, especially when the domains are large.

1 Introduction

Constraint programming has restricted itself largely to finding values for variables taken from given finite domains. However, we might want to consider variables whose values have more structure. We might, for instance, want to find a set of values for a variable [12, 13, 14, 15], a multiset of values for a variable [16], an ordered tuple of values for a variable, or a string of values for a variable. There are a number of reasons to want to enrich the type of values taken by a variable. First, we can reduce the space needed to represent possible domain values. For example, we can represent the exponential number of subsets for a set variable with just an upper and lower bound representing possible and definite elements in the set. Second, we can improve the efficiency of constraint propagators for such variables by exploiting the structure in the domain. For example, it might be sufficient to consider each of the possible elements in a set in turn, rather than the exponential number of subsets. Third, we inherit all the usual benefits of data abstraction like ease of debugging and code maintenance.

As an example, consider the round robin sports scheduling problem (prob026 in CSPLib). In this problem, we wish to find a game for each slot in the schedule. Each game is a pair of teams. There are a number of constraints that the schedule needs to satisfy including that all games are different from each other. We therefore would like a propagator which works on an ALL-DIFFERENT constraint posted on variables whose values are pairs (binary tuples). In this paper, we consider how to implement such constraints efficiently and effectively. We show how two of the most important constraint propagators, those for the ALL-DIFFERENT

B. Hnich et al. (Eds.): CSCLP 2005, LNAI 3978, pp. 1–13, 2006.

and the global cardinality constraint (*gcc*) can be extended to deal with variables whose values are sets, multisets or tuples.

2 Propagators for the ALL-DIFFERENT Constraint

Propagating the ALL-DIFFERENT constraint consists of detecting the values in the variable domains that cannot be part of an assignment satisfying the constraint. To design his propagator, Leconte [18] introduced the concept of *Hall set* based on Hall's work [1].

Definition 1. *A* Hall set *is a set H of values such that the number of variables whose domain is contained in H is equal to the cardinality of H. More formally, H is a Hall set if and only if $|H| = |\{x_i \mid dom(x_i) \subseteq H\}|$.*

Consider the following example.

Example 1. Let $\text{dom}(x_1) = \{3,4\}$, $\text{dom}(x_2) = \{3,4\}$, and $\text{dom}(x_3) = \{2,4,5\}$ be three variable domains subject to an ALL-DIFFERENT constraint. The set $H = \{3,4\}$ is a Hall set since it contains two elements and the two variable domains $\text{dom}(x_1)$ and $\text{dom}(x_2)$ are contained in H.

In Example 1, variables x_1 and x_2 must be assigned to values 3 and 4, making these two values unavailable for other variables. Therefore, value 4 should be removed from the domain of x_3.

To enforce domain consistency, it is necessary and sufficient to detect every Hall set H and remove its values from the domains that are not fully contained in H. This is exactly what Régin's propagator [4] does using matching theory to detect Hall sets. Leconte [18], Puget [20], López-Ortiz et al. [19] use simpler ways to detect Hall intervals in order to achieve weaker consistencies.

3 Beyond Integer Variables

A propagator designed for integer variables can be applied to any type of variable whose domain can be enumerated. For instance, let the following variables be sets whose domains are expressed by a set of required values and a set of allowed values.

$$\{\} \subseteq S_1, S_2, S_3, S_4 \subseteq \{1,2\} \text{ and } \{\} \subseteq S_5, S_6 \subseteq \{2,3\}$$

Variable domains can be expanded as follows:

$$S_1, S_2, S_3, S_4 \in \{\{\}, \{1\}, \{2\}, \{1,2\}\} \text{ and } S_5, S_6 \in \{\{\}, \{2\}, \{3\}, \{2,3\}\}$$

And then by enforcing GAC on the ALL-DIFFERENT constraint, we obtain

$$S_1, S_2, S_3, S_4 \in \{\{\}, \{1\}, \{2\}, \{1,2\}\} \text{ and } S_5, S_6 \in \{\{3\}, \{2,3\}\}$$

We can now convert the domains back to their initial representation.

$$\{\} \subseteq S_1, S_2, S_3, S_4 \subseteq \{1, 2\} \text{ and } \{3\} \subseteq S_5, S_6 \subseteq \{2, 3\}$$

This technique always works but is not tractable in general since variable domains might have exponential size. For instance, the domain of $\{\} \subseteq S_i \subseteq \{1, \ldots, n\}$ contains 2^n elements. The following important lemma allows us to ignore such variables and focus just on those with "small" domains.

Lemma 1. *Let n be the number of variables and let F be a set of variables whose domains are not contained in any Hall set. Let $x_i \notin F$ be a variable whose domain contains more than $n - |F|$ values. Then $dom(x_i)$ is not contained in any Hall set.*

Proof. The largest Hall set can contain the domain of $n - |F|$ variables and therefore has at most $n - |F|$ values. If $|\text{dom}(x_i)| > n - |F|$, then $\text{dom}(x_i)$ cannot be contained in any Hall set. □

Using Lemma 1, we can iterate through the variables and append to a set F those whose domain cannot be contained in a Hall set. A propagator for the ALL-DIFFERENT constraint can prune the domains not in F and find all Hall sets. Values in Hall sets can then be removed from the variable domains in F. This technique ensures that domains larger than n do not slow down the propagation. Algorithm 1 exhibits the process for a set of (possibly non-integer) variables X.

Algorithm 1. ALL-DIFFERENT propagator for variables with large domains

```
  F ← ∅
  Sort variables such that |dom(x_i)| ≥ |dom(x_{i+1})|
  for x_i ∈ X do
1 └ if |dom(x_i)| > n − |F| then F ← F ∪ {x_i}
2 Expand domains of variables in X − F.
  Find values H belonging to a Hall set and propagate the All-Different constraint
  on variables X − F.
  for x_i ∈ F do
  └ dom(x_i) ← dom(x_i) − H;
3 Collapse domains of variables in X − F.
```

To apply our new techniques, three conditions must be satisfied by the representation of the variables:

1. Computing the size of the domain must be tractable (Line 1).
2. Domains must be efficiently enumerable (Line 2).
3. Domains must be efficiently computed from an enumeration of values (Line 3).

The next sections describe how different representations of domains for set, multiset and tuple variables can meet these three conditions.

4 All-Different on Sets

Several representations of domains have been suggested for set variables. We show how their cardinality can be computed and their domain enumerated efficiently. One of the most common representations for a set are the required elements lb and the allowed elements ub, with any set S satisfying $lb \subseteq S \subseteq ub$ belongs to the domain [12, 14]. The number of sets in the domain is given by $2^{|ub-lb|}$. We can enumerate all these sets simply by enumerating all subsets of $ub - lb$ and adding them to the elements from lb. A set can be represented as a binary vector where each element is associated to a bit. A bit equals 1 if its corresponding element is in the set and equals 0 if its corresponding element is not in the set. Enumerating all subsets of $ub - lb$ is reduced to the problem of enumerating all binary vectors between 0 and $2^{|ub-lb|}$ exclusively which can be done in $O(2^{|ub-lb|})$ steps, i.e. $O(|\text{dom}(S_i)|)$ steps.

In order to exclude from the domain undesired sets, one can also add a cardinality variable [3]. The domain of a set variable is therefore expressed by $\text{dom}(S_i) = \{S \mid lb \subseteq S \subseteq ub, |S| \in \text{dom}(C)\}$ where C is an integer variable. We assume that C is consistent with lb and ub, i.e. $\min(C) >= |lb|$ and $\max(C) <= |ub|$. The size of the domain is given by Equation 1 where $\binom{a}{b}$ is the binomial coefficient.

$$|\text{dom}(S_i)| = \sum_{j \in C} \binom{|ub - lb|}{j - |lb|} \tag{1}$$

The binomial coefficients can efficiently be computed as explained in Chapter 6.1 of [10]. The identity $\binom{n}{k+1} = \frac{n-k}{k+1}\binom{n}{k}$ can be particularly useful to compute the summation when the domain of C is an interval. The number of steps required to compute $|\text{dom}(S_i)|$ is bounded by $O(|\text{dom}(C)|)$.

Algorithm 2 enumerates all combinations of t elements chosen from elements 0 to $n - 1$. Each element i in a combination is mapped to the ith element in $ub - lb$. By enumerating all t-combinations for $t \in \text{dom}(C)$ to which we add the required elements lb, we enumerate all sets in $|\text{dom}(S_i)|$. Algorithm 2 has a time complexity of $O(t + \binom{n}{t})$. Since we call it for each $t \in \text{dom}(C)$, the total time complexity simplifies to $O(\max(|ub - lb|, |\text{dom}(S_i)|))$.

Sadler and Gervet [7] suggest adding a lexicographic ordering constraint to the domain description. This gives more expressiveness to the domain representation and can eliminate more undesired sets. that We say that $S_1 < S_2$ holds if S_1 comes before S_2 in a lexicographical order. The new domain representation now involves two lexicographic bounds l and u.

$$\text{dom}(S_i) = \{S \mid lb \subseteq S \subseteq ub, |S| = C, l \leq S \leq u\} \tag{2}$$

Knuth [8] represents all subsets of a set using a binomial tree like the one in Figure 1. The empty set is the root of the tree to which we can add elements by branching to a child. One can list all sets in lexicographical order by visiting

Algorithm 2. Enumerate the $\binom{n}{t}$ combinations of t elements between 0 and $n-1$. (Source: Algorithm T, Knuth [8] p.5)

$c_j \leftarrow j-1, \forall j\ 1 \le j \le t$
$c_{t+1} \leftarrow n$
$c_{t+2} \leftarrow 0$
repeat
  visit $c_t, c_{t-1}, \dots, c_1$
  $j \leftarrow 1$
  while $c_j + 1 = c_{j+1}$ **do**
    $c_j \leftarrow j-1$
    $j \leftarrow j+1$
  $c_j \leftarrow c_j + 1$
until $j > t$

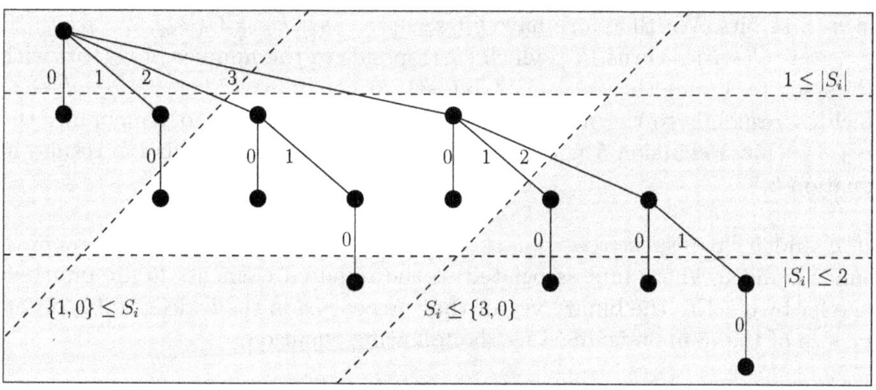

Fig. 1. Binomial tree representing the domain $\emptyset \subseteq S_i \subseteq \{0,1,2,3\}$, $1 \le |S_i| \le 2$, and $\{1,0\} \le S_i \le \{3,0\}$

the tree from left to right with a depth-first-search (DFS). We clearly see that the lexicographic constraints are orthogonal to the cardinality constraints.

Based on the binomial tree, we compute, level by level, the number of sets that belong to the domain. Notice that sets at level k have cardinality k. A set in the variable domain can be encoded with a binary vector of size $|ub - lb|$ where each bit is associated to a potential element in $ub - lb$. A bit set to one indicates the element belongs to the set while a bit set to zero means that the element does not belong to the set. The number of sets of cardinality k in the domain is equal to the number of binary vectors with k bits set to one and that lexicographically lie between l and u. Let $[u_m, \dots, u_1]$ be the binary representation of the lexicographic upper bound u. Assuming $\binom{b}{a} = 0$ for all negative values of a, function $C([u_m, \dots, u_1], k)$ returns the number of binary vectors that are lexicographically smaller than or equal to u and that have k bits set to one.

$$C([s_m, \ldots, s_1], k) = \sum_{i=1}^{m} s_i \binom{i-1}{k - \sum_{j=i+1}^{m} s_j} + \delta(s, k) \tag{3}$$

$$\delta([s_m, \ldots, s_1], k) = \begin{cases} 1 & \text{if } \sum_{i=1}^{m} s_i = k \text{ and } s_0 = 0 \\ 0 & \text{otherwise} \end{cases} \tag{4}$$

Lemma 2. *Equation 3 is correct.*

Proof. We prove correctness by induction on m. For $m = 1$, Equation 3 holds with both $k = 0$ and $k = 1$. Suppose the equation holds for m, we want to prove it also holds for $m + 1$. We have

$$C([s_{m+1}, \ldots, s_1], k) = s_{m+1}\binom{m}{k} + C([s_m, \ldots, s_1], k - s_{m+1}) \tag{5}$$

If $s_{m+1} = 0$, the lexicographic constraint is the same as if we only consider the m first bits. We therefore have $C([s_{m+1}, \ldots, s_1], k) = C([s_m, \ldots, s_1], k)$. If $s_{m+1} = 1$, $C(s, k)$ returns $\binom{m}{k}$ which corresponds to the number of vectors with k bits set to 1 and the $(m + 1)^{th}$ bit set to zero plus $C([s_m, \ldots, s_1], k - 1)$ which corresponds to the number of vectors with k bits set to 1 including the $(m + 1)^{th}$ bit. Recursion 5 is therefore correct. Solving this recursion results in Equation 3. □

Let a and b be respectively binary vectors associated to the lexicographical bounds l and u where bits associated to the required elements lb are omitted. We refer by $a - 1$ to the binary vector that precedes a in the lexicographic order. The size of the domain is given by the following equation.

$$|\text{dom}(S_i)| = \sum_{k \in C} (C(b, k) - C(a - 1, k))$$

Function C can be evaluated in $O(|ub - lb|)$ steps. The size of domain $\text{dom}(S_i)$ therefore requires $O(|ub - lb||C|)$ steps to compute. Enumerating can also proceede level by level without taking into account the required elements lb since they belong to all sets in the domain. The first set on level k can be obtained from the lexicographic lower bound l. If $|l| \neq k$, we have to find the first set l' of cardinality k that is lexicographically greater than l. If $|l| < k$, we simply add to set l the $k - |l|$ smallest elements in $ub - lb - l$. Suppose $|l| > k$ and consider the binary representation of l. Let p be the kth heaviest bit set to 1 in l. We add one to bit p and propagate carries and we set all bits before p to 0. We obtain a bit vector l' representing a set with no more than k elements. If $|l'| < k$, we add the first $k - |l'|$ elements in $ub - lb - l'$ to l' and obtain the first set of cardinality k.

Once the first set at level k has been computed, subsequent sets can be obtained using Algorithm 2. Obtaining the first set of each level costs $O(|\text{dom}(C)|$ $|ub - lb|)$ and cumulative calls to Algorithm 2 cost $O(\sum_{i \in \text{dom}(C)} i + |dom(S)|)$. Enumerating the domain therefore requires $O(|\text{dom}(C)||ub - lb| + |\text{dom}(S)|)$ steps.

5 All-Different on Tuples

A tuple t is an ordered sequence of n elements that allows multiple occurrences. Like sets, there are different ways to represent the domain of a tuple. The most common way is simply by associating an integer variable to each of the tuple components. A tuple of size n is therefore represented by n integer variables $x_1, \ldots, x_n$.

To apply an All-Different constraint to a set of tuples, a common solution is to create an integer variable t for each tuple. If each component x_i ranges from 0 to c_i exclusively, we add the following channeling constraint between tuple t and its components.

$$t = ((((x_1c_2 + x_2)c_3 + x_3)c_4 + x_4)\ldots)c_n + x_n = \sum_{i}^{n}\left(x_i \prod_{j=i+1}^{n} c_j\right)$$

This technique suffers from either inefficient or ineffective channeling between variable t and the components x_i. Most constraint libraries enforce bound consistency on t. A modification to the domain of x_i does not affect t if the bounds of $\text{dom}(x_i)$ remain unchanged. Conversely, even if all tuples encoded in $\text{dom}(t)$ have $x_i \neq v$, value v will most often not be removed from $\text{dom}(x_i)$. On the other hand, enforcing domain consistency typically requires $O(n^k)$ steps where k is the size of the tuple.

To address this issue, one can define a tuple variable whose domain is defined by the domains of its components.

$$\text{dom}(t) = \text{dom}(x_1) \times \ldots \times \text{dom}(x_n)$$

The size of such a domain is given by the following equation which can be computed in $O(n)$ steps.

$$|\text{dom}(t)| = \prod_{i=1}^{n} |\text{dom}(x_i)|$$

The domain of a tuple variable can be enumerated using Algorithm 3. Assuming the domain of all component variables have the same size, Algorithm 3 runs in $O(|dom(t)|)$ which is optimal.

As Sadler and Gervet [7] did for sets, we can add lexicographical bounds to tuples in order to better express the values the domain contains. Let l and u be these lexicographical bounds.

$$\text{dom}(t) = \{t \mid t[i] \in \text{dom}(x_i), l \leq t \leq u\}$$

Let $idx(v, x)$ be the number of values smaller than v in the domain of the integer variable x. More formally, $idx(v, x) = |\{w \in \text{dom}(x) \mid w < v\}|$. Assuming $idx(v, x)$ has a running time complexity of $O(\log(|\text{dom}(x)|))$, the size of

Algorithm 3. Enumerate tuples of size n in lexicographical order. (Source: Algorithm T, Knuth [8] p.2).

Initialize first tuple: $a_j \leftarrow \min(\text{dom}(x_j)), \forall j\ 1 \leq j \leq n$
repeat
  visit $(a_1, a_2, \ldots, a_n)$
  $j \leftarrow n$
  while $j > 0$ ***and*** $a_j = \max(dom(x_j))$ **do**
    $a_j \leftarrow \min(\text{dom}(x_j))$
    $j \leftarrow j - 1$
  $a_j \leftarrow \min(\{a \in \text{dom}(x_j) \mid a > a_j\})$
until $j = 0$

the domain can be evaluated in $O(n + \log(|\text{dom}(t)|))$ steps using the following equation.

$$|\text{dom}(t)| = 1 + \sum_{i=1}^{n} \left((idx(u[i], x_i) - idx(l[i], x_i)) \prod_{j=i+1}^{n} |\text{dom}(x_i)| \right)$$

We enumerate the domain of tuple variables with lexicographical bounds similarly as tuple variables without lexicographical bounds. We simply initialize Algorithm 3 with tuple l and stop enumerating when tuple u is reached. In average case analysis, this operation is performed in $O(|\text{dom}(t)|)$ steps.

6 All-Different on Multi-sets

Unlike sets, multi-sets allow multiple occurrences of the same element. We use $occ(v, S)$ to denote the number of occurrences of element v in multi-set S. An element v belongs to a multi-set A if and only if its number of occurrences $occ(v, A)$ is greater than 0. We say that set A is included in set B ($A \subseteq B$) if for all element v we have $occ(v, A) \leq occ(v, B)$. The domain representation of multi-sets is generally similar to the one for standard sets. We have a multi-set of essential elements lb and a multi-set of allowed elements ub. Equation 6 gives the domain of a multi-set and Equation 7 shows how to compute its size in $O(|ub|)$ steps.

$$\text{dom}(S_i) = \{S \mid lb \subseteq S \subseteq ub\} \tag{6}$$

$$|\text{dom}(S_i)| = \prod_{v \in ub} (occ(v, ub) - occ(v, lb) + 1) \tag{7}$$

Multisets can be represented by a vector where each component represents the number of occurrences of an element in the multi-set. Of course, for the multi-set to be in the domain, this number of occurrences must lie between $occ(v, lb)$ and $occ(v, ub)$. Therefore a multi-set variable is equivalent to a tuple variable where the domain of each component is given by the interval $[occ(v, lb), occ(v, ub)]$.

Enumerating the values in the domain is done as seen in Section 5. The same approach can be used to introduce lexicographical bounds to multi-sets.

7 Indexing Domain Values

Propagators for the ALL-DIFFERENT constraint, like the one proposed by Régin [4], need to store information about some values appearing in the variable domains. When values are integers, the simplest implementation is to create a table T where information related to value v is stored in entry $T[v]$. Algorithm 1 ensures that the propagator is called over a maximum of n variables each having no more than n (possibly distinct) values in their domain. We therefore have a maximum of n^2 values to consider. When these n^2 values come from a significantly greater set of values, table T becomes sparse. In some cases, it might not even be realistic to consider such a solution. To allow direct memory access when accessing the information of a value, we need to map the n^2 values to an index in the interval $[1, n^2]$.

We suggest to build an indexing tree able to index sets, multi-sets, tuples, or any other sequential data structure. Each node is associated to a sequence. The root of the tree is the empty sequence ($\emptyset$). We append an element to the current sequence by branching to a child of the current node. There are at most n^2 nodes corresponding to a value in a variable domain. These nodes are labeled with integers from 1 to n^2. Figure 2 shows the indexing tree based on the domain of 5 set variables.

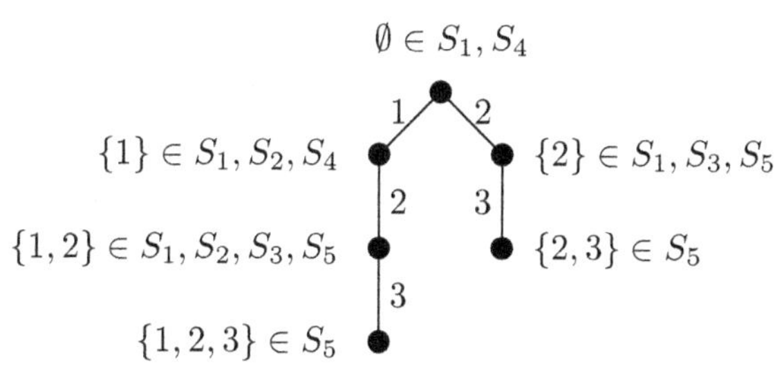

Fig. 2. Indexing tree representing the following domains: $\emptyset \subseteq S_1 \subseteq \{1,2\}, \{1\} \subseteq S_2 \subseteq \{1,2\}, \{2\} \subseteq S_3 \subseteq \{1,2\}, \emptyset \subseteq S_4 \subseteq \{1\}, \{2\} \subseteq S_5 \subseteq \{1,2,3\}$

This simple data structure allows to index and retrieve in $O(l)$ steps the number associated to a sequence of length l.

8 Global Cardinality Constraint

The global cardinality constraint (*gcc*) is a generalization of the ALL-DIFFERENT constraint. A value v must be assigned to at least $\lfloor v \rfloor$ variables and at most $\lceil v \rceil$ variables. Traditionally, the *lower capacity* $\lfloor v \rfloor$ and the *upper capacity* $\lceil v \rceil$ are given by look-up tables. When working with large domains, these look-up tables could require too much memory. We therefore assume that the lower and upper capacity of each value is returned by a function. For instance, the constant functions $\lfloor v \rfloor = 0$ and $\lceil v \rceil = 1$ define the ALL-DIFFERENT constraint. In order to be feasible, the following restrictions apply: $\sum_v \lfloor v \rfloor \leq n$ and $\sum_v \lceil v \rceil \geq n$. For efficiency reasons, we assume that the values L whose lower capacity is positive are known, i.e. $L = \{v \mid \lfloor v \rfloor > 0\}$ is known.

Based on the concept of upper capacity, we give a new definition to a Hall set.

Hall set [9]. A Hall set H is a set of values such that there are $\sum_{v \in H} \lceil v \rceil$ variables whose domains are contained in H; i.e., H is a Hall set iff $|\{x_i \mid \mathrm{dom}(x_i) \subseteq H\}| = \sum_{v \in H} \lceil v \rceil$.

Under *gcc*, Lemma 1 becomes the following lemma.

Lemma 3. *Let F be a set of variables whose domains are not contained in any Hall set and assume $\lceil v \rceil \geq k$ holds for all value v. If $x_i \notin F$ is a variable whose domain contains more than $\lfloor \frac{n-|F|}{k} \rfloor$ values, then dom(x_i) is not contained in any Hall set.*

Proof. The largest Hall set can contain the domain of $n - |F|$ variables and therefore has at most $\lfloor \frac{n-|F|}{k} \rfloor$ values. If $|\mathrm{dom}(x_i)| > \lfloor \frac{n-|F|}{k} \rfloor$, then $\mathrm{dom}(x_i)$ cannot be contained to any Hall set. □

Following [9], the *gcc* can be divided into two constraints: the lower bound constraint is only concerned with the lower capacities ($\lfloor v \rfloor$) and the upper bound constraint is only concerned with the upper capacities ($\lceil v \rceil$).

The upper bound constraint is similar to the ALL-DIFFERENT constraint. Up to $\lceil v \rceil$ variables can be assigned to a value v instead of only 1 with the ALL-DIFFERENT constraint. Lemma 3 suggests to modify Line 1 of Algorithm 1 by testing if $|\mathrm{dom}(x_i)| > \frac{|X|-|F|}{k}$ before inserting variable x_i in set F.

The lower bound constraint can easily be handled when variable domains are large. Consider the set L of values whose lower capacity is positive, i.e. $L = \{v \mid \lfloor v \rfloor > 0\}$. In order for the lower bound constraint to be satisfiable over n variables, the cardinality of L must be bounded by n. The values not in L can be assigned to a variable only if all values v in L have been assigned to at least $\lfloor v \rfloor$ variables. Since all values not in L are symmetric, we can replace them by a single value p such that $\lfloor p \rfloor = 0$. We now obtain a problem where each variable domain is bounded by $n + 1$ values. We can apply a propagator for the lower bound constraint on this new problem. Notice that if the lower bound constraint propagator removes p from a variable domain, it implies by symmetry that all values not in L should be removed from this variable domain.

9 Experiments

To test the efficiency and effectiveness of these generalizations to the propagator for the ALL-DIFFERENT constraint, we ran a number of experiments on a well known problem from design theory. A Latin square is an $n \times n$ table where cells can be colored with n different colors. We use integers between 1 and n to identify the n colors. A Graeco-Latin square is m Latin squares $A_1, \ldots, A_m$ such that the tuples $\langle A_1[i,j], \ldots, A_m[i,j] \rangle$ are all distinct. The following tables represent a Graeco-Latin square for $n = 4$ and $m = 2$.

1	2	3	4
2	1	4	3
3	4	1	2
4	3	2	1

3	4	1	2
1	2	3	4
2	1	4	3
4	3	2	1

We encode the problem using one tuple variable per cell. There is an ALL-DIFFERENT constraint on each row and each column. We add a redundant 0/1-CARDINALITY-MATRIX constraint on each value as suggested by Régin [11]. We use two different encodings for tuples: one is the tuple encoding where each component is an integer variable, the other is the factored representation. We enforce bounds consistency on the channeling constraints between the cell variables and the factored tuple variables. As suggested in [11], our heuristic chooses the variable with the smallest domain and we break ties on the variable that has the most bounded variables on its row and column. We use the same implementation of the ALL-DIFFERENT propagator for both tuple encodings.

Table 1 and Figure 3 clearly show that when tuples gets longer, our technique outperforms the factored representation of tuples. This is mainly due to space requirements since the factored representation of tuples requires more memory than the cache can contain.

Table 1. Time to solve a Graeco-Latin square using factored and tuple variables

n \ m	3		4		5		6	
	factored	tuple	factored	tuple	factored	tuple	factored	tuple
8	0.48	0.23	0.57	0.35	4.51	0.40	56.48	1.08
9	0.33	0.49	0.31	0.85	1.77	0.94	23.09	2.39
10	0.58	0.91	0.56	1.57	3.44	1.78	52.30	4.36
11	1.05	1.62	1.04	2.97	7.33	3.23	124.95	7.69
12	1.76	2.80	1.79	5.59	13.70	6.04	263.28	13.61
13	2.86	4.69	2.85	9.00	23.96	9.74	493.04	22.80
14	4.37	7.03	4.17	14.34	38.95	15.19		33.79
15	6.88	10.62	6.56	22.18	69.89	23.63		50.23
16	10.11	15.41	9.54	32.52	110.08	34.55		73.60
17	14.21	21.48	13.82	45.35	174.18	47.89		102.98
18	20.41	30.55	19.13	64.87	255.76	68.46		146.21
19	28.28	42.12	25.01	91.45	364.58	95.99		204.45
20	38.31	56.10	34.35	122.30	540.06	136.43		274.29

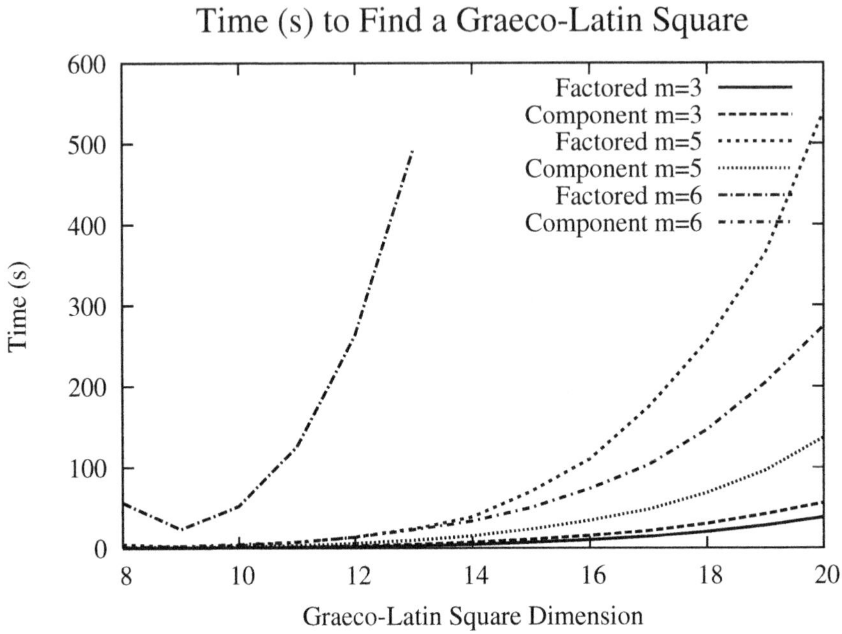

Fig. 3. Time in seconds to solve a Graeco-Latin square with m different square sizes. The data is extracted from Table 1. We see that for $m \geq 5$, the component encoding offers a better performance than the factored encoding.

10 Conclusions

We have described how Régin's propagator for the All-Different constraint can be generalized to prune variables whose domains are not just simple finite domains. In particular, we described how it can be used to propagate set variables, multiset variables and variables which represent tuples of values. We also described how the propagator for the global cardinality constraint can be generalized in a similar way. Experiments showed that such propagators can be beneficial in practice, especially when the domains are large. Many other global constraints still remain to be generalized to deal with other variable types than simple integer domains.

References

1. P. Hall, On representatives of subsets. *Journal of the London Mathematical Society*, pages 26–30, 1935.
2. J. Hopcroft and R. Karp, An $n^{5/2}$ algorithm for maximum matchings in bipartite graphs. *SIAM Journal of Computing*, volume 2 pages 225–231, 1973.
3. ILOG S. A., *ILOG Solver 4.2 user's manual.* 1998.

4. J.-C. Régin, A filtering algorithm for constraints of difference in CSPs. In *Proceedings of the Twelfth National Conference on Artificial Intelligence*, pages 362–367, Seattle, 1994.
5. J.-C. Régin, Generalized arc consistency for global cardinality constraint. In *Proceedings of the Thirteenth National Conference on Artificial Intelligence*, pages 209–215, Portland, Oregon, 1996.
6. K. Stergiou and T. Walsh, The difference all-difference makes. In *Proceedings of the Sixteenth International Joint Conference on Artificial Intelligence*, pages 414–419, Stockholm, 1999.
7. A. Sadler and C. Gervet, Hybrid Set Domains to Strengthen Constraint Propagation and Reduce Symmetries. In *In Proceedings of the 10th International Conference on Principles and Practice of Constraint Programming*, pages 604–618, Toronto, Canada, 2004.
8. D. Knuth, *Generating All Tuples and Permutations.* Addison-Wesley Professional, 144 pages, 2005.
9. A. López-Ortiz, C.-G. Quimper, J. Tromp, and P. van Beek, A fast and simple algorithm for bounds consistency of the alldifferent constraint. In *Proceedings of the Eighteenth International Joint Conference on Artificial Intelligence*, pages 245–250, Acapulco, Mexico, 2003.
10. W. H. Press, B. P. Flannery, S. A. Teukolsky, W. T. Vetterling, *Numerical Recipes in C: The Art of Scientific Computing, Second Edition,* Cambridge University Press, 1992.
11. J.-C. Régin and C. P. Gomes, The Cardinality Matrix Constraint. In *In Proceedings of the 10th International Conference on Principles and Practice of Constraint Programming*, pages 572–587, Toronto, Canada, 2004.
12. C. Gervet, Interval Propagation to Reason about Sets: Definition and Implementation of a Practical Language. *Constraints Journal,* 1(3) pages 191–244, 1997.
13. C. Gervet, *Set Intervals in Constraint Logic Programming: Definition and Implementation of a Language.* PhD thesis, Université de Franche-Comté, France, September 1995. European thesis, in English.
14. J.-F. Puget, Finite set intervals. In *Proceedings of Workshop on Set Constraints,* held at CP'96, 1996.
15. T. Müller and M. Müller, Finite set constraints in Oz. In François Bry,Burkhard Freitag, and Dietmar Seipel, editors, *13. Workshop Logische Programmierung,* pages 104–115, Technische Universität München, pages 17–19 September 1997.
16. T. Walsh, Consistency and Propagation with Multiset Constraints: A Formal Viewpoint. In *Proceedings of the 9th International Conference on Principles and Practice of Constraint Programming*, Kinsale, Ireland, 2003.
17. I.P. Gent and T. Walsh, CSPLib: a benchmark library for constraints. *Technical report APES-09-1999*, 1999.
18. M. Leconte, A bounds-based reduction scheme for constraints of difference. In *Proceedings of the Constraint-96 International Workshop on Constraint-Based Reasoning,* pages 19–28, 1996.
19. A. López-Ortiz, C.-G. Quimper, J. Tromp, and P. van Beek, A fast and simple algorithm for bounds consistency of the alldifferent constraint. in *Proceedings of the 18th International Joint Conference on Artificial Intelligence (IJCAI-03)* pages 245–250, 2003.
20. J.-F. Puget, A Fast Algorithm for the Bound Consistency of Alldiff Constraints. In *Proceedings of the 15th National Conference on Artificiel Intelligence (AAAI-98)* and the *10th Conference on Innovation Applications of Artificial Intelligence (IAAI-98)*", pages 359–366, 1998.

Complete Propagation Rules for Lexicographic Order Constraints over Arbitrary Domains

Thom Frühwirth

Faculty of Computer Science, University of Ulm, Germany
www.informatik.uni-ulm.de/pm/mitarbeiter/fruehwirth/

Abstract. We give an efficiently executable specification of the global constraint of lexicographic order in the Constraint Handling Rules (CHR) language. In contrast to previous approaches, the implementation is short and concise without giving up on the best known worst case time complexity. It is incremental and concurrent by nature of CHR. It is provably correct and confluent. It is independent of the underlying constraint system, and therefore not restricted to finite domains. We have found a direct recursive decomposition of the problem. We also show completeness of constraint propagation, i.e. that all possible logical consequences of the constraint are generated by the implementation. Finally, we report about some practical implementation experiments.

1 Introduction

Lexicographic orderings are common in everyday life as the alphabetical order used in dictionaries and listings (e.g., 'zappa' comes before 'zilch'). In computer science, lexicographic orders also play a central role in termination analysis, for example for rewrite systems [3]. In constraint programming, these orders have recently raised interest because of their use in symmetry breaking (e.g. [14]) and earlier in modelling preferences among solutions (e.g. [7]).

A natural question to ask is whether lexicographic orders can be implemented as constraints and what would be appropriate propagation algorithms. There are two approaches to this problem, starting with [8] and [6]. Both consider the case of finite domain constraints and (hyper/generalized) arc consistency algorithms, while our work is independent of the underlying constraint system and achieves complete constraint progagation as well. All approaches, including ours, yield algorithms with a worst-case time complexity that is linear in the size of the lexicographic ordering constraint.

The algorithms and their derivation are quite different, however. In [8] an algorithm based on two pointers that move along the elements of the sequences to be lexicographically ordered is given. The algorithm's description consists of five procedures with 45 lines of pseudo-code. In [6], a case analysis of the lexicographic order constraints yields 7 cases to distinguish, these are translated into a finite automaton that is then made incremental. The pseudo-code of the algorithm has 42 lines [5]. The manual derivation of the algorithm is made semi-automatic in a subsequent paper [4], that can deal with an impressive range

B. Hnich et al. (Eds.): CSCLP 2005, LNAI 3978, pp. 14–28, 2006.

of global constraints over sequences. The pseudo-code of a simple constraint checker is converted by hand into a corresponding automaton code (16 lines) that is automatically translated into automata constraints that allow incremental execution of the automaton and so enforce arc consistency. Note that the automaton code is interpreted at run-time.

We summarize that these approaches are based on imperative pseudo-code that seems either lengthy or requires subsequent translation into a different formalism. Their specifications seem hard to analyse and are not directly executable. In contrast, we give a short and concise executable specification in the Constraint Handling Rules (CHR) language that consists of 6 rules that derive from three cases. The problem is solved by recursive decomposition, no additional constraints need to be defined. The implementation is incremental and concurrent by nature of CHR. It is independent of the underlying constraint system, and therefore not restricted to finite domains. Its CHR rules can be analysed, for example we will show their confluence using a confluence checker, and prove their logical correctness. We derive worst-case time complexity that is parameterized by the cost of handling built-in constraints. We also show that the rules are complete, that they propagate as much information (constraints) as possible.

CHR [9, 13, 16] is a concurrent committed-choice constraint logic programming language consisting of guarded rules that transform multi-sets of constraints (atomic formulae) into simpler ones until they are solved. CHR was initially developed for writing constraint solvers, but has matured into a general-purpose concurrent constraint language over the last decade. Its main features are a kind of multi-set rewriting combined with propagation rules. The clean logical semantics of CHR facilitates non-trivial program analysis and transformation. Implementations of CHR now exist in many Prolog systems, also in Haskell and Java. Besides constraint solvers, applications of CHR range from type systems and time tabling to ray tracing and cancer diagnosis.

Overview of the Paper. After introducing CHR, we give our generic implementation of the global constraint for lexicographic orderings in Section 3. Then, in separate sections, we discuss confluence, logical correctness, completeness, worst-case time complexity and some implementation experiments before we conclude. This paper is a significantly revised and extended version of [12].

2 Preliminaries: Constraint Handling Rules

In this section we give an overview of syntax and semantics for constraint handling rules (CHR) [9, 13, 16]. Readers familiar with CHR can skip this section.

2.1 Syntax of CHR

We distinguish between two different kinds of constraints: *built-in (pre-defined) constraints* which are solved by a given constraint solver, and *CHR (user-defined) constraints* which are defined by the rules in a CHR program. This distinction allows one to embed and utilize existing constraint solvers as well as side-effect-free host language statements. Built-in constraint solvers are considered as black-box in whose behavior is trusted and that do not need to be modified or inspected. The solvers for the built-in constraints can be written in CHR itself, giving rise to a hierarchy of solvers [15].

Definition 1. A *CHR program* is a finite set of rules. There are two main kinds of rules:

$$\begin{array}{ll} \textit{Simplification rule: } & \textit{Name} \ @\ H \Leftrightarrow C \mid B \\ \textit{Propagation rule: } & \textit{Name} \ @\ H \Rightarrow C \mid B \end{array}$$

Name is an optional, unique identifier of a rule, the *head* H is a non-empty conjunction of CHR constraints, the *guard* C is a conjunction of built-in constraints, and the *body* B is a goal. A *goal* is a conjunction of built-in and CHR constraints. A trivial guard expression "*true* |" can be omitted from a rule.

Example 1. For example, let $\leq$ be a built-in constraint symbols with the usual meaning. Here is a rule for a CHR constraint `max`, where `max(X,Y,Z)` means that `Z` is the maximum of `X` and `Y`:

```
max(X,Y,Z) ⇔ X≤Y | Z =Y.
```

2.2 Declarative Semantics of CHR

The CHR rules have an immediate logical reading, where the guard implies a logical equality or implication between the l.h.s. and r.h.s. of a rule.

Definition 2. The logical meaning of a simplification rule is a logical equivalence provided the guard holds.

$$\forall (C \rightarrow (H \leftrightarrow \exists \bar{y}\ B)),$$

where $\forall$ denotes universal closure as usual and $\bar{y}$ are the variables that appear only in the body B.

The logical meaning of a propagation rule is an implication provided the guard holds

$$\forall (C \rightarrow (H \rightarrow \exists \bar{y}\ B)).$$

The logical meaning $\mathcal{P}$ of a CHR program P is the conjunction of the logical meanings of its rules united with a consistent *constraint theory* CT that defines the built-in constraint symbols.

Example 2. Recall the rule for `max` from Example 1. The rule means that `max(X,Y,Z)` is logically equivalent to `Z=Y` if `X≤Y`:

$$\forall (X{\leq}Y \rightarrow (max(X,Y,Z) \leftrightarrow Z{=}Y))$$

2.3 Operational Semantics of CHR

At runtime, a CHR program is provided with an initial state and will be executed until either no more rules are applicable or a contradiction occurs.

The operational semantics of CHR is given by a transition system (Fig. 1). Let P be a CHR program. We define the transition relation $\mapsto$ by two computation steps (transitions), one for each kind of CHR rule. *States* are goals, i.e. conjunctions of built-in and CHR constraints. States are also called *(constraint) stores*. In the figure, all upper case letters are meta-variables that stand for conjunctions of constraints. The constraint theory CT defines the semantics of the built-in constraints. G_{bi} denotes the built-in constraints of G.

Simplify

If	$(r@H \Leftrightarrow C \mid B)$ is a fresh variant with variables $\bar{x}$ of a rule named r in P
and	$CT \models \forall\,(G_{bi} \rightarrow \exists \bar{x}(H{=}H' \wedge C))$
then	$(H' \wedge G) \mapsto_r (B \wedge G \wedge H{=}H' \wedge C)$

Propagate

If	$(r@H \Rightarrow C \mid B)$ is a fresh variant with variables $\bar{x}$ of a rule named r in P
and	$CT \models \forall\,(G_{bi} \rightarrow \exists \bar{x}(H{=}H' \wedge C))$
then	$(H' \wedge G) \mapsto_r (H' \wedge B \wedge G \wedge H{=}H' \wedge C)$

Fig. 1. Computation Steps of Constraint Handling Rules

Starting from an arbitrary *initial goal (state, query, problem)*, CHR rules are applied exhaustively, until a fixpoint is reached. A *final state (answer, solution)* is one where either no computation step is possible anymore or where the built-in constraints are inconsistent.

A simplification rule $H \Leftrightarrow C \mid B$ *replaces* instances of the CHR constraints H by B provided the guard C holds. A propagation rule $H \Rightarrow C \mid B$ instead *adds* B to H. If new constraints arrive, rules are reconsidered for application. Computation stops if the built-in constraints become inconsistent. Trivial non-termination of the **Propagate** computation step is avoided by applying a propagation rule at most once to the same constraints (see the more concrete semantics in [1]).

In more detail, a rule is *applicable*, if its head constraints are matched by constraints in the current goal one-by-one and if, under this matching, the guard of the rule is logically implied by the built-in constraints in the goal. Any of the applicable rules can be applied, and the application cannot be undone, it is committed-choice.

Example 3. Here are some sample computations involving the rule for `max`:

$\texttt{max(1,2,M)} \mapsto \texttt{M=2.}$
$\texttt{max(A,B,M)} \wedge \texttt{A<B} \mapsto \texttt{M=B} \wedge \texttt{A<B.}$
$\texttt{max(A,A,M)} \mapsto \texttt{M=A.}$

3 The Lexicographic Order Constraint Solver

A lexicographic order allows one to compare sequences by pairwise comparing the elements of the sequences.

Definition 3. Given two sequences l_1 and l_2 of variables of the same length n, $[x_1, \ldots, x_n]$ and $[y_1, \ldots, y_n]$. Then l_1 is lexicographically smaller than or equal to l_2, written $l_1 \preceq_{lex} l_2$, iff either $n{=}0$ or $x_1{<}y_1$ or $x_1{=}y_1$ and $[x_2, \ldots, x_n] \preceq_{lex} [y_2, \ldots, y_n]$.

The corresponding logical specification of the `lex` constraint thus is:

$$\begin{aligned} l_1 \preceq_{lex} l_2 \leftrightarrow\ & (l_1{=}[] \wedge l_2{=}[]) \vee \\ & (l_1{=}[x|l_1'] \wedge l_2{=}[y|l_2'] \wedge x{<}y) \vee \\ & (l_1{=}[x|l_1'] \wedge l_2{=}[y|l_2'] \wedge x{=}y \wedge l_1' \preceq_{lex} l_2') \end{aligned}$$

In our CHR solver for the `lex` constraint we will use concrete syntax of Prolog implementations of CHR. Variables start with upper-case letters, constraint and function symbols with lower-case letters. Lists are enclosed in square brackets, with their elements seperated by commata, while after the symbol `''|''` the remainder of the list follows as a list. Conjunction $\wedge$ is written as comma `','`.

Our solver will be independent from the constraint system in which the built-in constraints (inequalities) are defined. Different list elements can be from different constraint domains if their inequalities are polymorphic. They can even be a (differently named) lexicographic constraint provided it is built-in.

The derivation of the following six rules for our lexicographic order constraint solver is explained in [12]. The solver consists of three pairs of rules, the first two corresponding to base cases of the recursion (garbage collection), then two rules performing forward reasoning (recursive traversal and implied inequality), and finally two for backward reasoning, covering a not so obvious special case when the lexicographic constraint has a unique solution.

```
l1 @ [] lex [] <=> true.
l2 @ [X|L1] lex [Y|L2] <=> X<Y | true.
l3 @ [X|L1] lex [Y|L2] <=> X=Y | L1 lex L2.
l4 @ [X|L1] lex [Y|L2] ==> X=<Y.

l5 @ [X,U|L1] lex [Y,V|L2] <=> U>V | X<Y.
l6 @ [X,U|L1] lex [Y,V|L2] <=> U>=V, L1=[_|_] |
                                [X,U] lex [Y,V], [X|L1] lex [Y|L2].
```

The first three rules `l1`, `l2` and `l3` are directly derived from the three disjuncts of the logical specification. The notation `[X|L]` refers to a list with first element `X` and the remainder of the list is the list `L`. The three rules will apply when the lists are empty or when the relationship between the leading list elements `X` and `Y` is sufficiently known. The built-in constraints `X<Y` and `X=Y` are in the guards, so they check if the appropriate relationship between the variables holds. When a rule is tried, the built-in constraint solver has to check if the guard is implied by the current built-in constraints.

For example, the three queries `[1] lex [2]`, `[X] lex [X]`, and `[X] lex [Y], X<Y` will all reduce to `true`. For finite domains, consider `X in {0,1}, Y in {2,3}, [X] lex [Y]`. Rule `12` asks in the guard if the constraint `X<Y` holds, i.e. if it is implied by the current built-in constraints. If the built-in finite domain solver is strong enough to infer `X<Y` from `X in {0,1}, Y in {2,3}`, then rule `12` is applicable and its application results in `X in {0,1}, Y in {2,3}`. For simplicity, we will just use explicit inequalities in our examples.

The propagation rule `14` implements a common consequence of the last two disjuncts of the logical specification. The built-in inequality constraint appears in the body of the rule and is thus enforced when the rule is applied.

For example, to the query `[R|Rs] lex [T|Ts], R<>T` only the propagation rule is applicable and adds `R=<T`. This results in `[R|Rs] lex [T|Ts], R<T` after simplification of the built-in constraints for inequality. Now rule `12` is applicable, the `lex`-constraint is removed and the final answer is the remaining `R<T`.

Rule `15` deals with the special case where the elements of the second pair of the sequence are related by a strict inequality in the wrong way such that the only (way to a) solution is to enforce a strict inequality on the first two elements. Note that rules `14` and `15` are the only ones that directly impose a built-in constraint. Rule `16` uses double recursion, but note that the first recursive `lex` constraint has a fixed, small list length. The rule deals with the case where the wrong inequality treated in `15` is further down the lists. The additional condition `L1=[_|_]` in the guard of rule `16` avoids non-termination in case `L1=[]`.

To see how rules `15` and `16` work together, consider the query `[R1,R2,R3] lex [T1,T2,T3], R2>=T2, R3>T3`. Since `R2>=T2`, rule `16` is applicable, and leads to `R2>=T2, R3>T3, [R1,R2] lex [T1,T2], [R1,R3] lex [T1,T3]`. Now rule `15` can be applied to the second `lex` constraint, and we arrive at `R2>=T2, R3>T3, [R1,R2] lex [T1,T2], R1<T1`. Because now `R1<T1` is enforced, rule `12` removes the remaining `lex` constraint and the final answer is `R2>=T2, R3>T3, R1<T1`.

4 Confluence

Typically, CHR programs for constraint solving are well-behaved, i.e. terminating and confluent. Confluence means that the result of a computation is independent from the order in which rules are applied to the constraints. This also implies that the order of constraints in a goal does not matter. Once termination has been established [10], there is a decidable, sufficient and necessary test for confluence [1, 2]. In the latter papers it is also shown that confluent CHR programs have a consistent logical reading.

Definition 4. A CHR program is *confluent* if for all computation states S, S_1, S_2: If $S \mapsto^* S_1$ and $S \mapsto^* S_2$ then there exist states T_1 and T_2 such that $S_1 \mapsto^* T_1$ and $S_2 \mapsto^* T_2$ and T_1 and T_2 are identical up to renaming of local variables and logical equivalence of built-in constraints.

For checking confluence, one takes copies (with fresh variables) of two rules (not necessarily different) from the program. The heads of the rules are *overlapped* by equating at least one head constraint from one rule with one from the other rule. For each overlap, one considers the two states resulting from applying one or the other rule. These two states form a so-called *critical pair*. One tries to *join* the states in the critical pair by finding two computations starting from the states that reach a common state. If a critical pair is not joinable, one has found a counterexample for confluence of the program.

We used and improved the confluence checker mentioned in [11] to check confluence of the `lex` constraint. The six rules for the lexicographic order constraint are confluent, the program code and its results are available at: `www.informatik.uni-ulm.de/pm/mitarbeiter/fruehwirth/more/conflexico.pl`

The rule `l1` cannot give rise to any critical pair. It does not overlap with any other rule, since it is the only one dealing with empty lists. The rules `l2` and `l3` are mutually exclusive. There are overlaps between all the remaining pairs of rules. If rule `l2` or rule `l4` is dropped, the solver becomes non-confluent, while the other rules can be dropped without hurting confluence.

Example 4. Consider the overlap between the rules

```
l3 @ [X|L1] lex [Y|L2] <=> X=Y | L1 lex L2.
l5 @ [X,U|L1] lex [Y,V|L2] <=> U>V | X<Y.
```

which is `[X,U|L1] lex [Y,V|L2], U>V, X=Y` and which leads to the following confluence check:

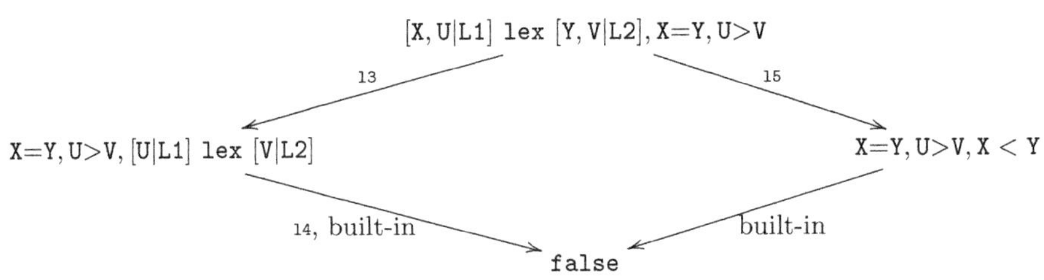

Using the first rule, we arrive at `X=Y, U>V, [U|L1] lex [V|L2]`. Using the second rule, we arrive at `X=Y, U>V, X<Y`. These two states form the critical pair. The propagation rule `l4` is applicable to the first state `X=Y, U>V, [U|L1] lex [V|L2]` and leads to `X=Y, U>V, [U|L1] lex [V|L2], U=<V`, which fails due to the contradicting constraints on `U` and `V`. The second state immediately fails due to the contradicting constraints on `X` and `Y`. Hence, this critical pair is joinable, in both cases we finally fail (independent of the order of rule applications).

Example 5. Another confluence check involves the rules `l5` and `l6`.

```
l5 @ [X,U|L1] lex [Y,V|L2] <=> U>V | X<Y.
l6 @ [X,U|L1] lex [Y,V|L2] <=> U>=V, L1=[_|_] |
                                [X,U] lex [Y,V], [X|L1] lex [Y|L2].
```

Their overlap is

```
[X,U|L1] lex [Y,V|L2], U>V, L1=[_|_].
```

The resulting critical pair is

```
U>V, L1=[_|_], X<Y   vs.
U>V, L1=[_|_], [X,U] lex [Y,V], [X|L1] lex [Y|L2].
```

The first state of the critical pair is already a final state, in the second one, rule `15` can be applied to the first `lex` constraint resulting in `U>V, L1=[_|_], X<Y, [X|L1] lex [Y|L2]`. Now, since `X<Y`, rule `12` can be applied to remove the remaining `lex` constraint, the two states of the critical pair are joinable.

5 Logical Correctness

CHR programs can be formally verified on the basis of their logical reading. Recall that the logical meaning of a CHR program is the logical meaning of its rules united with the constraint theory CT for the built-in constraints.

Definition 5. Let $\mathcal{P}$ be the logical meaning of a CHR program P. Let $\mathcal{S}$ be a *logical specification* for P, i.e. a consistent theory for the CHR constraints in P. Then program P is *logically correct* with respect to specification $\mathcal{S}$ iff

$$\mathcal{S} \cup CT \models \mathcal{P}.$$

The logical reading of the six rules for the lexicographic order constraint solver is as follows.

$$\begin{array}{rl}
 & ([] \preceq_{lex} []) \\
X{<}Y \rightarrow & ([X|L1] \preceq_{lex} [Y|L2]) \\
X{=}Y \rightarrow & ([X|L1] \preceq_{lex} [Y|L2] \leftrightarrow L1 {\preceq_{lex}} L2) \\
 & ([X|L1] \preceq_{lex} [Y|L2] \rightarrow X{\leq}Y) \\
U{>}V \rightarrow & ([X,U|L1] \preceq_{lex} [Y,V|L2] \leftrightarrow X{<}Y) \\
(U{\geq}V \wedge L1{=}[_|_]) \rightarrow & ([X,U|L1] \preceq_{lex} [Y,V|L2] \leftrightarrow \\
 & \quad ([X,U] {\preceq_{lex}} [Y,V] \wedge [X|L1] {\preceq_{lex}} [Y|L2]))
\end{array}$$

For logical correctness, we have to show that these formulas are logical consequences of the logical specification given by

$$\begin{array}{rl}
l_1 {\preceq_{lex}} l_2 \leftrightarrow & (l_1{=}[] \wedge l_2{=}[]) \vee \\
 & (l_1{=}[x|l_1'] \wedge l_2{=}[y|l_2'] \wedge x{<}y) \vee \\
 & (l_1{=}[x|l_1'] \wedge l_2{=}[y|l_2'] \wedge x{=}y \wedge l_1' {\preceq_{lex}} l_2')
\end{array}$$

For example, it is easy to see that the logical reading of propagation rule `14` is a common consequence of the last two disjuncts of the specification,

$$(l_1{=}[x|l_1'] \wedge l_2{=}[y|l_2'] \wedge x{<}y) \;\vee\; (l_1{=}[x|l_1'] \wedge l_2{=}[y|l_2'] \wedge x{=}y \wedge l_1' {\preceq_{lex}} l_2') \quad \rightarrow$$

$$l_1{=}[x|l_1'] \wedge l_2{=}[y|l_2'] \wedge x{\leq}y.$$

Proof for Rule `16`. As a more involved example, we prove that the logical reading of propagation rule `16` is a logical consequence of the specification. From the specification it follows

$$[X|L1] \preceq_{lex} [Y|L2] \leftrightarrow (X{<}Y \ \vee \ X{=}Y \wedge L1 \preceq_{lex} L2)$$

For the rule `16`, we will actually prove a slightly stronger result by removing $L1{=}[\_|\_]$ from the precondition (the condition was introduced to ensure termination). Instead of $C \ \rightarrow \ (H \ \leftrightarrow \ B)$ we use the logically equivalent $(H \wedge C) \leftrightarrow (C \wedge B))$.

To show the equivalence of the l.h.s. and r.h.s. of the formula, we will now replace the `lex` constraints in the logical reading of the rule according to the specification, distribute conjunction over disjunction and simplify by removing unsatisfiable disjuncts.

The l.h.s. of the rule, $[X,U|L1] \preceq_{lex} [Y,V|L2] \wedge U{\geq}V$, becomes

$$U{\geq}V \wedge (X{<}Y \ \vee \ X{=}Y \wedge U{<}V \ \vee \ X{=}Y \wedge U{=}V \wedge L1 \preceq_{lex} L2) \leftrightarrow$$
$$(U{\geq}V \wedge X{<}Y \ \vee \ X{=}Y \wedge U{=}V \wedge L1 \preceq_{lex} L2)$$

The r.h.s. $U{\geq}V \wedge [X,U] \preceq_{lex} [Y,V] \wedge [X|L1] \preceq_{lex} [Y|L2]$ becomes

$$U{\geq}V \wedge (X{<}Y \vee X{=}Y \wedge U{<}V \vee X{=}Y \wedge U{=}V) \wedge (X{<}Y \vee X{=}Y \wedge L1 \preceq_{lex} L2) \leftrightarrow$$
$$U{\geq}V \wedge (U{\geq}V \wedge X{<}Y \vee X{=}Y \wedge U{=}V) \wedge (U{\geq}V \wedge X{<}Y \vee U{\geq}V \wedge X{=}Y \wedge L1 \preceq_{lex} L2)$$
$$\leftrightarrow (U{\geq}V \wedge X{<}Y \ \vee \ X{=}Y \wedge U{=}V \wedge L1 \preceq_{lex} L2)$$

Both sides, l.h.s. and r.h.s., are equivalent.

6 Worst-Case Time Complexity

We would like to give a complexity result that is independent from the constraint system in which the built-in constraints (inequalities) are defined. The reason is that most constraint systems, such as Booleans, finite domains, and linear polynomials, admit these inequalities, but the typical algorithms used (e.g. arc and path consistency, simplex) have different time complexities and achieve different degrees of completeness (local or global). We therefore give our complexity result in the number of atomic built-in constraints that are checked and imposed, respectively.

Lemma 1. For the rules of the `lex` constraint, the number of checks and additions of built-in constraints is proportional to the number of rule applications.

Proof. Head matching can be done in constant time, guards contain at most one built-in inequality constraint to check, and rule bodies directly impose at most one built-in inequality constraint.

We show now that an upper bound on the number of rule applications r depends on the list lengths only. We treat `lex` constraints with list arguments up to two elements separately, because they play a special role in rule `16`.

Lemma 2. The number of checks and additions of built-in inequality constraints is linear in the length of the list.

Proof. By Lemma 1, it suffices to consider the number of rule applications. We use the following recurrence equations generated from the rules of the `lex` constraint solver. The number of rule applications involving a list of some given length is computed as follows in the equations below: We charge 1 (unit) cost for applying one of the applicable rules and add the number of rule applications caused by the body of the respective rule. The unit costs are represented by constants $l1$ to $l6$ to indicate which rule is applied. From all the potential rule applications, the maximum is taken. Since the propagation rule is always applicable to non-empty lists, its cost is added outside of the maximum expression.

$$
\begin{array}{rl}
 & l1 = l2 = l3 = l4 = l5 = l6 = 1 \\
\hline
r(0) = & l1 = 1 \\
r(1) = & max(l2, l3{+}r(0), l5){+}l4 = 3 \\
r(2) = & max(l2, l3{+}r(1), l5){+}l4 = 5 \\
 & \vdots \\
r(n) = & max(l2, l3{+}r(n{-}1), l5, l6{+}r(2){+}r(n{-}1)){+}l4 = 7{+}r(n{-}1) < 7n{-}8
\end{array}
$$

To empty lists, only the rule `l1` is applicable. To lists with one or two elements, the rules `l2` up to `l5` are applicable, but not rule `l6`. The propagation rule `l4` can be applied at most once to each `lex` constraint. The recursive rules `l3` and `l6` dominate the costs.

For lists of length n less than or equal to 2, the number of rule applications is bounded by a constant (at most 5). For lists of length greater than 2, the number of rule applications is linear in the length of the list.

For the overall complexity, we should not forget about waking: If a variable of a pending `lex` constraint gets more constrained by a built-in constraint, the `lex` constraint will be woken. Then the results hold even if the built-in constraints are imposed incrementally, as is standard in constraint programming applications.

Theorem 1. The overall worst case time complexity is linear modulo the cost of handling the built-in constraints. At most $O(n + w)$ built-in constraints are checked, imposed or woken where n is the list length and w is the number of wake (propagation) events caused by the built-in constraint solver.

Proof. The result follows from Lemma 2 and the following observation: If a CHR constraint is woken, it's rules will be re-checked for applicability. If a rule is applicable, the cost of the continuation of the computation on the `lex` constraint has already been accounted for in the above calculations. But what is the cost of waking `lex` in vain, i.e. if no rule turns out to be applicable? Then a constant number of head matchings and guard checks has been performed if rules are tried.

7 Completeness

In this section we discuss completeness of the constraint solver for the lexicographic order constraint, i.e. if it produces all built-in constraints, i.e. inequalities, that logically follows from the `lex` constraint and some given inequalities.

We already know that the solver is correct and confluent. Thus it cannot propagate incorrect conctraints and starting from a given goal it will always propagate the same constraints, no matter which of the applicable rules are applied. Thus what is left to show for completeness is that all possible propagations are performed, not just a few.

Of course, also the completeness result is relative to the built-in constraint solver. In particular, if its entailment check is too weak to detect all cases where guard inequalities are implied, the `lex` constraint solver will also become incomplete. This is the case for finite domains, since the underlying arc consistency algorithm only provides local completeness.

Definition 6. A *solution* of a lexicographic order constraint $[x_1, \ldots, x_n] \preceq_{lex} [y_1, \ldots, y_n]$ is of the form

$$x_1{=}y_1 \wedge x_2{=}y_2 \wedge \ldots \wedge x_{i-1}{=}y_{i-1}[\wedge x_i{<}y_i] \quad (1 \leq i \leq n{+}1),$$

where $x_i{<}y_i$ is dropped from the conjunction if $i = n{+}1$. We describe a solution to `lex` by an expression $(=)^{i-1}[<]$ and we identify it by the position i of the strict inequality $<$. The resulting sequence of inequalities is meant to hold between the respective pairs of variables from the two lists of the `lex` constraint. $[e]$ means that expression e is dropped if its position in the sequence is greater than n. An expression e^0 is also dropped.

We argue for completeness based on the following observations:

- There can be at most $n + 1$ solutions to a given `lex` constraint over lists of length n.
- The disjunction of all solutions of a `lex` constraint is logically equivalent to the constraint.
- Inequality constraints can be added to a `lex` constraint so that any subset of solutions is possible:
  - Imposing $x_i < y_i$ or $x_i \neq y_i$ means there can be a solution at position i, but not at any greater position, since equality is not possible anymore at position i.
  - Imposing $x_i = y_i$ or $x_i \geq y_i$ means there cannot be a solution at position i, but possibly at greater positions.
  - Imposing $x_i \leq y_i$ means there can be a solution at position i or any greater position.
  - Imposing $x_i > y_i$ means there cannot be a solution at position i or any greater position.
- Hence the smallest position that admits a solution is the first position i that admits $<$ (i.e. $<, \leq, \neq,$ *true*) or where $i{=}n{+}1$, provided all previous positions admitted $=$ but not $<$ (i.e. $=, \geq$). If there is no such smallest position, then there is no solution.

Based on these observations, we distinguish two kinds of propagation.

Forward Propagation. The new inequalities that we can propagate from a disjunction of the solutions of a given `lex` constraint together with some inequalities, i.e. all those built-in constraints that are implied, that must hold no matter which disjunct (solution) is chosen, are simply and only $(=)^{i-1}[\leq]$, where i is the first, smallest position of a solution.

Thus a complete implementation has to turn leading $\geq$ inequalities into equalities $=$, proceed over $=$ and impose $\leq$ on the first remaining other inequality. In our constraint solver implementation this is achieved by the propagation rule `14` that imposes $\leq$ on any current first position and the recursive simplification rule `13` that removes leading $=$.

Backward Propagation. A special case arises if there is exactly one solution, in that case obviously the last inequality that we have to propagate can be made strict, $(=)^{i-1}[<]$. We have exactly one solution if there are no more solutions after the smallest position that admits a solution. This is the case if the smallest position is followed by a sequence of zero or more $=$ or $\geq$ constraints that is ended by $>$.

This special one-solution case is handled by the simplification rules `15` and `16`. Rule `15` covers the case where $>$ holds for the second position, so $<$ must hold for the first position to ensure a solution. Rule `16` allows one to reduce the other instances of the special case, where there is an arbitrary number of $=$ or $\geq$ constraints between the unique position for a solution and the $>$ inequality (that could also come from a $\geq$ being strenghened), to the situation in rule `15`.

Note that the rules `11` and `12` are not needed for completeness of propagation, simply because they do not propagate anything except the trivial *true*. But the two rules are useful for garbage collection and `12` is also needed for confluence.

8 Implementation Experiments

In the literature so far, the `lex` constraint has only been used for finite domains, so a comparison is only possible when this constraint system is chosen as built-in one. While the implementation of [8] seems not to be public domain, the implementation of [6] is included in the latest Sicstus Prolog releases.

We tested our CHR implementation of `lex` with the CHR library in Sicstus Prolog, while Tom Schrijvers was so kind to test it in SWI Prolog. The implementations are not incremental at this point, but can be made so by a tighter coupling. While some readers may be impressed with benchmark tables, we have omitted them for space reasons. The interested reader can find more detailed measures that would fit a paper online. The main test file with code and results for both Prolog implementations is available online (further test files are mentioned in that file):
`www.informatik.uni-ulm.de/pm/mitarbeiter/fruehwirth/more/lextest.pl`

For our tests we have used Sicstus 3.11 Prolog with standard settings running on a Suse Linux PC with medium overall work load. We compiled our code with the 'compactcode' option of Sicstus. In the implemented rules, we used a straightforward coupling between the CHR `lex` constraint utilizing the `chr` library of Sicstus and the finite domain built-in constraints of the Sicstus `clpfd` library, where we inspect domains in the guards to perform the necessary checks.

After some initial experiments we found that the propagation rule `l4` of the solver exhibits a non-linear (quadratic) behavior instead of a linear one. One reason is because every time a `lex` constraint suspends, all its variables in the constraint are scanned, while it would only be necessary to scan the first two variable pairs. We avoided this bottleneck by rewriting the propagation rule into a guarded simplification rule.

We compared our CHR implementation of `lex` with the built-in `lex_chain` constraint [6] of the Sicstus `clpfd` constraint library. This unary constraint takes a list of lists of domain variables with finite bounds or integers. The constraint holds if the lists are in ascending lexicographic order.

We considered lists up to 40000 elements, at around 50000 elements memory problems occurred. Garbage collection was never performed by the system. In our experiments, both lexicographic constraints showed a complete propagation behavior and linear time complexity. The number of rule applications in our solver is linear in the list length as calculated. Run-times were less than a second for the CHR `lex` constraint for simpler test cases. While forward propagation in CHR was just 3 times slower than built-in `lex_chain`, backward propagation proved to be 10–20 times slower, possibly because the recursive decomposition in the CHR solver generates many small `lex` constraints.

Tom Schrijvers has run the tests in his K.U. Leuven CHR system in an experimental version of SWI Prolog that will be included in the development version in early 2006. Due to compile-time suspension variable inference in that CHR implementation, scanning is improved so that the original propagation rule of the lexicographic constraint solver can be run without run-time penalty in linear time. In tests with up to 4000 list elements, a linear-time behavior was observed. Some additional time is spend in garbage collection.

9 Conclusions

Just six CHR rules correctly and efficiently specify and implement an incremental and concurrent, logical algorithm to maintain consistency of the lexicographic ordering constraint. Previous approaches presented algorithms for the lexicographic order constraint in pseudo-code that seems hard to analyse or use an automata formalism that seems hard to re-implement, while our solver program is simple, short, concise and directly executable. We have found a direct recursive decomposition of the problem that does not need additional constraints and performs all possible propagations. Moreover, our solver is independent of the underlying constraint system that provides inequalities between the elements of the sequences to be compared lexicographically, and therefore our solver is not restricted to finite domains.

Our solver consists of three pairs of rules, the first two corresponding to base cases of the recursion (garbage collection), then two rules performing forward reasoning (recursive traversal and implied inequality), and finally two for backward reasoning, covering a special case when the lexicographic constraint has a unique solution. We have proven the rules to be confluent using our semi-automatic confluence checker. We showed logical correctness, completeness of constraint propagation and worst-case time complexity linear in the cost of handling the built-in inequality constraints.

We already know that, at least in theory, CHR can implement any algorithm in best-known space and time complexity [17], and many CHR constraint solvers including the `lex` constraint discussed here are practical proof that it is indeed possible. The remaining constant-factor slow-down observed in the implementation experiments is the price one currently has to pay for using a very high-level language as CHR in contrast to a low-level hard-wired implementation. Since the run-time increase is by a constant factor only, we can hope that compiler optimization will further close the performance gap.

Future work should consider extensions of the lexicographic ordering constraint that can be found in the recent literature, e.g. using it in chains or with a summation constraint, or simplifying `lex` constraints for symmetry breaking. As for the instantiations of the generic constraint solver to specific built-in constraint systems, several issues are open: To show that the finite domain instance maintains generalized arc consistency, to use other underlying built-in constraint systems such as linear polynomials or temporal constraints, and to give an implementation that does not rely on built-in constraints for inequality, but rather uses existing CHR solvers. Finally, a hard, challenging question is if and how rules such as the ones presented here can be derived automatically from inductive definitions.

Acknowledgements. The author would like to thank Marc Meister and Tom Schrijvers for discussions and help with implementation and testing, and the reviewers for their helpful comments.

References

1. S. Abdennadher. Operational semantics and confluence of constraint propagation rules. In *3rd International Conference on Principles and Practice of Constraint Programming*, LNCS 1330. Springer, 1997.
2. S. Abdennadher, T. Frühwirth, and H. Meuss. Confluence and semantics of constraint simplification rules. *Constraints Journal, Special Issue on the 2nd International Conference on Principles and Practice of Constraint Programming*, 4(2):133–165, 1999.
3. F. Baader and T. Nipkow. *Term Rewriting and All That.* Cambridge Univ. Press, 1998.
4. N. Beldiceanu, M. Carlsson, and T. Petit. Deriving filtering algorithms from constraint checkers. In M. Wallace, editor, *CP'2004, Principles and Practice of Constraint Programming*, volume 3258 of LNCS, Berlin, Heidelberg, New York, 2004. Springer.

5. M. Carlsson and N. Beldiceanu. Revisiting the lexicographic ordering constraint. Technical Report T2002-17, Swedish Institute of Computer Science, 2002.
6. M. Carlsson and N. Beldiceanu. From constraints to finite automata to filtering algorithms. In D. Schmidt, editor, *ESOP2004*, volume 2986 of *LNCS*, pages 94–108, Berlin, Heidelberg, New York, 2004. Springer.
7. H. Fargier, J. Lang, and T. Schiex. Selecting preferred solutions in fuzzy constraint satisfaction problems. In *1st European Congress on Fuzzy and Intelligent Technologies (EUFIT)*, 1993.
8. A. Frisch, B. Hnich, Z. Kiziltan, I. Miguel, and T. Walsh. Global constraints for lexicographic orderings. In P. V. Hentenryck, editor, *CP'2002, Int. Conf. on Principles and Practice of Constraint Programming*, volume 2470 of *LNCS*, pages 93–108, Berlin, Heidelberg, New York, 2002. Springer.
9. T. Frühwirth. Theory and Practice of Constraint Handling Rules, Special Issue on Constraint Logic Programming. *Journal of Logic Programming*, 37(1–3):95–138,1998.
10. T. Frühwirth. As time goes by: Automatic complexity analysis of simplification rules. In *8th International Conference on Principles of Knowledge Representation and Reasoning*, Toulouse, France, 2002.
11. T. Frühwirth. Parallelizing union-find in constraint handling rules using confluence. In M. Gabbrielli and G. G., editors, *Logic Programming: 21st International Conference, ICLP 2005*, volume 3668 of *Lecture Notes in Computer Science*, pages 113–127. Springer, Oct. 2005.
12. T. Frühwirth. Complete propagation rules for lexicographic order constraints over arbitrary domains. In *Recent Advances in Constraints, CSCLP 2005*, LNAI. Springer, 2006. To appear.
13. T. Frühwirth and S. Abdennadher. *Essentials of Constraint Programming.* Springer, 2003.
14. B. Hnich, Z. Kiziltan, and T. Walsh. Combining symmetry breaking with other constraints: Lexicographic ordering with sums. In *AMAI 2004 Eighth International Symposium on Artificial Intelligence And Mathematics*, 2004.
15. T. Schrijvers, B. Demoen, G. Duck, P. Stuckey, and T. Frühwirth. Automatic implication checking for chr constraints. In *6th International Workshop on Rule-Based Programming*, volume 147 of *Electronic Notes in Theoretical Computer Science*, pages 93–111, Jan. 2006.
16. T. Schrijvers and T. Frühwirth. CHR Website, `www.cs.kuleuven.ac.be/~dtai/projects/CHR/`, 2006.
17. J. Sneyers, T. Schrijvers, and B. Demoen. The Computational Power and Complexity of Constraint Handling Rules. In *Second Workshop on Constraint Handling Rules, at ICLP05,* Sitges, Spain, October 2005.

Among, Common and Disjoint Constraints

Christian Bessiere[1], Emmanuel Hebrard[2], Brahim Hnich[3], Zeynep Kiziltan[4], and Toby Walsh[2]

[1] LIRMM, CNRS/University of Montpellier, France
bessiere@lirmm.fr
[2] NICTA and UNSW, Sydney, Australia
{ehebrard, tw}@cse.unsw.edu.au
[3] Izmir University of Economics, Turkey
brahim.hnich@ieu.edu.tr
[4] University of Bologna, Italy
zkiziltan@deis.unibo.it

Abstract. AMONG, COMMON and DISJOINT are global constraints useful in modelling problems involving resources. We study a number of variations of these constraints over integer and set variables. We show how computational complexity can be used to determine whether achieving the highest level of consistency is tractable. For tractable constraints, we present a polynomial propagation algorithm and compare it to logical decompositions with respect to the amount of constraint propagation. For intractable cases, we show in many cases that a propagation algorithm can be adapted from a propagation algorithm of a similar tractable one.

1 Introduction

Global constraints are an essential aspect of constraint programming. See, for example, [8, 3, 9, 2]. They specify patterns that occur in many problems, and exploit efficient and effective propagation algorithms to prune search. In problems involving resources, we often need to constrain the number of variables taking particular values. For instance, we might want to limit the number of night shifts assigned to a given worker, to ensure some workers are common between two shifts, or to prevent any overlap in shifts between workers who dislike each other. The AMONG, COMMON and DISJOINT constraints respectively are useful in such circumstances. The AMONG, COMMON and DISJOINT constraints are useful in such circumstances.

The AMONG constraint was first introduced in CHIP to model resource allocation problems like car sequencing [3]. It counts the number of variables using values from a given set. A generalization of the AMONG and ALLDIFFERENT constraints is the COMMON constraint [2]. Given two sets of variables, this counts the number in each set which use values from the other set. A special case of the COMMON constraint also introduced in [2] is the DISJOINT constraint. This ensures that no value is common between two sets of variables. We study these three global constraints as well as seven other variations over integer and set variables. For each case, we present a polynomial propagation algorithm, and identify when achieving a higher level of local consistency is intractable. For example,

B. Hnich et al. (Eds.): CSCLP 2005, LNAI 3978, pp. 29–43, 2006.

rather surprisingly, even though the DISJOINT constraint is closely related to (but somewhat weaker than) the ALLDIFFERENT constraint, it is NP-hard to achieve generalised arc consistency on it.

The rest of the paper is oragnised as follows. We first present the necessary formal background in Section 2. Then, in Section 3 and Section 4 we study various generalisations and specialisations of the AMONG, COMMON, and DISJOINT constraints on integer and set variables. Finally, we review related work in Section 5 before we conclude and present our future plans in Section 6.

2 Formal Background

A constraint satisfaction problem consists of a set of variables, each with a finite domain of values, and a set of constraints specifying allowed combinations of values for given subsets of variables. A solution is an assignment of values to the variables satisfying the constraints. We consider both integer and set variables. A set variable S can be represented by a lower bound $lb(S)$ which contains the definite elements and an upper bound $ub(S)$ which contains the definite and potential elements. We use the following notations: X, Y, N, and M (possibly with subscripts) denote integer variables; S and T (again possibly with subscripts) denote set variables; $\mathcal{S}$ (possibly with a subscript) and $\mathcal{K}$ denote sets of integers; and v and k (possibly with a subscript) denote integer values. We write $\mathcal{D}(X)$ for the domain of a variable X. For integer domains, we write $min(X)$ and $max(X)$ for the minimum and maximum elements in $\mathcal{D}(X)$. Throughout the paper, we consider constraint satisfaction problems in which a constraint contains no repeated variables.

Constraint solvers often search in a space of partial assignments enforcing a local consistency property. A *bound support* for a constraint C is a partial assignment which satisfies C and assigns to each integer variable in C a value between its minimum and maximum, and to each set variable in C a set between its lower and upper bounds. A bound support in which each integer variable takes a value in its domain is a *hybrid support.* If C involves only integer variables, a hybrid support is a *support.* A constraint C is *bound consistent* (BC) iff for each integer variable X, $min(X)$ and $max(X)$ belong to a bound support, and for each set variable S, the values in $ub(S)$ belong to S in at least one bound support and the values in $lb(S)$ are those from $ub(S)$ that belong to S in all bound supports. A constraint C is *hybrid consistent* (HC) iff for each integer variable X, every value in $D(X)$ belongs to a hybrid support, and for each set variable S, the values in $ub(S)$ belong to S in at least one hybrid support and the values in $lb(S)$ are those from $ub(S)$ that belong to S in all hybrid supports. A constraint C over integer variables is *generalized arc consistent* (GAC) iff for each variable X, every value in $D(X)$ belongs to a support. If all variables in C are integer variables, HC is equivalent to GAC, whilst if all variables in C are set variables, HC is equivalent to BC. Finally, we will compare local consistency properties applied to (sets of) logically equivalent constraints. A local consistency property Φ on C_1 is *strictly stronger* than Ψ on C_2 iff, given any domains, Φ removes all values Ψ removes, and sometimes more.

3 Integer Variables

3.1 Among Constraint

The AMONG constraint counts the number of variables using values from a given set [3]. More formally, we have:

$$\text{AMONG}([X_1, .., X_n], [k_1, .., k_m], N) \text{ iff } N = |\{i \mid \exists j \,.\, X_i = k_j\}|$$

For instance, we can use this constraint to limit the number of tasks (variables) assigned to a particular resource (value). Enforcing GAC on such a constraint is polynomial. Before we give an algorithm to do this, we establish the following theoretical results.

Lemma 1. *Given $\mathcal{K} = \{k_1, .., k_m\}$, $lb = |\{i \mid \mathcal{D}(X_i) \subseteq \mathcal{K}\}|$, and $ub = n - |\{i \mid \mathcal{D}(X_i) \cap \mathcal{K} = \emptyset\}|$, a value $v \in \mathcal{D}(N)$ is GAC for* AMONG *iff $lb \leq v \leq ub$.*

Proof. At most ub variables in $[X_1, .., X_n]$ can take a value from $\mathcal{K}$ and lb of these take values only from $\mathcal{K}$. Hence v is inconsistent if $v < lb$ or $v > ub$. We now need to show any value between lb and ub is consistent. We have $ub - lb$ variables that can take a value from $\mathcal{K}$ as well from outside $\mathcal{K}$. A support for $lb \leq v \leq ub$ can be constructed by assigning v variables to a value from $\mathcal{K}$ and $ub - v$ variables to a value from outside $\mathcal{K}$. □

Lemma 2. *Given $\mathcal{K} = \{k_1, .., k_m\}$, $lb = |\{i \mid D(X_i) \subseteq \mathcal{K}\}|$, $ub = n - |\{i \mid D(X_i) \cap \mathcal{K} = \emptyset\}|$, and $lb \leq min(N) \leq max(N) \leq ub$, a value in $D(X_i)$ may not be GAC for* AMONG *iff $lb = min(N) = max(N)$ or $min(N) = max(N) = ub$.*

Proof. The variables $[X_1, .., X_n]$ can be divided into three categories: 1) those whose domain contains values only from $\mathcal{K}$ (lb of them), 2) those whose domain contains both values from $\mathcal{K}$ and from outside ($ub - lb$ of them), and 3) those whose domain does not intersect with $\mathcal{K}$ ($n - ub$ of them). If $lb = min(N) = max(N)$ then exactly lb variables must take a value from $\mathcal{K}$. These variables can then only be those of the first category and thus $\mathcal{K}$ cannot be in the domains of the second category. If $min(N) = max(N) = ub$ then exactly ub variables must take a value from $\mathcal{K}$. These variables can then only be those of the first and the second category and thus any value $v \notin \mathcal{K}$ cannot be in the domains of the second category. We now need to show this is the only possibility for inconsistency. Consider an assignment to the constraint. Due to the variables of the first and the third category we have lb values from $\mathcal{K}$ and $n - ub$ values from outside $\mathcal{K}$. If $lb < max(N)$ then in the second category we can have at least one variable assigned to a value from $\mathcal{K}$, the rest assigned to a value outside $\mathcal{K}$ and satisfy the constraint. Similarly, if $min(N) < ub$ then in the second category we can have at least one variable assigned to a value outside of $\mathcal{K}$, the rest assigned to a value from $\mathcal{K}$ and satisfy the constraint. Hence, all values are consistent when $lb < max(N)$ or $min(N) < ub$. □

We now give an algorithm for the AMONG constraint.

Algorithm 1. GAC for $\text{AMONG}([X_1,..,X_n],\mathcal{K},N)$.

1 $lb := |\{i \mid D(X_i) \subseteq \mathcal{K}\}|$;
2 $ub := n - |\{i \mid D(X_i) \cap \mathcal{K} = \emptyset\}|$;
3 $min(N) := max(min(N), lb)$;
4 $max(N) := min(max(N), ub)$;
5 **if** $(max(N) < min(N))$ **then** fail;
6 **if** $(lb = min(N) = max(N))$ **then**
  foreach $X_i \;.\; \mathcal{D}(X_i) \not\subseteq \mathcal{K}$ **do** $\mathcal{D}(X_i) := \mathcal{D}(X_i) \setminus \mathcal{K}$;
7 **if** $(min(N) = max(N) = ub)$ **then**
  foreach $X_i \;.\; \mathcal{D}(X_i) \cap \mathcal{K} \neq \emptyset$ **do** $\mathcal{D}(X_i) := \mathcal{D}(X_i) \cap \mathcal{K}$;

Theorem 1. *Algorithm 1 maintains GAC on* $\text{AMONG}([X_1,..,X_n],[k_1,..,k_m],N)$ *and runs in $O(nd)$ where d is the maximum domain size.*

Proof. (Sketch) By Lemmas 1 and 2, the algorithm maintains GAC. Computing lb and ub is in $O(nd)$. Updating the bounds of N is constant time. Updating $\mathcal{D}(X_i)$ is in $O(d)$. Since there are n variables, pruning X_i's is in $O(nd)$. Thus, GAC on AMONG is in $O(nd)$. □

The behaviour of the algorithm can be simulated by encoding the AMONG constraint using the sum constraint:

$$\text{AMONG}([X_1,\ldots,X_n],\mathcal{K},N) \text{ iff}$$
$$\forall i \in \{1,..,n\}\; B_i = 1 \leftrightarrow X_i \in \mathcal{K} \wedge \sum_{i\in\{1,..,n\}} B_i = N$$

where each B_i is a Boolean variable with the domain $\{0,1\}$. In the algorithm, lb corresponds to the number of Boolean variables assigned 1, and ub to the number of Boolean variables not assigned 0 (that is, either assigned 1 or having the domain {0,1}). Lines 3 and 4 of the algorithm can be seen as the propagation of the sum constraint: $min(N)$ is computed by taking the maximum of $min(N)$ and the sum of $min(B_i)$ which is equivalent to lb; similarly $max(N)$ is computed by taking the minimum of $max(N)$ and the sum of $max(B_i)$ which is equivalent to ub. If $lb = min(N) = max(N)$, all the Booleans having the $\{0,1\}$ domain will be assigned 0, meaning that the associated variables do not take values from $\mathcal{K}$. Likewise, if $min(N) = max(N) = ub$, all the Booleans having the $\{0,1\}$ domain will be assigned 1, meaning that the associated variables take values only from $\mathcal{K}$. Otherwise, no propagation will occur. Consequently, the sum decomposition maintains GAC.

An alternative method of propagating an AMONG constraint is using the global cardinality constraint GCC [9]:

$$\text{AMONG}([X_1,\ldots,X_n],[k_1,..,k_m],N) \text{ iff}$$
$$\text{GCC}([X_1,\ldots,X_n],[k_1,..,k_m],[O_1,..,O_m]) \wedge$$
$$\sum_{i\in\{1,..,m\}} O_i = N$$

As shown in [6], this decomposition may not always achieve GAC.

Even if GAC on AMONG can be maintained by a simple decomposition, the presented algorithm is useful when we consider a number of extensions of the AMONG constraint. An interesting extension is when we count not the variables taking some given values but those taking values taken by other variables. This is useful when, for example, the resources to be used are not initially known. We consider here two such extensions in which we replace $[k_1, .., k_m]$ either by a set variable S or by a sequence of variables $[Y_1, .., Y_m]$

AMONG($[X_1, .., X_n], S, N$) holds iff N variables in X_i take values in the set S. That is, $N = |\{i \mid X_i \in S\}|$. Enforcing HC on this constraint is NP-hard in general.

Theorem 2. *Enforcing HC on* AMONG($[X_1, .., X_n], S, N$) *is NP-hard.*

Proof. We reduce 3-SAT to the problem of deciding if such an AMONG constraint has a satisfying assignment. Finding hybrid support is therefore NP-hard. Consider a formula φ with n variables (labelled from 1 to n) and m clauses. Let k be $m + n + 1$. To construct the AMONG constraint, we create $2k + 1$ variables for each literal i in the formula such that $X_{i1}..X_{ik} \in \{i\}$, $X_{i(k+1)}..X_{i(2k)} \in \{-i\}$, and $X_{i(2k+1)} \in \{i, -i\}$. We create a variable Y_j for each clause j in φ and let $Y_j \in \{x, -y, z\}$ where the jth clause in φ is $x \vee \neg y \vee z$. We let $N = n(k + 1) + m$ and $\{\} \subseteq S \subseteq \{1, -1, .., n, -n\}$. The constraint AMONG($[X_{11}, .., X_{1(2k+1)}, .., X_{n1}, .., X_{n(2k+1)}, Y_1, .., Y_m]$, S, N) has a solution iff φ has a satisfying assignment. ♡

In Algorithm 2, we give a propagation algorithm for this AMONG constraint. Notice that we assume all values are strictly positive. We highlight the differences with Algorithm 1. The first modification is to replace each occurrence of $\mathcal{K}$ by either $lb(S)$ or $ub(S)$. As a consequence, instead of a single lower bound and upper bound on N, we have now two pairs of bounds, one under the hypothesis that S is fixed to its lower bound ($lb[0]$ and $glb[0]$), and one under the hypothesis that S is fixed to its upper bound ($lub[0]$ and $ub[0]$). Moreover, in loop 1, we compute the contingent values of lb (resp. ub) when a value v is added to $lb(S)$ (resp. removed from $ub(S)$) and store the results in $lb[v]$ (resp. $ub[v]$). These arrays are necessary for pruning N (lines 3, 4, 6, 7), when the minimum (resp. maximum) value of N cannot be achieved with the current lower (resp. upper) bound of S (conditionals 2 and 5). In this case, we know that at least one of these values must be added to $lb(S)$ (resp. removed from $ub(S)$). Therefore the smallest value $lb[v]$ (resp. greatest value $ub[v]$) is a valid lower bound (resp. upper bound) on N. We also use them for pruning S (lines 8 and 9). Finally, we need to compute lb and ub, as they may have been affected by the pruning on S. This is done in line 10. The worst case time complexity is unchanged, as loop 1 can be done in O(nd).

The level of consistency achieved by this propagation algorithm is incomparable to BC. The following example shows that BC is not stronger: $X_1 \in \{2, 3\}$, $X_2 \in \{2, 3\}$, $X_3 \in \{1, 2, 3, 4\}$, $lb(S) = ub(S) = \{2, 3\}$, $min(N) = max(N) = 2$. The algorithm will prune $\{2, 3\}$ from X_3, whereas a BC algorithm will not do

Algorithm 2. Propagation for $\text{AMONG}([X_1, .., X_n], S, N)$.

$lb[0] := |\{X_i \mid D(X_i) \subseteq lb(S)\}|$;
$glb[0] := n - |\{X_i \mid D(X_i) \cap lb(S) = \emptyset\}|$;
$ub[0] := n - |\{X_i \mid D(X_i) \cap ub(S) = \emptyset\}|$;
$lub[0] := |\{X_i \mid D(X_i) \subseteq ub(S)\}|$;
foreach $v \in ub(S) \setminus lb(s)$ **do**
  $lb[v] := |\{X_i \mid D(X_i) \subseteq (lb(S) \cup \{v\})\}|$;
  $ub[v] := n - |\{X_i \mid D(X_i) \cap (ub(S) \setminus \{v\}) = \emptyset\}|$;
if $glb[0] < min(N)$ **then**
  $LB := \{lb[v] \mid v \in (ub(S) \setminus lb(S))\}$;
  if $(LB \neq \emptyset)$ **then** $min(N) = min(LB)$;
else
  $min(N) := max(min(N), lb[0])$;
if $lub[0] > max(N)$ **then**
  $UB := \{ub[v] \mid v \in (ub(S) \setminus lb(S))\}$;
  if $(UB \neq \emptyset)$ **then** $max(N) = max(UB)$;
else
  $max(N) := min(max(N), ub[0])$;
if $(max(N) < min(N))$ **then** fail;
$lb(S) := lb(S) \cup \{v \mid ub[v] < min(N)\}$;
$ub(S) := ub(S) \setminus \{v \mid lb[v] > max(N)\}$;
if $(min(N) = max(N))$ **then**
  $lb := |\{i \mid \mathcal{D}(X_I) \subseteq lb(S)\}|$;
  $ub := |\{i \mid \mathcal{D}(X_I) \cap ub(S) \neq \emptyset\}|$;
  if $(lb = min(N))$ **then**
    foreach $X_i \,.\, \mathcal{D}(X_i) \not\subseteq lb(S)$ **do** $\mathcal{D}(X_i) := \mathcal{D}(X_i) \setminus lb(S)$;
  if $(ub = max(N))$ **then**
    foreach $X_i \,.\, \mathcal{D}(X_i) \cap ub(S) \neq \emptyset$ **do** $\mathcal{D}(X_i) := \mathcal{D}(X_i) \cap ub(S)$;

any pruning. On the other hand, the following example shows that this algorithm does not enforce BC. Consider $X_1 \in \{1,2\}$, $X_2 \in \{1,2\}$, $X_3 \in \{3\}$, $X_4 \in \{3\}$, $X_5 \in \{4\}$, $X_6 \in \{4\}$, $X_6 \in \{5\}$, $X_8 \in \{5\}$, $lb(S) = \{1,2\}$, $ub(S) = \{1,2,3,4,5\}$, $N \in \{5,6,7,8\}$. The algorithm will not do any pruning whereas a BC algorithm will prune 5 from N.

We can again use the sum constraint to encode the AMONG constraint:

$$\text{AMONG}([X_1, .., X_n], S, N) \;\text{ iff}$$
$$\forall i \in \{1, .., n\}\; B_i = 1 \leftrightarrow X_i \in S \wedge \sum_{i \in \{1,..,n\}} B_i = N$$

where each B_i is a Boolean variable with the domain $\{0,1\}$. Algorithm 2 is strictly stronger than such a decomposition. It is easy to see that whenever the decomposition prunes a value from N, X_i's, or S, our algorithm also can detect these inconsistencies. However, Algorithm 2 might detect more inconsistent values than the decomposition. For instance, consider $X_1 \in \{1,2\}$, $X_2 \in \{1,2\}$, $X_3 = 3$, $X_4 = 3$, $X_5 = 4$, $X_6 = 4$, $lb(S) = \{1,2\}$, $ub(S) = \{1,2,3,4\}$, and $N \in \{2,3\}$. Algorithm 2 prunes 3 and 4 from $ub(S)$ but the decomposition does not.

The level of consistency achieved by this decomposition is also incomparable to BC. The example which demonstrates the incomparability of Algorithm 2 and BC also shows that the decomposition is incomparable to BC.

It remains an open question, however, whether BC on such a constraint is tractable or not.

We now consider the second generalization. $\text{AMONG}([X_1, .., X_n], [Y_1, .., Y_m], N)$ holds iff N variables in X_i take values in common with Y_j. That is, $N = |\{i \mid \exists j \, . \, X_i = Y_j\}|$. As before, we cannot expect to enforce GAC on this constraint.

Theorem 3. *Enforcing GAC on* $\text{AMONG}([X_1, .., X_n], [Y_1, .., Y_m], N)$ *is NP-hard.*

Proof. We again use a transformation from 3-SAT. Consider a formula φ with n variables (labelled from 1 to n) and m clauses. We construct the constraint $\text{AMONG}([Y_1, .., Y_m], [X_1, .., X_n], M)$ in which X_i represents the variable i and Y_j represents the clause j in φ. We let $M = m$, $X_i \in \{i, -i\}$ and $Y_j \in \{x, -y, z\}$ where the jth clause in φ is $x \vee \neg y \vee z$. The constructed AMONG constraint has a solution iff φ has a model. ♡

To propagate $\text{AMONG}([X_1, .., X_n], [Y_1, .., Y_m], N)$, we can use the following decomposition:

$$\text{AMONG}([X_1, .., X_n], [Y_1, .., Y_m], N) \text{ iff}$$
$$\text{AMONG}([X_1, .., X_n], S, N) \wedge \bigcup_{j \in \{1,..,m\}} \{Y_j\} = S$$

We can therefore use the propagation algorithm proposed for $\text{AMONG}([X_1, .., X_n], S, N)$. However, even if we were able to enforce HC on the decomposition (which is NP-hard in general to do), we may not make the original constraint GAC.

Theorem 4. *GAC on* $\text{AMONG}([X_1, .., X_n], [Y_1, .., Y_m], N)$ *is strictly stronger than HC on the decomposition.*

Proof: It is at least as strong. To show the strictness, consider $Y_1 \in \{1, 2, 3\}$, $X_1 \in \{1, 2\}$, $X_2 \in \{1, 2, 3\}$, $N = 2$. We have $\{\} \subseteq S \subseteq \{1, 2, 3\}$, hence the decomposition is HC. However, enforcing GAC on $\text{AMONG}([X_1, X_2], [Y_1], N)$ prunes 3 from Y_1 and X_2. ♡

Again, we still do not know whether BC on such a constraint is tractable or not.

3.2 Common Constraint

A generalization of the AMONG and ALLDIFFERENT constraints introduced in [2] is the following COMMON constraint:

$$\text{COMMON}(N, M, [X_1, .., X_n], [Y_1, .., Y_m]) \text{ iff}$$

$$N = |\{i \mid \exists j \, . \, X_i = Y_j\}| \wedge M = |\{j \mid \exists i \, . \, X_i = Y_j\}|$$

That is, N variables in X_i take values in common with Y_j and M variables in Y_j take values in common with X_i. Hence, the AllDifferent constraint is a special case of the Common constraint in which the Y_j enumerate all the values j in X_i, $Y_j = \{j\}$ and $M = n$. Not surprisingly, enforcing GAC on Common is NP-hard in general, as the result immediately follows from the intractability of the related Among constraint.

Theorem 5. *Enforcing GAC on* Common *is NP-hard.*

Proof. Consider the reduction in the proof of Theorem 3. We let $N \in \{1,..,n\}$. The constructed Common constraint has a solution iff the original 3-Sat problem has a model. ♡

As we have a means of propagation for Among$([X_1,..,X_n],[Y_1,..,Y_m],N)$, we can use it to propagate the Common constraint using the following decomposition:

$$\begin{aligned}&\textsc{Common}(N, M, [X_1,..,X_n], [Y_1,..,Y_m]) \text{ iff}\\ &\textsc{Among}([X_1,..,X_n],[Y_1,..,Y_m],N) \ \wedge\\ &\textsc{Among}([Y_1,..,Y_m],[X_1,..,X_n],M)\end{aligned}$$

In the next theorem, we prove that we might not achieve GAC on Common even if we do so on Among.

Theorem 6. *GAC on* Common *is strictly stronger than GAC on the decomposition.*

Proof: It is at least as strong. To show the strictness, consider $N = 2$, $M = 1$, $X_1, Y_1 \in \{1,2\}$, $X_2 \in \{1,3\}$, $Y_2 \in \{1\}$, and $Y_3 \in \{2,3\}$. The decomposition is GAC. However, enforcing GAC on Common$(N, M, [X_1, X_2], [Y_1, Y_2, Y_3])$ prunes 2 from X_1, 3 from X_2, and 1 from Y_1. ♡

Similar to the previous cases, the tractability of BC on such a constraint needs further investigation.

3.3 Disjoint Constraint

We may require that two sequences of variables be disjoint (i.e. have no value in common). For instance, we might want the sequence of shifts assigned to one person to be disjoint from those assigned to someone who dislikes them. The Disjoint$([X_1,..,X_n],[Y_1,..,Y_m])$ constraint introduced in [2] is a special case of the Common constraint where $N = M = 0$. It ensures $X_i \neq Y_j$ for any i and j. Surprisingly, enforcing GAC remains intractable even in this special case.

Theorem 7. *Enforcing GAC on* Disjoint *is NP-hard.*

Proof: We again use a transformation from 3-Sat. Consider a formula φ with n variables (labelled from 1 to n) and m clauses. We construct the Disjoint constraint in which X_i represents the variable i and Y_j represents the clause j in φ.

We let $X_i \in \{i, -i\}$ and $Y_j \in \{-x, y, -z\}$ where the jth clause in φ is $x \vee \neg y \vee z$. The constructed DISJOINT constraint has a solution iff φ has a model. ♡

An obvious decomposition of the DISJOINT constraint is to post an inequality constraint between every pair of X_i and Y_j, for all $i \in \{1, .., n\}$ and for all $j \in \{1, .., m\}$. Not surprisingly, the decomposition hinders propagation (otherwise we would have a polynomial algorithm for a NP-hard problem).

Theorem 8. *GAC on* DISJOINT *is strictly stronger than AC on the binary decomposition.*

Proof: It is at least as strong. To show the strictness, consider $X_1, Y_1 \in \{1, 2\}$, $X_2, Y_2 \in \{1, 3\}$, $Y_3 \in \{2, 3\}$. Then all the inequality constraints are AC. However, enforcing GAC on DISJOINT($[X_1, X_2], [Y_1, Y_2, Y_3]$) prunes 2 from X_1, 3 from X_2, and 1 from both Y_1 and Y_2. ♡

This decomposition is useful if we want to maintain BC on DISJOINT.

Theorem 9. *BC on* DISJOINT *is equivalent to BC on the decomposition.*

Proof. It is at least as strong. To show the equivalence, we concentrate on X_i's, but the same reasoning applies to Y_j's. Given X_k where $k \in \{1, .., n\}$, we show that for any bound b_k of X_k ($b_k = min(X_k)$ or $b_k = max(X_k)$) there exists a bound support containing it. We partition the integers as follows. S_X contains all integers v such that $\exists X_i,\ D(X_i) = \{v\}$, S_Y contains all integers w such that $\exists Y_j,\ D(Y_j) = \{w\}$, and T contains the remaining integers. T inherits the total ordering on the integers. So, we can partition T in two sets T_1 and T_2 such that no pair of integers consecutive in T belong both to T_1 or both to T_2. T_1 denotes the one containing b_k if $b_k \in T$. The four sets S_X, S_Y, T_1, T_2 all have empty intersections. Hence, if all X_i can take their value in $S_X \cup T_1$ and all Y_j in $S_Y \cup T_2$, we have a bound support for (X_k, b_k) on the DISJOINT constraint. We have to prove that $[min(X_i)..max(X_i)]$ intersects $S_X \cup T_1$ for any $i \in \{1, .., n\}$ (and similarly for Y_j and $S_Y \cup T_2$). Since $X_i \neq Y_j$ is BC for any j, $min(X_i)$ and $max(X_i)$ cannot be in S_Y. If $min(X_i)$ or $max(X_i)$ is in S_X or T_1, we are done. Now, if both $min(X_i)$ and $max(X_i)$ are in T_2, this means that there is a value between $min(X_i)$ and $max(X_i)$, which is in T_1, by construction of T_1 and T_2. As a result, any bound is BC on DISJOINT if the decomposition is BC. ♡

From Theorem 9, we deduce that BC can be achieved on DISJOINT in polynomial time. In fact, we can achieve more than BC in polynomial time.

Theorem 10. *AC on the binary decomposition is strictly stronger than BC on* DISJOINT.

Proof. AC on the decomposition is at least as strong BC on the decomposition which is equivalent to BC on the original constraint. The following example shows strictness. Consider $X_1 \in \{1, 2, 3\}$ and $Y_1 \in \{2\}$. The constraint DISJOINT($[X_1], [Y_1]$) is BC whereas GAC on the decomposition prunes 2 from X_1. ♡

Algorithm 3. BC for $\text{AMONG}([S_1,..,S_n],\mathcal{K},N)$.

$InLb := f([lb(S_1,..,lb(S_n))],\mathcal{K})$;
$InUb := f([ub(S_1,..,ub(S_n))],\mathcal{K})$;
$min(N) := max(min(N), InLb)$;
$max(N) := min(max(N), InUb)$;
if $min(N) > max(N)$ **then** fail;
if $max(N) = InLb$ **then**
  foreach S_i . $lb(S_i) \cap \mathcal{K} = \emptyset$ **do** $ub(S_i) := ub(S_i) \setminus \mathcal{K}$;
if $min(N) = InUb$ **then**
  foreach S_i . $lb(S_i) \cap \mathcal{K} = \emptyset \wedge |\mathcal{K} \cap ub(S_i)| = 1$ **do**
    $lb(S_i) := lb(S_i) \cup \mathcal{K} \cap ub(S_i)$;

4 Set Variables

Many problems involve finding a set of values (for example, the set of nurses on a particular shift). It is useful therefore to have global constraints over set variables [10]. For instance, we might want to count the number of times each nurse has a shift during the monthly roster where each shift is a set variable listing the nurses on duty. This could be achieved with a global constraint that counted the values occurring in a sequence of set variables.

4.1 Among Constraint

We consider an AMONG constraint over set variables that counts the number of these variables which contain one of the given values. More formally, we have:

$$\text{AMONG}([S_1,..,S_n],[k_1,..,k_m],N) \text{ iff } N = |\{i \mid \exists j \,.\, k_j \in S_i\}|$$

Enforcing BC on such a constraint is polynomial. We propose an algorithm to do this where we define the function $f([S_1,..,S_n],\mathcal{K})$ to be $|\{i \mid S_i \cap \mathcal{K} \neq \emptyset\}|$.

Theorem 11. *Algorithm 3 maintains BC on* $\text{AMONG}([S_1,.., S_n],\mathcal{K},N)$ *and runs in* $O(nd)$ *where* d *is the size of the maximum upper bound of the* S_i .

Proof. Soundness is relatively immediate. N cannot be greater than the number of variables having k_j's in their upper bounds or smaller than the number of variables having k_j's in their lower bounds. Furthermore, if $max(N)$ is equal to the number of variables having k_j's in their lower bound, there is no hope to satisfy the AMONG constraint if we use a value k_j in another variable. If $min(N) = InUb$, then for each S_i, if there exists only one element in its upper bound (but not in its lower bound) which is also in $\mathcal{K}$, then that element has necessarily to belong to the lower bound of S_i as it cannot be covered by another S_j otherwise $min(N) < InUb$. Finally, if $min(N) > max(N)$ we necessarily fail.

To show completeness, we need that when we do not fail, the domains returned are bound consistent. Consider an integer k such that $InLb \leq k \leq InUb$. We can construct an assignment of S_i's where exactly k of them take a value in $\mathcal{K}$. We first assign all S_i's with their lower bound. $InLb$ of the S_i's necessarily contain some k_j since their lower bound overlaps $\mathcal{K}$. For $k - InLb$ variables among the $InUb - InLb$ variables with some k_j in their upper bound but none in their lower bound, we take some k_j from their upper bound to obtain a satisfying assignment with $N = k$. Since $min(N) \geq InLb$ and $max(N) \leq InUb$ (lines 3 and 4), N is BC. Suppose now a value v in $ub(S_i)$. The only case in which v should not belong to $ub(S_i)$ is when v is in the k_j's, none of the k_j's appear in $lb(S_i)$, and no more variable can take values in the k_j's, i.e., $InLb = max(N)$. Then, v will have been removed from $ub(S_i)$ (line 6). In addition, suppose v should belong to $lb(S_i)$. This is the case only if there is no k_j in $lb(S_i)$, and v is the only value in $ub(S_i)$ appearing in the k_j's, and $InUb = min(N)$. Then, v will have been added in $lb(S_i)$ (line 7).

Computing the counters $InLb$ and $InUb$ is in $O(nd)$. Updating the bounds on N is constant time. Deleting values that are not bound consistent in a $ub(S_i)$ or adding a value in $lb(S_i)$ is in $O(d)$. Since there are n variables, this phase is again in $O(nd)$. Bound consistency on AMONG is in $O(nd)$. ♡

Note we can also add non-empty or cardinality conditions to the S_i without making constraint propagation intractable.

We again consider an extension in which we replace $[k_1, .., k_m]$ by a set variable S. Unlike the previous AMONG constraint, enforcing BC on AMONG$([S_1, .., S_n], S, N)$ is NP-hard in general.

Theorem 12. *Enforcing BC on* AMONG$([S_1, .., S_n], S, N)$ *is NP-hard.*

Proof. We reuse the reduction from the proof of Theorem 2 with minor modifications. We create $2k + 1$ set variables for each literal i in the formula such that $S_{i1}..S_{ik} \in \{i\}..\{i\}$, $S_{i(k+1)}..S_{i(2k)} \in \{-i\}..\{-i\}$, and $S_{i(2k+1)} \in \{\}..\{i, -i\}$. We create a set variable T_j for each clause j in φ and let $T_j \in \{\}..\{x, -y, z\}$ where the jth clause in φ is $x \vee \neg y \vee z$. We let $N = n(k + 1) + m$ and $\{\} \subseteq S \subseteq \{1, -1, .., n, -n\}$. The constraint AMONG$([S_{11}, .., S_{1(2k+1)}, .., S_{n1}, .., S_{n(2k+1)}, T_1, .., T_m], S, N)$ has a solution iff φ has a model. ♡

Note that the constraint remains intractable if the S_i are non-empty or have a fixed cardinality. We can easily modify the reduction by adding distinct "dummy" values to S_i and T_j respectively. We also add these dummy values to the lower bound of S.

Despite this intractability result, we can easily modify Algorithm 3 to derive a filtering algorithm for AMONG$([S_1, .., S_n], S, N)$ without changing the complexity. We use the lower bound of S (resp. $ub(S)$) in the computation of $InLb$ (resp. $InUb$). Also, instead of $\mathcal{K}$ in line 6 (resp. line 7), we use $lb(S)$ (resp. $ub(S)$). Finally, we need to consider the bounds of S. We remove v from $ub(S)$ if $|\{i \mid lb(S_i) \subseteq lb(S) \cup \{v\}\}| > max(N)$. Similarly, we add v to $lb(S)$ if $|\{i \mid ub(S_i) \cap ub(S) \setminus \{v\} \neq \emptyset\}| < min(N)$. We can easily extend the soundness proof of Theorem 11 for this algorithm as well. Such an algorithm does not achieve BC (otherwise we would have a polynomial algorithm for a NP-hard problem).

Finally, the constraint AMONG$([S_1, .., S_n], [T_1, .., T_m], N)$ is very similar to the previous one since several set variables $[T_1, \ldots, T_m]$ behave like their union. That

Algorithm 4. BC for DISJOINT($[S_1, .., S_n], [T_1, .., T_m]$).

1 $S := \bigcup_{i \in \{1,..,n\}}(lb(S_i))$;
2 $T := \bigcup_{i \in \{1,..,m\}}(lb(T_i))$;
3 **if** $S \cap T \neq \emptyset$ **then** fail;
4 **foreach** S_i **do** $ub(S_i) := ub(S_i) \setminus T$;
5 **foreach** T_j **do** $ub(T_j) := ub(T_j) \setminus S$;

is, AMONG($[S_1, .., S_n], [T_1, .., T_m], N$) is similar to AMONG($[S_1, .., S_n], T, N$) with $T = \bigcup_{j \in \{1..m\}} T_j$.

4.2 Common Constraint

We may also want to post a COMMON constraint on set variables. We have:

$$\text{COMMON}(N, M, [S_1, .., S_n], [T_1, .., T_m]) \text{ iff}$$

$$N = |\{i \mid \exists j \,.\, S_i \cap T_j \neq \emptyset\}| \wedge M = |\{j \mid \exists i \,.\, S_i \cap T_j \neq \emptyset\}|$$

Enforcing BC on such a constraint is intractable as it is an extension of the previous AMONG constraint. We can reduce AMONG($[S_1, .., S_n], [T_1, .., T_m], N$) to COMMON($N, M$, $[S_1, .., S_n], [T_1, .., T_m]$) by setting M to $\{0, .., m\}$.

Since we have a means of propagation for AMONG($[S_1, .., S_n], [T_1, .., T_m], N$), we can use it to propagate the COMMON constraint by decomposing it into two such AMONG constraints. However, such a decomposition hurts propagation. Consider the set variables S_1, S_2, S_3, T_1, T_2 and T_3 with $\{i\} \subseteq S_i \subseteq \{i\}$, $N = 1$, $\{\} \subseteq T_i \subseteq \{i\}$, and $M = 2$. The two AMONG constraints of the decomposition are BC while COMMON is inconsistent.

4.3 Disjoint Constraint

We finally consider DISJOINT($[S_1, .., S_n], [T_1, .., T_m]$). Unlike GAC on DISJOINT with integer variables, we can maintain BC on DISJOINT($[S_1, .., S_n], [T_1, .., T_m]$) in polynomial time.

Theorem 13. *Algorithm 4 maintains BC on* DISJOINT($[S_1, .., S_n], [T_1, .., T_m]$) *and runs in* $O((n + m)d)$.

Proof. We first show that the algorithm is sound. If there exists one value which occurs both in the lower bound of one of S_i and in the lower bound of one of the T_j, then we necessarily fail (Line 3). If a value is consumed by one of the T_j, then we cannot satisfy the constraint if this value is allowed to be consumed by one of the S_i (Line 4). Similarly, if a value is consumed by one of the S_i, then we cannot satisfy the constraint if this value is allowed to be consumed by one of the T_j (Line 5).

To show completeness, we prove that either we fail or we return bound consistent domains. We only consider the S_i as the reasoning is analogous for the T_j.

First, if the lower bounds of the S_i do not overlap those of the T_j, then assigning all S_i and T_j to their lower bound is a solution. Thus, the lower bounds are BC. Now, for each value in the upper bound of each S_i, we can construct a satisfying assignment involving v by assigning all other S_i to their lower bounds, S_i to its lower bound plus the element v, and all the T_j to their corresponding lower bounds as none has v as an element.

If d is the total number of values appearing in the upper bounds of the set variables, then at worst case the complexity of line 4 is $O(nd)$ and of line 5 is $O(md)$. Hence, the algorithm runs in $O((n+m)d)$. ♡

Note that if we add a cardinality restriction to the size of the set variables, it becomes NP-hard to enforce BC on this constraint.

5 Related Work

AMONG($[X_1, .., X_n], [k_1, .., k_m], N$) was first introduced in CHIP by [3]. A closely related constraint is the COUNT constraint [11]. COUNT($[X_1, .., X_n], v, op, N$) where $op \in \{\leq, \geq, <, >, \neq, =\}$ holds iff $N \; op \; |\{i \mid X_i = v\}|$. The AMONG constraint is more general as it counts the variables taking values from a set whereas COUNT counts those taking a given value. The algorithm of AMONG can easily be adapted to cover the operations considered in COUNT.

There are other counting and related constraints for which there are specialised propagation algorithms such as GCC [9], NVALUE [1], SAME and USEDBY [4].

In [6], a wide range of counting and occurrence constraints are specified using two primitive global constraints, ROOTS and RANGE. For instance, the AMONG on integer variables constraint is decomposed into a ROOTS and set cardinality constraint. Similarly, the COMMON constraint is decomposed into two ROOTS, two RANGE and two set cardinality constraints. However, ROOTS and RANGE cannot be used to express the AMONG, COMMON, and DISJOINT constraints on set variables.

Finally our approach to the study of the computational complexity of reasoning with global constraints has been proposed in [5]. In particular, as in [5], we show how computational complexity can be used to determine when a lesser level of local consistency should be enforced and when decomposing constraints will lose pruning.

6 Conclusions

We have studied a number of variations of the AMONG, COMMON and DISJOINT constraints over integer and set variables. Such constraints are useful in modelling problems involving resources. Our study shows that whether a global constraint is tractable or not can be easily affected by a slight generalization or specialization of the constraint. However, a propagation algorithm for an intractable constraint can often be adapted from a propagation algorithm of a

Table 1. Summary of complexity results

Constraint	Tractability
Integer Variables	
AMONG($[X_1,..,X_n],\mathcal{K},N$)	GAC is in P
AMONG($[X_1,..,X_n],S,N$)	HC is NP-hard
AMONG($[X_1,..,X_n],[Y_1,..,Y_m],N$)	GAC is NP-hard
COMMON($N,M,[X_1,..,X_n],[Y_1,..,Y_m]$)	GAC is NP-hard
DISJOINT($[X_1,..,X_n],[Y_1,..,Y_m]$)	GAC is NP-hard, BC is in P
Set Variables	
AMONG($[S_1,..,S_n],\mathcal{K},N$)	BC is in P
AMONG($[S_1,..,S_n],S,N$)	BC is NP-hard
AMONG($[S_1,..,S_n],[T_1,..,T_m],N$)	BC is NP-hard
COMMON($N,M,[S_1,..,S_n],[T_1,..,T_m]$)	BC is NP-hard
DISJOINT($[S_1,..,S_n],[T_1,..,T_m]$)	BC is in P

similar tractable one. In Table 1, we present a summary of our complexity results. For integer variables, we propose a polynomial time propagation algorithm for the AMONG constraint that achieves GAC. We prove that AMONG is intractable when we count the number of variables using values from *a set variable* or a *sequence of integer variables*. Nevertheless, we propose a polynomial algorithm to propagate the former and show how this algorithm can be used to propagate the latter. We also show that the COMMON constraint is intractable in general, and this holds even in the special case of the DISJOINT constraint when the number of values in common is zero. The last result is somewhat surprising, since the DISJOINT constraint is related to (and weaker than) the ALLDIFFERENT constraint. When we demonstrate the intractability of a constraint like DISJOINT, we also present a polynomial method to propagate the constraint. Finally, we consider AMONG, COMMON and DISJOINT constraints over set variables rather than integer variables. We show that most of the results on integer variables hold for set variables with the exception that the DISJOINT constraint now becomes tractable.

In future work, we will focus on determining whether BC on AMONG($[X_1,..,X_n],S,N$) is tractable or not. Such a result will also help us answer the still open questions of whether BC on the related AMONG($[X_1,..,X_n],[Y_1,..,Y_m],N$) and COMMON($N,M,[X_1,..,X_n],[Y_1,..,Y_m]$) is tractable or not. We will also implement these constraints and see their value in practice.

Acknowledgements

Hebrard and Walsh are supported by the National ICT Australia, which is funded through the Australian Government's *Backing Australias Ability* initiative, in part through the Australian Research Council. Hnich received support from Science Foundation Ireland (Grant 00/PI.1/C075). We would like to thank our reviewer for helping to improve the paper.

References

1. Beldiceanu, N. 2001. Pruning for the minimum constraint family and for the number of distinct values constraint family. In *Proc. of CP 2001*, 211–224. Springer.
2. Beldiceanu, N. 2000. Global constraints as graph properties on a structured network of elementary constraints of the same type. Technical report T2000/01, Swedish Institute of Computer Science.
3. Beldiceanu, N., and Contegean, E. 1994. Introducing global constraints in CHIP. *Mathematical Computer Modelling* 20(12):97–123.
4. Beldiceanu, N., Katriel, I., and Thiel, S. 2004. Filtering algorithms for the *same* and *usedby* constraints. MPI Technical Report MPI-I-2004-1-001.
5. Bessiere, C., Hebrard, E., Hnich, B. and Walsh, T. 2004. The Complexity of Global Constraints. In *Proc. of AAAI 2004*. AAAI Press / The MIT Press.
6. Bessiere, C., Hebrard, E., Hnich, B., Kizilitan Z. and Walsh, T. 2005. The Range and Roots Constraints: Specifying Counting and Occurrence Problems. In *Proc. of IJCAI 2005*, 60–65. Professional Book Center.
7. Cheng, B.M.W., Choi, K.M.F., Lee, J.H.M. and Wu, J.C.K. 1999. Increasing Constraint Propagation by Redundant Modeling: an Experience Report. *Constraints* 4(2): 167–192.
8. Régin, J.-C. 1994. A filtering algorithm for constraints of difference in CSPs. In *Proc. of AAAI 1994*, 362–367. AAAI Press.
9. Régin, J.-C. 1996. Generalized arc consistency for global cardinality constraints. In *Proc. of AAAI 1996*, 209–215. AAAI Press / The MIT Press.
10. Sadler, A., and Gervet, C. 2001. Global reasoning on sets. In *Proc. of Workshop on Modelling and Problem Formulation (FORMUL'01)*. Held alongside CP 2001.
11. Swedish Institue of Computer Science. 2004. *SICStus Prolog User's Manual, Release 3.12.0*. Available at `http://www.sics.se/sicstus/docs/latest/pdf/sicstus.pdf`.

Partitioning Based Algorithms for Some Colouring Problems

Ola Angelsmark[1] and Johan Thapper[2]

[1] Department of Computer Science,
Box 118, Lund University,
S-221 00 Lund, Sweden
olaan@cs.lth.se

[2] Department of Mathematics,
Linköpings Universitet,
S-581 83 Linköping, Sweden
jotha@mai.liu.se

Abstract. We discuss four variants of the *graph colouring problem,* and present algorithms for solving them. The problems are k-COLOURABILITY, MAX IND k-COL, MAX VAL k-COL, and, finally, MAX k-COL, which is the unweighted case of the MAX k-CUT problem. The algorithms are based on the idea of *partitioning* the domain of the problems into disjoint subsets, and then considering all possible instances were the variables are restricted to values from these partitions. If a pair of variables have been restricted to different partitions, then the constraint between them is always satisfied since the only allowed constraint is disequality.

1 Introduction

The graph colouring problem is probably one of the most well-studied graph problem. While it is conceptually easy to understand — colour the vertices of a graph such that if there is an edge between two vertices, then they must have different colours — it is *NP*-complete for more than two colours [15]. It has been studied for a long time, and was actually the 12th problem in the list of *NP*-complete problems presented in Karp [18]. One reason for studying this problem is, of course, that it regularly appears as a natural problem in a wide range of areas, such as register allocation in compiler construction [8], and frequency assignment in mobile communication [14].

The graph colouring problem is nicely formulated as a constraint satisfaction problem; it is the (very) restricted CSP in which we only allow the constraint *disequality*, i.e. given two vertices of a graph, the only requirement we can have is that they have different colours if there is an edge between them.

In this paper, we will discuss a number of different versions of the graph colouring problem. Our results are based on an idea which was first formalised in Angelsmark & Jonsson [2]. This method, which is called the *partitioning method*, works by partitioning the domain of the problem into a number of (disjoint) subsets, and then solving a number of restricted instances in order to find a

B. Hnich et al. (Eds.): CSCLP 2005, LNAI 3978, pp. 44–58, 2006.

solution. The idea is of course not restricted to the problems we discuss in this paper; in [2] it was used to construct an algorithm for #CSP (i.e. the problem of *counting* the solutions to a CSP) and it turned out to be very successful when applied to the problem of counting graph colourings.

Problems where the only allowed constraint is disequality have the property that once a pair of variables have been restricted to assume values from different partitions they cannot be assigned a common value in any solution to this instance and thus the constraint between them, if there was one, 'disappears.' Consequently, we can consider those variables that have been assigned the same partition in isolation, thereby reducing the problem to one with a smaller domain. We can also introduce a hierarchy of partitions — the instance arising from the partition can be partitioned further — and at the bottom level we can apply an algorithm specialised for solving problems with small domains. Of course, any improvement in this specialised algorithm will also improve the overall algorithm.

The first problem we look at is the *k-colouring problem*, where the aim is to decide if it is possible to colour a given graph using at most k colours. As was mentioned earlier, this problem is *NP*-complete for $k > 2$. Interestingly enough, for $k > 6$, the fastest algorithm for this problem is the general, exponential space algorithm for CHROMATIC NUMBER; the original version by Lawler [20] has a running time of $\mathcal{O}\left((1 + \sqrt[3]{3})^n\right) \in \mathcal{O}\left(2.4423^n\right)$. This was later improved to $\mathcal{O}\left(2.4151^n\right)$ by Eppstein [12], and, recently, to $\mathcal{O}\left(2.4023^n\right)$ by Byskov [5].

The algorithm we present for this problem uses polynomial space, and while it is not faster than the CHROMATIC NUMBER algorithm, it is faster than the currently fastest polynomial space algorithm, which is due to Feder & Motwani [13], and has a running time of $\mathcal{O}\left(\left(\min\left(k/2, 2^{\phi_k}\right)\right)^n\right)$, where ϕ_k is given by

$$\frac{1}{k+1}\sum_{i=0}^{k-1}\left(1 + \frac{i}{\binom{k}{2}}\right)\log_2(k-i).$$

Asymptotically, 2^{ϕ_k} is bounded from above by k/e, where $\mathsf{e} \approx 2.7182$ as usual. In contrast, the algorithm we propose runs $\mathcal{O}\left(\alpha_k^n\right)$, $k > 6$, where n is the number of vertices in the graph and

$$\alpha_k = \begin{cases} i - 2 + \beta_5 \text{ if } 2^i < k \leq 2^i + 2^{i-2} \\ i - 1 + \beta_3 \text{ if } 2^i + 2^{i-2} < k \leq 2^i + 2^{i-1} \\ i - 1 + \beta_4 \text{ if } 2^i + 2^{i-1} < k \leq 2^{i+1} \end{cases}$$

for $i \geq 2$, assuming we can solve 3-, 4-, and 5-colourability in $\mathcal{O}\left(\beta_3^n\right), \mathcal{O}\left(\beta_4^n\right)$, and $\mathcal{O}\left(\beta_5^n\right)$ time, respectively. See Table 1 for a comparison. (Throughout the paper, we will omit polynomial factors in time and space complexities.)

MAX IND $(d, 2)$-CSP is, basically, the problem of finding a satisfiable *subinstance* of the original problem which contains as many variables as possible (we let (d, l)-CSP denote a CSP where the domain has size at most d, and the constraints have arity l.) A subinstance is here a subset of the variables, together with the constraints which only involve these variables. (For example, if we have the variables x, y in the subset, then the constraint $R(x, y)$ would be included,

Table 1. Comparison between our k-colouring algorithm and that of Feder & Motwani

	$k=6$	$k=7$	$k=8$	$k=9$	$k=10$
F & M [13]	2.8277^n	3.2125^n	3.5956^n	3.9775^n	4.3581^n
New result	2.3290^n	2.7505^n	2.7505^n	3.1021^n	3.1021^n

but the constraint $R'(x, y, z)$ would not, since z is not in the subset.) MAX IND $(d, 2)$-CSP is, in some sense, dual to the classical MAX CSP in that it does not maximise the number of satisfied *constraints*, but instead tries to maximise the number of *variables* that are assigned values without violating any constraints.

The colouring version of this problem is called the MAXIMUM INDUCED k-COLOURABLE SUBGRAPH, or MAX IND k-COL for short. Using the partitioning method, we arrive at an algorithm which has a running time of $\mathcal{O}(\alpha_k^n)$, where

$$\alpha_k = \begin{cases} i - 1 + \beta_3 & \text{if } 2^i < k \leq 2^i + 2^{i-1} \\ i + \beta_2 & \text{if } 2^i + 2^{i-1} < k \leq 2^{i+1} \end{cases}$$

with $\beta_2 = 1.4460$, $\beta_3 = 1.7388$ and $i \geq 1$. We get the values of β_2 and β_3 are by applying the MAXIMUM INDEPENDENT SET algorithm from Robson [21] to the microstructure of the instances witg domain sizes 2 and 3 (see [4].)

Next, we consider the MAX VALUE problem, which (somewhat simplified) is the problem of maximising the sum of the variable values. We first construct a specialised algorithm for the MAX VALUE 3-COLOURING problem, which runs in $\mathcal{O}(1.6181^n)$ time, and end up with a running time of $\mathcal{O}(\alpha_k^n)$, where

$$\alpha_k = \begin{cases} i - 1 + \beta_3 & \text{if } 2^i < k \leq 2^i + 2^{i-1} \\ i + 1 & \text{if } 2^i + 2^{i-1} < k \leq 2^{i+1} \end{cases}$$

with $\beta_3 = 1.6180$ and $i \geq 1$, for the general MAX VALUE k-COLOURING problem.

For our final problem we consider the MAXIMUM k-COLOURABLE SUBGRAPH, or MAX k-COL, problem. This is also known as the unweighted case of the well-known MAX k-CUT problem. The currently fastest algorithm for this problem is the $\mathcal{O}\left(k^{\omega n/3}\right)$ time algorithm presented in Williams [22], which utilises exponential space. Here, $\omega \in \mathbb{R}$ is the exponent in matrix multiplication over a ring, and has been shown to be less than 2.376 [9].

Using cases $k = 2$ and $k = 3$ from [22], we apply the partitioning method to get an algorithm for MAX k-COL with a running time of $\mathcal{O}(\alpha_k^n)$, where

$$\alpha_k = \begin{cases} i - 1 + \beta_3 & \text{if } 2^i < k \leq 2^i + 2^{i-1} \\ i + \beta_2 & \text{if } 2^i + 2^{i-1} < k \leq 2^{i+1} \end{cases}$$

for $i \geq 1$, assuming we can solve for domain sizes 2 and 3 in $\mathcal{O}(\beta_2^n)$ and $\mathcal{O}(\beta_3^n)$ time. The underlying algorithms uses exponential space, and this will also be the case for our algorithm. However, since we only use the algorithms for $k = 2$ and $k = 3$, we only need the space required for these. For larger values of k, this is considerably less than the $\mathcal{O}\left(k^{n/3}\right)$ required by the algorithm from [22].

This result also holds for the *counting* problem #MAX k-COL, by simply replacing the underlying algorithms with their counting versions.

2 Preliminaries

A (d, l)*-constraint satisfaction problem* ((d, l)-CSP) is a triple (X, D, C) where

- X is a finite set of variables,
- D a finite set of domain values, with $|D| = d$, and
- C is a set of constraints $\{c_1, c_2, \ldots, c_k\}$.

Each constraint $c_i \in C$ is a structure $R(x_{i_1}, \ldots, x_{i_j})$ where $j \le l, x_{i_1}, \ldots, x_{i_j} \in X$ and $R \subseteq D^j$. A *solution* to a CSP instances is a function $f : X \to D$ s.t. for each constraint $R(x_{i_1}, \ldots, x_{i_j}) \in C$, $(f(x_{i_1}, \ldots, f(x_{i_j}))) \in R$. Given a (d, l)-CSP, the basic computational problem is to decide whether it has a solution or not — to determine if it is *satisfiable*. If the function does not assign values to every variable, but only a subset of them, it will be referred to as a *partial* solution, provided no constraints are violated by these assignments.

The special case (2, 2)-CSP is equivalent to 2-SATISFIABILITY, or 2-SAT. An instance of 2-SAT, a 2-SAT *formula*, consists of the conjunction of a set of clauses, where each clause is the disjunction of (at most) 2 literals. (A literal is either a variable or its negation.) We will be interested in *weighted* instances of 2-SAT, and define them as follows:

Definition 1 (Dahllöf *et al.* [10]). *Let Γ be a 2-SAT formula and let L be the set of all literals for all variables occurring in Γ. Given a weight vector* $\mathbf{w}$*, and a solution M to Γ, we define the* weight $W(M)$ of M *as*

$$W(M) = \sum_{\{l \in L \ \mid \ l \text{ is true in } M\}} \mathbf{w}(l)$$

Dahllöf *et al.* [10] presents an algorithm for counting the number of maximum weighted solutions to 2-SAT instances. This algorithm has a running time of $\mathcal{O}(1.2561^n)$, and it can easily be modified to return one of the solutions. We will denote this modified algorithm *2-SAT*$_w$.

A *graph* G consists of a set $V(G)$ of *vertices*, and a set $E(G)$ of *edges*, where each element of $E(G)$ is an unordered pair of vertices. The *size* of a graph, denoted $|G|$ is the number of vertices. The *neighbourhood* of a vertex $v \in V(G)$ is the set of all vertices adjacent to v, v itself excluded, denoted $N_G(v)$; $N_G(v) = \{w \in V(G) \mid (v, w) \in E(G)\}$. The *degree* $\deg_G(v)$ of a vertex v is the size of its neighbourhood, $|N_G(v)|$ (note that we do not consider graphs which allow 'self-loops,' i.e. edges of the form $\{v, v\}$.) When G is obvious from the context, it can be omitted as a subscript. If we pick a subset S of the vertices of a graph together with the edges between them (but no other edges), then we get the *subgraph of G induced by S*, $G(S)$. $G(S)$ has vertex set S and edge set $\{(v, u) \mid v, u \in S, (v, u) \in E(G)\}$. If the induced subgraph has empty edge set, then it forms an *independent set*.

Definition 2 (Jégou [16]). *Given a binary CSP $\Theta = (X, D, C)$, i.e. a CSP with binary constraints, the* microstructure *of Θ is an undirected graph G defined as follows:*

1. *For each variable $x \in X$, and domain value $a \in D$, there is a vertex $x[a]$ in G.*
2. *There is an edge $(x[a], y[b]) \in E(G)$ iff (a, b) violates the constraint between x and y, i.e. if xRy and $(a, b) \notin R$.*

We assume there is exactly one constraint between any pair of variables; any variables without explicit constraints are assumed to be constrained by the universal constraint which allows all values.

For readers familiar with the original formulation, the graph given by this construction is actually the complement of the one given in Jégou [16]. This is mostly a matter of convenience; the algorithms we present are easier formulated in terms of independent sets than maximum cliques.

3 Partitioning and Colouring Problems

We now present the method behind the algorithms for the colouring problems in this paper. We begin by defining what a partitioning is, and briefly discuss the partitioning based method for construction algorithms, before investigating how it applies to colouring problems.

Definition 3. *A* partitioning $P = \{P_1, P_2, \ldots, P_m\}$ *of a domain D is a division of D into m disjoint subsets such that $\bigcup P = D$. A* k-partition *is an element of P with k elements. Given a partitioning P, we let $\sigma(P, k)$ denote the number of k-partitions in P. Since the actual elements in the subset $P_i \in P$ is often less interesting than their number, we let the multiset $[|P_1|, \ldots, |P_m|]$ represent P.*

As an example of how the partitioning method could be used to construct an algorithm for solving CSPs, consider the following: An algorithm for solving (4, 2)-CSPs has a running time of $\mathcal{O}\left(1^{n_1+n_2} \cdot \alpha^{n_3} \cdot \beta^{n_4}\right)$, where n_i is the number of variables with domain size i. Thus for problems with domains of sizes 1 and 2 it is polynomial (recall that we have omitted polynomial factors), for domain size 3 it runs in $\mathcal{O}(\alpha^n)$, and for domain size 4, it runs in $\mathcal{O}(\beta^n)$.

Using this algorithm, we want to solve, say, a (7, 2)-CSP. First, we split the domain of each variable into one part with 3 elements and one part with 4 elements. So if the original domain is $\{1, 2, 3, 4, 5, 6, 7\}$, we could, for example, use the partitioning $P_1 = \{1, 2, 3, 4\}$ and $P_2 = \{5, 6, 7\}$. Next, we consider each possible way of restricting the variables to only take values from one of these partitions. With n variables in the original problem we get k variables restricted to P_1 and $n - k$ restricted to P_2, and thus get a total running time of

$$\mathcal{O}\left(\sum_{k=0}^{n} \alpha^k \cdot \beta^{n-k}\right) = \mathcal{O}\left((\alpha + \beta)^n\right).$$

When we apply this to colouring problems, we exploit the fact that if two variables are assigned different partitions, then any constraint between them is trivially satisfied.

Let $\Theta = (X, D, C)$ and $\Theta' = (X', D', C')$ be two CSPs with the property that given solutions f to Θ and f' to Θ', they can be combined to get a solution to $\Theta_{\cup} = (X \cup X', D \cup D', C \cup C')$ (possibly modulo renaming of the variables and domain values.) Conversely, the two subinstances Θ and Θ' correspond to a partitioning of $\Theta_{\cup}$; the partitioning is $[|D|, |D'|]$, and the variables in X are mapped to D, while those in X' are mapped to D'.

We will let $Col(k, n)$ denote an arbitrary instance of a problem with domain size k and n variables which can be partitioned in this way.

Theorem 1 (Angelsmark [1]). *Let $A_1, \ldots, A_m$ be algorithms for the problems $Col(k_1, n)$, ..., $Col(k_m, n)$, respectively, with running times in $\mathcal{O}(\alpha^n)$. Given a partitioning $P = \{P_1, \ldots, P_p\}$ of the set $\{1, \ldots, k\}$ such that for any partition P_i, we have an algorithm for solving problems with this domain size, i.e. $|P_i| \in \{k_1, k_2 \ldots, k_m\}$, there exists a partitioning based algorithm for solving $Col(k, n)$ which has a running time of*

$$\mathcal{O}\left(\left(|P| - 1 + \alpha\right)^n\right).$$

We note that the running time given by Theorem 1 is largely dependent on *the number of partitions* and less so on the running times of the algorithms for the different partitions. Consequently, in order to minimise the running times, we want to use as few partitions as possible. First, note that if we have an algorithm for $Col(k, n)$, then we can of course get an algorithm for $Col(2k, n')$ by using the partitioning $[k, k]$. The idea here is to use a *recursive* partitioning to build the $Col(k, n)$-algorithm bottom up; to get an algorithm for $Col(4k, n)$, we first create an algorithm for domains of size $2k$ from a $Col(k, n)$ algorithm together with the partitioning $[k, k]$, provided we have an algorithm for $Col(k, n)$. If this is not the case, then we have to construct one by using the partitioning $[\lceil k/2 \rceil, \lfloor k/2 \rfloor]$, etc. Whether this partitioning is *optimal* is still an open question.

In general, given algorithms for instances with domain sizes $k_1, \ldots, k_m$, with running times $\mathcal{O}\left(\beta_{k_i}^n\right)$, $i \in \{1, \ldots, m\}$, if it is faster to use the available algorithm for size k_i than using the partitioning $[\lceil k_{i/2} \rceil, \lfloor k_{i/2} \rfloor]$, i.e. $T([k_i]) < T([\lceil k_i/2 \rceil, \lfloor k_i/2 \rfloor])$, then there exists a partitioning based algorithm for solving for domain size k which has a running time of $\mathcal{O}\left(\alpha_k^n\right)$, where α_k is the solution to the following recurrence:

$$\alpha_k = \begin{cases} \beta_k & \text{if } k \in \{k_1, \ldots, k_m\} \\ 1 + \alpha_{\lceil k/2 \rceil} & \text{otherwise.} \end{cases}$$

Solving this equation is straightforward, albeit tedious, thus we will omit this part of the proofs.

4 *k*-Colouring Algorithm

We will now show how the partitioning method applies to the problem of finding a k-colouring of a graph. This being the first of the problems, we will describe it in more detail than the remaining problems. For a further discussion of the method, see Angelsmark [1]. Formally, we define the problem as follows:

Table 2. The fastest polynomial space algorithms for k-colouring, $k < 7$

k	Time	Reference
3	$\mathcal{O}(1.3289^n)$	Eppstein [11]
4	$\mathcal{O}(1.7504^n)$	Byskov [5]
5	$\mathcal{O}(2.1020^n)$	Byskov & Eppstein [7]
6	$\mathcal{O}(2.3289^n)$	Byskov [5]

Definition 4. *Let G be an arbitrary graph and k a natural number. The k-*Colouring *problem consists of finding a function $f : V(G) \to \{1, \ldots, k\}$ which assigns 'colours' to the vertices in such a way that for $v, w \in V(G)$, $f(v) \neq f(w)$ if $\{v, w\} \in E(G)$, i.e. adjacent vertices are given different colours.*

Before we can apply Theorem 1, we need to show that the k-colouring problem is a $Col(k, n)$ problem. To see this, note that if the vertices of a graph G are partitioned into two disjoint subsets, S_1, S_2, and the subgraphs induced by these can be coloured using the colours $\{1, \ldots, k_1\}$, and $\{k_1 + 1, \ldots, k_2\}$, respectively, then G can be coloured using the colours $\{1, \ldots, k_2\}$, since any assignment made by the colourings of S_1 and S_2 will also be allowed in G.

Once we know that Theorem 1 is applicable, it is straightforward to get an algorithm for the problem, shown in Algorithm 1. The running time of the algorithm is of course the one given in Theorem 1.

Theorem 2. *Algorithm 1 correctly solves the k-colouring problem.*

Proof. Let P be a partitioning of the domain values as given in Theorem 1, i.e., for any partition $P_i \in P$, there exists an algorithm $A_{|P_i|}$ for determining $|P_i|$-colourability of graphs with n variables in $\mathcal{O}(\alpha^n)$ time. Next, let G be a graph and f an arbitrary total function from $V(G)$ to P — i.e. a function which assigns the vertices to partitions.

Lines 3 to 6 work as follows: The vertices restricted to partition P_i induces a subgraph, and we can determine $|P_i|$-colourability of this subgraph in $\mathcal{O}(\alpha^n)$ time. Obviously, if we have two of these induced subgraphs, and we know that we can colour them using, say, k_1 and k_2 colours, respectively, then we can colour the union of them using $k_1 + k_2$ colours. So, by induction, the variable a will, once all of the induced subgraph have been examined, be **true** iff the graph is k-colourable. Repeating this for all total functions ensures that we will examine all possible restrictions of vertices to partitions. □

Algorithm 1 only determines the existence of a k-colouring (returning "yes" if one exists), but it is of course straightforward to change it to return an explicit colouring.

In the literature, we find a number of different algorithms for determining k-colourability of a graph. Table 2 contains the currently fastest polynomial space algorithms for $k \leq 6$. For $k > 6$, the most efficient polynomial space algorithm for k-colouring is the $\mathcal{O}((k/c_k)^n)$ time algorithm by Feder & Motwani [13]. We will not get an improvement over the bounds in Table 2 from the partitioning

Algorithm 1. Partitioning based k-COLOURING algorithm

```
k-COL (G, P)
for each total function f : V(G) → P do
   a := true
   for each P_i ∈ P do
      G' := G|{v ∈ V(G) | f(v) = P_i}
      a := a ∧ A_{|P_i|}(G')
   end for
   if a then
      return "yes"
end for
return "no"
```

method, but we do get a way of constructing algorithms for *any* $k > 6$, which is faster than $\mathcal{O}((k/c_k)^n)$.

As we noted earlier, the *number* of partitions has a large impact on the running time of the algorithm. For example, if we want an algorithm for, say, 8-colouring, it is tempting to use the partitioning $[2, 2, 2, 2]$, since 2-colouring is polynomial. This, however, gives a running time of $\mathcal{O}(4^n)$, while if we use the partitioning $[4, 4]$, we get a running time of $\mathcal{O}(((2-1) + 1.7504)^n) = \mathcal{O}(2.7504^n)$, which is an enormous improvement. Using the partitioning $[3, 3]$ we get a 6-colouring algorithm with the same running time as in [5], $\mathcal{O}((2 - 1 + 1.3289)^n) = \mathcal{O}(2.3289^n)$.

Now let β_i^n, $i \in \{3, 4, 5\}$ denote the running times of the 3-, 4- and 5-colouring algorithms in Table 2.

Theorem 3. *If we can solve 3-, 4-, 5-*COLOURING *in* $\mathcal{O}(\beta_i^n)$ *time, for* $i = 3, 4, 5$, *respectively, then there exists a partitioning based algorithm for solving* k-COLOURING, $k > 6$, *which has a running time of* $\mathcal{O}(\alpha_k^n)$, *where*

$$\alpha_k = \begin{cases} i - 2 + \beta_5 \text{ if } 2^i < k \leq 2^i + 2^{i-2} \\ i - 1 + \beta_3 \text{ if } 2^i + 2^{i-2} < k \leq 2^i + 2^{i-1} \\ i - 1 + \beta_4 \text{ if } 2^i + 2^{i-1} < k \leq 2^{i+1} \end{cases}$$

for $i \geq 2$.

Proof. Using the partitioning $[\lfloor k/2 \rfloor, \lceil k/2 \rceil]$ recursively, together with the colouring algorithms above, a partitioning based algorithm will have a running time of $\mathcal{O}(\alpha_k^n)$, where α_k is given by the solution to the following recurrence:

$$\alpha_k = \begin{cases} \beta_k & \text{if } k \in \{3, 4, 5\} \\ 1 + \alpha_{\lceil k/2 \rceil} & \text{otherwise} \end{cases}$$

Solving the equation gives the result. □

Thus if we wish to determine 14-colourability of a graph, we start with the pre-existing algorithms for 3- and 4- colourability, and let them be parts of a 7-colourability algorithm which uses the partitioning $[3, 4]$. From this we get an algorithm for 14-colourability which works with the partitioning $[7, 7]$. The running time, given by Theorem 3, is then $\mathcal{O}((2 + \beta_4)^n) \approx \mathcal{O}(3.7504^n)$.

5 Max Ind k-Colouring Algorithm

The general MAX IND $(d, 2)$-CSP is defined as follows:

Definition 5 (Jonsson & Liberatore [17]). *Let $\Theta = (X, D, C)$ be an instance of (d, l)-CSP. The* MAX IND *(d, l)-CSP problem consists of finding a maximal subset $X' \subseteq X$ such that $\Theta|X'$ is satisfiable.*

Here, $\Theta|X' = (X', D, C')$ is the *subinstance of Θ induced by X'*, i.e. the CSP we get when we restrict Θ to the variables in X' and the constraints which involve only variables from X', viz.,

$$C' := \{c \in C \mid c(x_1, x_2, \ldots, x_l) \in C, x_1, \ldots, x_l \in X'\}.$$

When we restrict this problem to colourings, we get the MAX IND k-COL problem, which is the problem of assigning colours to as many vertices as possible without having neighbours of the same colours. Unlike the k-colouring problem, not every vertex is necessarily assigned a colour.

Definition 6. *Given a graph G and a natural number k, the* MAX IND *k-COL problem is to find a subset $S \subseteq V(G)$ such that the induced subgraph $G(S)$ is k-colourable and $|S|$ is maximised.*

The problem is still *NP*-complete even under this restriction (see Jonsson & Liberatore [17]). Theorem 1 is of course applicable to this problem, and it has been shown that MAX IND 2-COL and MAX IND 3-COL can be solved in $\mathcal{O}\left(1.2025^{2n}\right) = \mathcal{O}\left(1.4460^{n}\right)$ and $\mathcal{O}\left(1.2025^{3n}\right) = \mathcal{O}\left(1.7388^{n}\right)$ time, respectively [4], thus we can combine this with the following theorem to get an algorithm for MAX IND k-COL.

Theorem 4. *Given that we can solve* MAX IND 2-COL *and* MAX IND 3-COL *in time $\mathcal{O}\left(\beta_2^n\right)$ and $\mathcal{O}\left(\beta_3^n\right)$, respectively, there exists a partitioning based algorithm for solving* MAX IND *k-COL which has a running time of $\mathcal{O}\left(\alpha_k^n\right)$, where*

$$\alpha_k = \begin{cases} i - 1 + \beta_3 & \text{if } 2^i < k \leq 2^i + 2^{i-1} \\ i + \beta_2 & \text{if } 2^i + 2^{i-1} < k \leq 2^{i+1} \end{cases}$$

for $i \geq 1$.

Proof. We use the partitioning $[\lfloor k/2 \rfloor, \lceil k/2 \rceil]$ recursively, and we get from Theorem 1 that a partitioning based algorithm will have a running time of $\mathcal{O}\left(\alpha_k^n\right)$, where α_k is given by the following recurrence:

$$\alpha_k = \begin{cases} \beta_2 & \text{if } k = 2 \\ \beta_3 & \text{if } k = 3 \\ 1 + \alpha_{\lceil k/2 \rceil} & \text{otherwise} \end{cases}$$

Solving the equation gives the result. □

Algorithm 2. Algorithm for MAX VALUE 2-COL

MaxVal 2-COL $(\Theta, \mathbf{w})$

1. Let G be the microstructure of Θ.
2. $m := 0$
3. **if** G is 2-colourable **then**
4. Let $f : V(G) \to \{1, 2\}$ be a 2-colouring of G
5. **for each** connected component c of G **do**
6. $m := m+$

$$\max_{v \in c} \left(\sum_{f(v)=1} \mathbf{w}(v), \sum_{f(v)=2} \mathbf{w}(v) \right)$$

7. **end for**
8. **end if**
9. **return** m

6 Max Value k-Colouring

The MAX VALUE problem for CSPs has been studied in, e.g. Angelsmark *et al.* [3], and is formally defined as follows:

Definition 7 (Angelsmark *et al.* [3]). *Let* $\Theta = (X, D, C)$ *be an instance of* (d, l)*-CSP, where* $D = \{a_1, a_2, \ldots, a_d\} \subseteq \mathbb{R}$, $X = \{x_1, x_2, \ldots, x_n\}$. *Given a real vector* $\mathbf{w} = (w_1, \ldots, w_n) \in \mathbb{R}^n$, *the* MAX VALUE *problem for* Θ *consists in finding a solution* $f : X \to D$ *which maximises*

$$\sum_{i=1}^{n} w_i \cdot f(x_i)$$

The colouring version of the MAX VALUE problem, the MAX VALUE k-COL problem, is defined as follows:

Definition 8. *Given a graph* G, *with* $|V(G)| = n$, *a real vector of weights* $\mathbf{w} = (w_1, \ldots, w_n) \in \mathbb{R}^n$ *and a natural number* k, *the* MAX VALUE k-COL *problem consists in finding a function* $f : V(G) \to \{1, \ldots, k\}$, *with* $f(v) \neq f(v')$ *if* $(v, v') \in E(G)$, *such that*

$$\sum_{v \in V(G)} w_v \cdot f(v)$$

is maximised.

For clarity, we let $(\Theta, \mathbf{w})$, where $\Theta = (X, D, C)$, denote an instance of MAX VALUE 2-COL. Now let G be the microstructure graph of Θ, and, for $x \in X$, let $\eta(x)$ be the number of constraints x is involved in (in the microstructure, this corresponds to $\deg(x[i]) - 1$).

Theorem 5. *There exists an algorithm for solving the* MAX VALUE 2-COL *problem which runs in polynomial time.*

Proof. We show that Algorithm 2 correctly solves the MAX VALUE 2-COL problem.

First of all, we note that if the microstructure graph is *not* 2-colourable, then the MAX VALUE 2-COL instance has the trivial solution 0, since there are no colourings, and this is what the algorithm returns.

Next we observe that *if* a 2-colouring exists, then for each of the connected component in G, there are exactly two possible colourings. Consequently, since we can choose the colour with largest weight for each connected component in isolation, when the algorithm reaches line 9, m will contain the weight of the maximum solution. □

In order to successfully apply the partitioning method here, we need to take care of odd-sized colourings, and thus we need an algorithm for the MAX VALUE 3-COL problem.

In the analysis of this algorithm, we encounter a recursion on the form $T(n) = \sum_{i=1}^{k} T(n - r_i) + p(n)$, where $p(n)$ is a polynomial in n, and $r_i \in \mathbb{N}^+$. These equations satisfy $T(n) \in \mathcal{O}(\tau(r_1, \ldots, r_k)^n)$, where $\tau(r_1, \ldots, r_k)$ is the largest real-valued root to $1 - \sum_{i=1}^{k} x^{-r_i}$ (see Kullmann [19].) Note that this bound does not depend on neither $p(n)$ nor the boundary conditions $T(1) = b_1, \ldots, T(k) = b_k$. We call τ the *work factor.*

First, some additional definitions: A variable having three possible domain values we call a 3-variable, and a variable having two possible values will be called a 2-variable. The size of an instance is defined as $m(\Theta) = n_2 + 2n_3$, where n_i denotes the number of i-variables in Θ. Consequently, the size of an instance can be decreased by either removing a 2-variable or eliminating one of the possible values for a 3-variable, turning it into a 2-variable.

Given a variable x with three possible values, $\{d_1, d_2, d_3\}$, ordered in such a way that $w(x, d_1) > w(x, d_2) > w(x, d_3)$, let $\delta(x) := (c_1, c_2, c_3)$ where $c_i = \deg_G(x[d_i])$, G being the microstructure graph. If x is a 2-variable then, similarly, we define $\delta(v) := (c_1, c_2)$. The *maximal* weight of a variable x, i.e. the domain value d for which $w(x, d)$ is maximal, will be denoted $x_{\max}$.

Since the only allowed constraint is disequality, it is never the case that a 3-variable has two unconstrained values — for example, if $x[d_1]$ had an edge to $y[d_1]$, but $x[d_2]$ and $x[d_3]$ had no edges to y, this would mean that vertices $y[d_2]$ and $y[d_3]$ had already been removed, and thus we could propagate $y[d_1]$, the only possible value for y.

Lemma 1. *If there is a variable x with $\delta(x) = (\geq 3, \cdot, \cdot)$, we can reduce the instance with a work factor of $\tau(4, 2)$.*

Proof. If $x_{\max}$ is chosen, then we remove x together with its two external neighbours, thus reducing the size of the instance by (at least) 4. The only reason *not* to choose $x_{\max}$ is, of course, that one of its external neighbours has alread been chosen, reducing the size of the instance by 2. □

Algorithm 3. Algorithm for MAX VALUE 3-COL

MaxVal 3-COL $(G, \mathbf{w})$

1. **if** at any time, the domain of a variable becomes empty,
   this branch can be pruned.
2. Apply Lemma 2, keeping track of eliminated variables.
3. **if** Lemma 1 applies **then**
4.   **return** the maximum of the branches described in Lemma 1
5. **else**
6.   Let Γ_w be the weighted 2-SAT instance corresponding to G.
7.   **return** $\mathit{2\text{-}SAT}_w(\Gamma_w)$
8. **endif**

After applying the reduction in this lemma, it is holds that *no* variable x has $x_{\max}$ with degree greater than 2. This means that either the neighbours of $x_{\max}$ are the other possible values of x, leaving x unconstrained, or one of the other values has been eliminated, and there are only two possible values for x. We can apply the following lemma to get rid of all of the cases of unconstrained variables, and what we have left is an instance of weighted 2-SAT.

Lemma 2 (Angelsmark & Thapper [4]). *For any instance Θ, we can find an instance Θ' with the same optimal solution as Θ, with size smaller than or equal to that of Θ and to which* none *of the following cases apply.*

1. *There is a 2-variable x for which $\delta(x) = (2, \geq 1)$.*
2. *There is a variable x for which the maximal weight is unconstrained.*

Thus, we get the following theorem:

Theorem 6. MAX VALUE 3-COL *can be solved by a deterministic algorithm in time $\mathcal{O}(1.6181^n)$.*

Proof. Algorithm 3 has, apart from the call to $\mathit{2\text{-}SAT}_w$, a work factor of $\tau(4, 2) \leq 1.2721$. Since we used $m(\Theta) = n_2 + 2n_3$ as the measure of size, the size of an instance is $2n$. Consequently, the algorithm has a running time of

$$\mathcal{O}\left((\max(1.2721, 1.2561))^{2n}\right)$$

i.e. $\mathcal{O}(1.6181^n)$. □

Since we are only considering colourings, we can apply Theorem 1 and get:

Theorem 7. *If we can solve* MAX VALUE 2-COL *in polynomial time, and* MAX VALUE 3-COL *in $\mathcal{O}(\beta_3^n)$ time, respectively, then there exists a partitioning based algorithm for solving* MAX VALUE k-COL *which has a running time of $\mathcal{O}(\alpha_k^n)$, where*

$$\alpha_k = \begin{cases} i - 1 + \beta_3 & \text{if } 2^i < k \leq 2^i + 2^{i-1} \\ i + 1 & \text{if } 2^i + 2^{i-1} < k \leq 2^{i+1} \end{cases}$$

and $i \geq 1$.

Proof. Again, we recursively use the partitioning $[\lfloor k/2 \rfloor, \lceil k/2 \rceil]$, and from Theorem 1 we get an algorithm which will have a running time of $\mathcal{O}(\alpha_k^n)$, where α_k is given by the solution to the following recurrence:

$$\alpha_k = \begin{cases} 1 & \text{if } k = 2 \\ \beta_3 & \text{if } k = 3 \\ 1 + \alpha_{\lceil k/2 \rceil} & \text{otherwise} \end{cases}$$

Solving the equation gives the result. □

7 Max k-COL and #Max k-COL Algorithms

Max CSP is probably one of the most widely studied optimisation problems for CSPs. Williams [22] presents an impressive algorithm for this problem, the first to run in provably less than $\mathcal{O}(d^n)$ time, as well as the *counting* version of this problem, i.e. the problem of finding *how many* solutions there are, usually denoted #Max CSP. Formally, we define the problem as follows:

Definition 9. *Given an instance $\Theta = (X, D, C)$ of $(d, 2)$-CSP, the* Max $(d, 2)$-*CSP problem is to find an assignment $f : X \to D$ which satisfies the maximum number of constraints.*

If we restrict Max CSP to colouring problems, we get the Maximum k-Colourable Subgraph problem, or Max k-COL — also known as the unweighted case of the Max k-CUT problem. Note the difference to the Max Ind k-COL problem; there, we were dealing with an *induced* subgraph.

Definition 10. *Given a graph G and a natural number k, the* Max k-COL *problem is to find a subset E' of $E(G)$ such that the graph $(V(G), E')$ is k-colourable and $|E'|$ maximised. The problem of determining the* number *of such subsets is denoted* #Max k-COL.

Williams [22] shows that Max k-COL can be solved in $\mathcal{O}\left(k^{\omega n/3}\right)$ time, where $\omega < 2.376$, but we can improve this bound using the partitioning method:

Theorem 8. *Given that we can solve* Max 2-COL *and* Max 3-COL *(*#Max 2-COL *and* #Max 3-COL*) in time $\mathcal{O}(\beta_2^n)$ and $\mathcal{O}(\beta_3^n)$, respectively, there exists a partitioning based algorithm for solving* Max k-COL *(*#Max k-COL*) which has a running time of $\mathcal{O}(\alpha_k^n)$, where*

$$\alpha_k = \begin{cases} i - 1 + \beta_3 & \text{if } 2^i < k \le 2^i + 2^{i-1} \\ i + \beta_2 & \text{if } 2^i + 2^{i-1} < k \le 2^{i+1} \end{cases}$$

for $i \ge 1$. Furthermore, the space requirement is equal to that of the most demanding of the given algorithms.

Proof. Again, we use the partitioning $[\lfloor k/2 \rfloor, \lceil k/2 \rceil]$ recursively. From Theorem 1, we know that a partitioning based algorithm will have a running time of $\mathcal{O}(\alpha_k^n)$, where α_k is given by the solution to the following recurrence:

$$\alpha_k = \begin{cases} \beta_2 & \text{if } k = 2 \\ \beta_3 & \text{if } k = 3 \\ 1 + \alpha_{\lceil k/2 \rceil} & \text{otherwise} \end{cases}$$

Solving the equation gives the time complexity stated in the theorem.

As for the space complexity, the algorithms for MAX 2-COL and MAX 3-COL are applied in sequence, and thus their space requirement remains unchanged. □

Combining this theorem with the algorithms for MAX 2-COL (#MAX 2-COL) and MAX 3-COL (#MAX 3-COL) with running times of $\mathcal{O}(1.7315^n)$ and $\mathcal{O}(2.3872^n)$, respectively, utilising $\mathcal{O}(2^{n/3})$ and $\mathcal{O}(3^{n/3})$ space, gives an algorithm for the general MAX k-COL (#MAX k-COL) problem.

Acknowledgements

Johan Thapper is supported by the *Programme for Interdisciplinary Mathematics* at the Department of Mathematics, Linköpings universitet.

The authors would like to thank Peter Jonsson for interesting and fruitful discussions during the writing of this paper, and the anonymous reviewers for insightful comments.

References

1. Ola Angelsmark. *Constructing Algorithms for Constraint Satisfaction and Related Problems.* PhD thesis, Department of Computer and Information Science, Linköpings Universitet, Sweden, 2005.
2. Ola Angelsmark and Peter Jonsson. Improved algorithms for counting solutions in constraint satisfaction problems. In Francesca Rossi, editor, *Principles and Practice of Constraint Programming, 9th International Conference (CP-2003), Kinsale, Ireland, September 29 - October 3, 2003, Proceedings*, volume 2833 of *Lecture Notes in Computer Science*, pages 81–95. Springer–Verlag, 2003.
3. Ola Angelsmark, Peter Jonsson, and Johan Thapper. Two methods for constructing new CSP algorithms from old. Unpublished manuscript, 2004.
4. Ola Angelsmark and Johan Thapper. A microstructure based approach to constraint satisfaction optimisation problems. In Ingrid Russell and Zdravko Markov, editors, *Recent Advances in Artificial Intelligience. Proceedings of the Eighteenth International Florida Artificial Intelligence Research Society Conference (FLAIRS-2005), 15-17 May, 2005, Clearwater Beach, Florida, USA*, pages 155–160. AAAI Press, 2005.
5. Jesper Makholm Byskov. Enumerating maximal independent sets with applications to graph colouring. *Operations Research Letters*, 32(6):547–556, November 2004.

6. Jesper Makholm Byskov. *Exact Algorithms for Graph Colouring and Exact Satisfiability.* PhD thesis, Basic Research In Computer Science (BRICS), Department of Computer Science, University of Aarhus, Denmark, August 2004.
7. Jesper Makholm Byskov and David Eppstein. An algorithm for enumerating maximal bipartite subgraphs. Unpublished manuscript (see also [6]), 2004.
8. Gregory J. Chaitin, Marc A. Auslander, Ashok K. Chandra, John Cocke, Martin E. Hopkins, and Peter W. Markstein. Register allocation via coloring. *Computer Languages*, 6:47–57, 1981.
9. Don Coppersmith and Shmuel Winograd. Matrix multiplication via arithmetic progressions. *Journal of Symbolic Computation*, 9(3):251–280, 1990.
10. Vilhelm Dahllöf, Peter Jonsson, and Magnus Wahlström. Counting models for 2SAT and 3SAT formulae. *Theoretical Computer Science*, 332(1–3):265–291, February 2005.
11. David Eppstein. Improved algorithms for 3-coloring, 3-edge-coloring, and constraint satisfaction. In *Proceedings of the Twelfth Annual ACM-SIAM Symposium on Discrete Algorithms (SODA-2001), January 7-9, 2001, Washington, DC, USA*, pages 329–337. ACM/SIAM, 2001.
12. David Eppstein. Small maximal independent sets and faster exact graph coloring. *Journal of Graph Algorithms and Applications*, 7(2):131–140, 2003.
13. Tomás Feder and Rajeev Motwani. Worst-case time bounds for coloring and satisfiability problems. *Journal of Algorithms*, 45(2):192–201, November 2002.
14. Andreas Gamst. Some lower bounds for a class of frequency assignment problems. *IEEE Transactions on Vehicular Technology*, 35(1):8–14, 1986.
15. Michael R. Garey and David S. Johnson. *Computers and Intractability: A Guide to the Theory of NP-Completeness.* W.H. Freeman and Company, New York, 1979.
16. Philippe Jégou. Decomposition of domains based on the micro-structure of finite constraint-satisfaction problems. In *Proceedings of the 11th (US) National Conference on Artificial Intelligence (AAAI-93)*, pages 731–736, Washington DC, USA, July 1993. American Association for Artificial Intelligence (AAAI).
17. Peter Jonsson and Paolo Liberatore. On the complexity of finding satisfiable subinstances in constraint satisfaction. Technical Report TR99-038, Electronic Colloquium on Computational Complexity, 1999.
18. Richard M. Karp. Reducibility among combinatorial problems. In Raymond E. Miller and James W. Thatcher, editors, *Complexity of Computer Computations*, pages 85–103. Plenum Press, 1972.
19. Oliver Kullmann. New methods for 3-SAT decision and worst-case analysis. *Theoretical Computer Science*, 223(1–2):1–72, 1999.
20. Eugene L. Lawler. A note on the complexity of the chromatic number problem. *Information Processing Letters*, 5(3):66–67, August 1976.
21. Mike Robson. Finding a maximum independent set in time $O(2^{n/4})$. Technical report, LaBRI, Université Bordeaux I, 2001.
22. Ryan Williams. A new algorithm for optimal constraint satisfaction and its implications. In Josep Díaz, Juhani Karhumäki, Arto Lepistö, and Donald Sanella, editors, *Automata, Languages and Programming: 31st International Colloquium (ICALP-2004), July 12-16, 2004, Turku, Finland. Proceedings*, volume 3142 of *Lecture Notes in Computer Science*, pages 1227–1237. Springer–Verlag, 2004.

A CSP Search Algorithm with Reduced Branching Factor

Igor Razgon and Amnon Meisels

Department of Computer Science,
Ben-Gurion University of the Negev,
Beer-Sheva, 84-105, Israel
{irazgon, am}@cs.bgu.ac.il

Abstract. This paper presents an attempt to construct a "practical" CSP algorithm that assigns a variable with 2 values at every step. Such a strategy has been successfully used for construction of "theoretical" constraint solvers because it decreases twice the base of the exponent of the upper bound of the search algorithm.

We present a solver based on the strategy. The pruning mechanism of the algorithm resembles Forward Checking (FC), therefore we term it 2FC. According to our experimental evaluation, 2FC outperforms FC on graph coloring problems and on non-dense instances of randomly generated CSPs.

1 Introduction

Partition of domains is a strategy that allows to reduce the size of the search space explored by a constraint solver. Consider a method based on the strategy that partitions the domain of every variable into subsets of two values (if a domain has an odd size than one subset is a singleton). The algorithm scans all constraint networks obtained by restriction of the domain of every variable to one of the partition classes. If at least one constraint network being scanned is soluble, the algorithm returns the solution found. Otherwise, it reports failure.

Assume that the considered constraint network has n variables and the maximal domain size is d. Then a simple analysis shows that the algorithm scans $O((d/2)^n)$ constraint networks if d is even and $O(((d+1)/2)^n)$ if d is odd. Taking into account that constraint networks with domains of size at most two can be solved efficiently [1], we get that these upper bounds determine the search space size of the considered algorithm. Clearly, this size is much smaller than $O(d^n)$ of FC, MAC, and others.

The strategy of domain partition has been successfully applied to the design of constraint solvers with exact upper bounds. Sophisticated techniques based on the strategy are presented in [2, 3]. However, the strategy attracted little attention of researchers that investigate "practical" approaches to construction of complete constraint solvers.

This paper introduces an attempt to construct a "practical" complete constraint solver based on domain partition. The main problem with the strategy

B. Hnich et al. (Eds.): CSCLP 2005, LNAI 3978, pp. 59–72, 2006.

is that the resulting algorithm is not guaranteed to have a solution when all variables are assigned. Therefore the algorithm could generate many "long" insoluble 2-CNs (constraint networks with domain sizes at most 2) which makes the actual time of its work close to the theoretical upper bound. To overcome this difficulty, we introduce the following modifications.

- Variables are assigned one by one. A variable is assigned with 2 values if its current domain contains at least 2 values. Otherwise, the variable is assigned with one value. To present this situation in a more general form, we say that at every step of the algorithm, a variable v is assigned with a subset S of its current domain.
- Whenever a variable v is assigned with a set of values S, the algorithm removes all values of unassigned variables that are incompatible with all the values of S.
- The algorithm backtracks when the current domain of some variable becomes empty.
- Whenever a variable v is assigned with a set $\{val_1, val_2\}$, a new conflict is added between any pair $(\langle v_1, val'_1\rangle, \langle v_2, val'_2\rangle)$ of values of different unassigned variables v_1 and v_2 such that $\langle v_1, val'_1\rangle$ conflicts with $\langle v, val_1\rangle$ and $\langle v_2, val'_2\rangle$ conflicts with $\langle v, val_2\rangle$.

The proposed algorithm resembles FC with the main difference that a variable can be assigned with 2 values. Therefore we call the algorithm 2FC. The main property of 2FC is that whenever all variables are assigned, the resulting 2-CN is *guaranteed* to have a solution.

In our experimental analysis, we compared 2FC to FC. The main experimental observation is that 2FC strictly outperforms FC on graph k-coloring problem. The rate of runtime improvement changes from a factor of 2 to 10. 2FC also outperforms FC on randomly generated constraint networks with low density.

The experimental result suggest that the proposed approach could be useful in the area of graph coloring. Another possible application of 2FC follows from the fact that it returns a 2-CN which could have many solutions that can be efficiently generated. Therefore the algorithm could be useful for dynamic environments where constraints frequently change: it might allow quick replacing of an inconsistent solution by another solution without performing search.

The rest of the paper is organized as follows. Section 2 provides necessary background. Section 3 presents the 2FC algorithm. Section 4 proves correctness of the 2FC algorithm. Section 5 demonstrates result of experimental evaluation. Section 6 outlines directions of further investigation.

2 Preliminaries

The model we consider in the paper is binary constraint network (CN). A CN $Z = \langle V, D, C\rangle$ is a triple consisting of a set of *variables* V, a set of *domains* D and a set of *constraints* C. Let $V = \{v_1, \ldots, v_n\}$. Then $D = \{D(v_1), \ldots, D(v_n)\}$, where $D(v_i)$ is the domain of values of v_i, $C = \{C(v_i, v_j) | i \neq j, 1 \leq i, j \leq n\}$, where $C(v_i, v_j) \subseteq D(v_i) \times D(v_j)$ is the set of all *compatible* pairs of values of v_i and v_j. We refer to the parts of Z as V_Z, D_Z, and C_Z. To emphasize that a value *val* belongs to the domain of a variable v, we refer to this value as $\langle v, val \rangle$. In this paper we consider a special case of constraint network, *2-CN*, that is a CN for which every domain has at most 2 values.

Given a CN Z as above, the task of Constraint Satisfaction Problem (CSP) is to find a set $P = \{\langle v_1, val_1 \rangle, \ldots, \langle v_n, val_n \rangle\}$ such that every val_i belongs to the domain of v_i and all values of P are mutually compatible (consistent), or to report that there is no such a set. The set P is called a *solution* of Z.

A typical CSP search algorithm like Forward Checking (FC) [4] usually creates a solution in an iterative manner. During its work it maintains a consistent set of values of a subset of variables and tries to extend it to a solution. This set of values is called a *partial* solution. Variables whose values are contained in the partial solution are called *assigned.* Other variables are called *unassigned.* The present paper introduces an algorithm that can assign a variable with more than one value. We refer to a set of assigned values maintained by the algorithm as an *extended partial solution.* When all variables are assigned, the algorithm has an *extended solution.*

The following notion is frequently used further in the paper.

Definition 1. *Let Z be a CN and let S be a set of values of Z. A subnetwork Z' of Z induced by S is obtained as follows:*

- *take to Z' only those variables of Z whose values appear in S;*
- *the domain of every variable v of Z' is the intersection of the domain of v in Z with S;*
- *two values are compatible in Z' if and only if they are compatible in Z.*

To illustrate the notion, consider Figure 1. On the left side of the figure there is a CN Z. Ellipses represent variables, black points represent values, conflicting values are connected by arcs. The CN Z' is a subnetwork of Z induced by the set of values encircled by additional circles. Note that Z' does not contain variable V_4 because no value of the domain of V_4 is included in the inducing set of values. Also note that there are conflicts between $\langle V_1, 2 \rangle$ and $\langle V_2, 2 \rangle$ and between $\langle V_2, 3 \rangle$ and $\langle V_3, 3 \rangle$ because these conflicts appear in the original CN.

Finally, we recall the notions of directional arc and path-consistency.

Definition 2. *A value $\langle v_i, val \rangle$ is consistent with a set of values S if it is compatible with at least one value of S.*

Definition 3. *A CN Z is called directionally arc-consistent with respect to an order $v_1, \ldots, v_n$ of its variables if every value $\langle v_i, val \rangle$ is consistent with a domain of a variable v_k whenever $k < i$.*

Definition 4. *A pair of values $\{\langle v_i, val_i \rangle, \langle v_k, val_k \rangle\}$ is consistent with a set of values S if at least one value of S is compatible with both $\langle v_i, val_i \rangle$ and $\langle v_k, val_k \rangle$.*

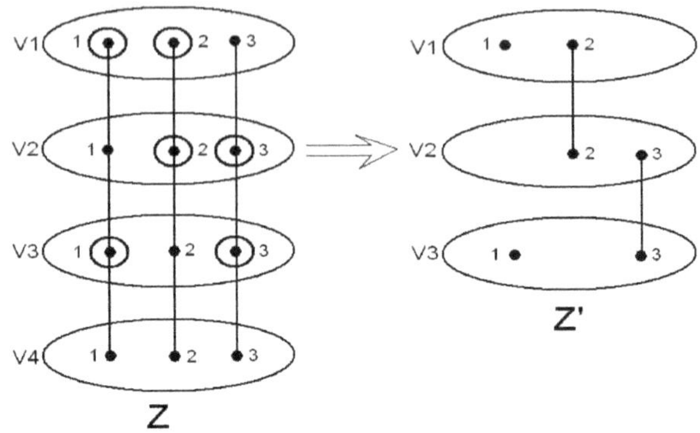

Fig. 1. Illustration of a CN induced by a set of values

Definition 5. *A CN Z is called directionally path-consistent with respect to the order* $v_1, \ldots, v_n$ *of its variables if every pair of compatible values* $\{\langle v_i, val_i \rangle, \langle v_k, val_k \rangle\}$ *is consistent with the domain of a variable* v_l *whenever* $l < i$ *and* $l < k$.

3 The 2FC Algorithm

In this section we introduce a modification of FC that explores much smaller search space than FC. In particular, processing a CN with n variables and maximal domain size d, the algorithm generates a search tree with $O((d/2)^n)$ nodes if d is even and $O(((d+1)/2)^n)$ nodes if d is odd.

The first 3 steps of the modification are the following.

1. Variables are assigned with subsets of their current domains. In particular, let v be the variable being assigned currently. If the current domain of v is of size at least 2 then v is assigned with a subset S of its domain such that $|S| = 2$. Otherwise, if the domain is a singleton, v is assigned with the domain itself.
2. Once a variable v is assigned with a set S, the algorithm removes from the domains of unassigned variables all the values that are incompatible with all the values of S.
3. Unassigning a variable v at the backtrack stage, the algorithm removes from the current domain of v *all* values of the set assigned to v.

These 3 steps naturally generalize FC, providing the ability to assign a variable with one value as well as with two values. However the resulting algorithm has an essential drawback: when all variables are assigned, the CN induced by the assigned values may be insoluble and this is in contrast to the standard FC that has a solution when all variables are assigned. Thus the modified FC has a restricted ability of early recognition of dead-ends.

To illustrate this drawback, consider a CN with variables $\{v_1, v_2, v_3, v_4\}$ and the domain of every variable $\{1, 2, 3\}$. Every 2 variables are connected by the inequality constraint. Assume that the algorithm assigns v_1 with $\{1, 2\}$. No value is deleted from the domains of the unassigned variables because there are values incompatible with 1, values incompatible with 2, but none that are incompatible with both of them. In the same way, the algorithm can assign v_2, v_3, v_4 with $\{1, 2\}$. The CN induced by the assigned values is clearly insoluble.

The following claim (proved in the next section) suggests a simple way to overcome the drawback.

Lemma 1. *Let Z be a 2-CN with no empty domain which is directionally arc-consistent and directionally path consistent with respect to an order $v_1, \dots, v_n$ of variables of Z. Then Z is soluble.* [1]

Thus, to guarantee that whenever all the variables are assigned, the CN induced by the assigned values is soluble, it is enough to ensure that it is directionally arc-consistent and directionally path-consistent.

Note that directional arc-consistency is already ensured by the modification number 2 described above. To ensure directional path-consistency, it is possible to perform the following operation: *Every time a variable v is assigned with a set S, add a conflict between every pair P of compatible assignments of future variables such that P is inconsistent with S.*

We call the resulting algorithm 2FC. Algorithm 1 introduces its pseudocode.

The algorithm is presented in the form of a recursive procedure that gets a CN Z as input. In the first 6 lines the termination conditions are checked. In particular, if Z has no variables, the procedure returns $\emptyset$ (lines 1-3), if Z has a variable with the empty domain, the procedure returns $FAIL$.

In line 7 a variable u is selected. In line 8 a CN Z' is created by removing from Z the variable u and all its values. Before exploring the domain of u, the algorithm removes from it all values that conflict with domains of some other unassigned variable (line 9).

The loop described in lines 10-27 explores the domain of u. In lines 11-15 a subset S of the current domain of u is selected. The set S contains 2 values unless there is only one value in the current domain of u. After u is assigned by S, the algorithm removes from the domains of variables of Z' all values inconsistent with S (line 16). If the size of S is 2, the algorithm adds conflicts between compatible pairs of values of Z' that are inconsistent with S (lines 18-20). Then the function 2FC is applied recursively to Z' (line 22). If the output of the recursive application is not $FAIL$, the procedure returns the union of the output with S (line 24). (The operation is correct because the output of 2FC is either $FAIL$ or a set of values.) Otherwise, if the recursive application returns $FAIL$, the algorithm removes S from the domain of u (line 26) and starts a new iteration of the loop or finishes it if the domain of u is wiped out. In the latter case the algorithm returns $FAIL$ in line 28.

Note that when 2FC returns a set of values, a solution can from it by the process described in the proof of Lemma 1. (See the next section.)

---

[1] Note that the suggested sufficient condition of solubility of 2-CNs is weaker than path-consistency whose sufficiency is proved in [1].

Algorithm 1. FUNCTION 2FC(Z)

```
if V_Z = ∅ then
    Return ∅
end if
if There is a variable with the empty domain then
    Return FAIL
end if
Select a variable u
Z' ← Z \ u
Remove from D_z(u) all values that are inconsistent with domains of unassigned
variables
while D_z(u) ≠ ∅ do
    if |D_z(u)| ≥ 2 then
        S ← {val_1, val_2}, where val_1 and val_2 are two values of D_z(u)
    else
        S ← D_z(u)
    end if
    Remove from the domains of Z' the values that are inconsistent with S
    if |S| ≤ 2 then
        for every pair {⟨v_1, val'_1⟩, ⟨v_2, val'_2⟩} of compatible values of Z' that is incon-
        sistent with S do
            C_Z'(v_1, v_2) ← C_Z'(v_1, v_2) \ {{⟨v_1, val_1⟩, ⟨v_2, val_2⟩}}
        end for
    end if
    R ← 2FC(Z')
    if R ≠ FAIL then
        Return R ∪ S
    end if
    D_Z(u) = D_Z(u) \ S
end while
Return FAIL
```

Consider an example of application of 2FC. Let Z be the CN described above with variables $\{v_1, \dots, v_4\}$, each domain equal $\{1, 2, 3\}$ and variables connected by inequality constraint. Assume that v_1 is assigned with $\{1, 2\}$. Then 2FC adds conflicts between every pair of values 1 and 2 of different unassigned variables, that is between $\langle v_2, 1\rangle$ and $\langle v_3, 2\rangle$, between $\langle v_2, 2\rangle$ and $\langle v_3, 1\rangle$ and so on. Assume that in the next iteration, variable v_2 is assigned with $\{1, 2\}$. Then values 1 and 2 are deleted from the current domains of v_3 and v_4. In the next iteration, trying to assign v_3, 2FC backtracks, because the only remaining values $\langle v_3, 3\rangle$ wipes out the current domain of v_4. As a result of backtrack, 2FC unassigns v_2. The only possible next assignment is $\{3\}$. After the assignment, 2FC removes 3 from the domains of v_3 and v_4. In the next iteration, 2FC tries again to assign v_3, but backtracks because both remaining values 1 and 2 wipe out the domain of v_4. This time, after unassigning v_2, the current domain of v_2 is finished; therefore

2FC backtracks again and changes the assignment of v_1 to $\{3\}$. In a few iteration the algorithm finishes with FAIL because of wiping out of the current domain of v_1.

A drawback of 2FC is large overhead spent to addition of conflicts between values of unassigned variables. It is not hard to show that $O(n^2d^2)$ additional consistency checks per iteration must be spent. The overhead can be reduced if we observe that 2FC checks compatibility of values of two variables only if one of these variables is either assigned or selected to be assigned.

Based on the observation we suggest a procedure of adding new conflicts based on the notion of *critical value.* Let u be a variable assigned with a set $\{val_1, val_2\}$. We say that $\langle u, val_1 \rangle$ is critical with respect to a value $\langle v, val \rangle$ if $\langle v, val \rangle$ conflicts with $\langle u, val_2 \rangle$. Instead of performing lines 18-19 in Algorithm 1, new conflicts can be added in the following "lazy" way. *Whenever a new variable v is selected to be assigned, a conflict is added between every pair of compatible values $\langle v, val \rangle, \langle w, val' \rangle$ that satisfies the following conditions:*

- *w is an unassigned variable other than u;*
- *val' belongs to the current domain of w;*
- *$\langle w, val' \rangle$ conflicts with at least one critical value with respect to $\langle v, val \rangle$.*

One can calculate that the suggested technique of updating of constraints takes $O(n^2d)$ consistency checks per iteration. We use the technique in our implementation of 2FC. We decided not to describe the method directly in the pseudocode because it reduces readability of the code and makes the correctness proof more complicated.

4 Theoretical Analysis

In this section we prove correctness of 2FC. We start from proving Lemma 1.

Proof of Lemma 1. By induction on n, the number of variables of Z. It is trivial for $n = 1$. For $n > 1$, assign v_n with a value val_n that belongs to its domain. Let Z' be a 2-CN obtained from Z by removing v_n and deleting from the domains of the rest of variables all values that are incompatible with $\langle v_n, val_n \rangle$. Observe the following properties of Z'.

- The domains of all variables of Z' are not empty. Really, an empty domain of some variable v in Z' would mean that $\langle v_n, val_n \rangle$ conflicts with all the values of the domain of v in Z in contradiction to the directional arc-consistency of Z.
- Z' is directionally arc-consistent with respect to the order $v_1, \dots, v_{n-1}$. Assume by contradiction that a value $\langle v_k, val \rangle$ is inconsistent with the domain of v_i, $i < k$. If the domain of v_i in Z' is the same as in Z, $\langle v_k, val \rangle$ is inconsistent with v_i in Z in contradiction to our assumption about directional arc-consistency of Z. Otherwise, one of the values of the domain of v_i is incompatible with $\langle v_n, val_n \rangle$, the other is incompatible with $\langle v_k, val \rangle$, while $\langle v_n, val_n \rangle$ and $\langle v_k, val \rangle$ are compatible. In this case we get contradiction with out assumption about directional path-consistency of Z.

– Z' is directionally path-consistent. For otherwise, if we have two compatible values $\langle v_k, val_k \rangle$ and $\langle v_l, val_l \rangle$ that wipe out the domain of some variable v_i, $(i < k, l)$, the same situation occurs in Z in contradiction to directional path-consistency of Z.

Thus Z' satisfies all conditions of the lemma and has $n-1$ variables, therefore it is soluble by the induction assumption. Let S be a solution of Z'. Note that all values of Z' are compatible with $\langle v_n, val_n \rangle$. Therefore $S \cup \{\langle v_n, val_n \rangle\}$ is a solution of Z. □.

The next lemma claims that every extended partial solution generated by 2FC satisfies the conditions of Lemma 1.

Lemma 2. *Every extended partial solution generated by 2FC induces a 2-CN without empty domains, directionally arc-consistent with respect to the chronological order of assignment of variables, and directionally path consistent with respect to the same order.*

Proof. By induction on the length n of the extended partial solution. It is clear that the lemma is valid for $n = 1$. For $n > 1$, let S be the considered extended partial solution and let $v_1, \ldots, v_n$ be the order according to which the variables were assigned. By the induction assumption, the extended partial solution obtained by removing v_n satisfies the conditions of the lemma. Therefore, if S violates these conditions then the values assigned to v_n violate either the directional arc-consistency or the directional path-consistency. Assume that the former holds. That is, a value val of assigned to v_n is inconsistent with all values assigned to v_k $(k < n)$. However, such a situation cannot happen because 2FC would remove val from the current domain of v_n when v_k has been assigned. For the latter, assume that a value val assigned to v_n, together with a compatible value val' assigned to some v_k are inconsistent with the set of values assigned to some v_i $(i < k, n)$. However, such a situation cannot happen as well because 2FC would add a conflict between $\langle v_k, val' \rangle$ and $\langle v_n, val \rangle$ when v_i was selected to be assigned. Thus the lemma holds for S. □

Now we are ready to claim the correctness of 2FC.

Theorem 1. *The 2FC algorithm is correct.*

Proof. To prove correctness, we have to prove that the algorithm terminates and also that it is sound and complete.

Termination is easy to verify by induction. If the underlying CN has 0 variables, the algorithm clearly terminates. Otherwise, 2FC selects a variable, assigns it with some partition class of its domain, and applies recursively to a CN created by the rest of variables (with updated constraints). By the induction assumption, every recursive application eventually finishes and also the number of partition classes in the first variable is finite so the algorithm terminates.

Soundness (solubility of an extended solution returned by 2FC) directly follows from Lemmas 1 and 2.

It follows from termination and soundness that 2FC always returns $FAIL$ when processes an insoluble CN. It remains to prove completeness, that is to show that 2FC always returns a solution when processes a soluble CN. In essence, all we have to show is that the additional conflicts generated by 2FC do not cause missing of a solution.

We prove completeness by induction on the number n of variables of the CN. Completeness follows immediately for $n = 1$. For $n > 1$, let v be the variable that 2FC selects to be assigned first. If the underlying CN is soluble then 2FC eventually assigns v with a set of values S that belongs to an extended solution. Then 2FC removes from the domains of the rest of variables all values that are inconsistent with S and adds conflicts between pairs of compatible values that wipe S out. Note that neither the removed values can be in the same solution with any value of S nor pairs of values that are made incompatible. Therefore 2FC is applied recursively to a soluble CN where it finds an extended solution by the induction assumption. □

5 Experimental Evaluation

It is not hard to show that 2FC explores $O(\lceil d/2 \rceil^n)$ nodes of the search tree and its running time is the bound multiplied by a polynomial. Clearly, this bound is much smaller than $O(d^n)$ upper bound for FC. However, we are interested to evaluate the practical merits of 2FC. To do this we compare in this section actual running times of 2FC and FC.

We implemented the algorithms in Microsoft Visual C++ 6.0 and tested them on a computer with CPU 2.4GHz and 0.2GB RAM. We used two measures of computation effort: the number of nodes visited and runtime (in seconds). For every tuple of parameters of the tested instances, the computation effort measures were obtained as average of 50 runs.

In our implementation, variables are ordered by the Fail-First heuristic [5] which takes first a variable with the smallest domain. The values of the variable being assigned are ordered according to the min-conflict heuristic, that is, values that conflict with the less number of values in the domains of unassigned variables are assigned first. (FC assigns the values one by one, while 2FC assigns them in pairs.)

We compared these algorithms on graph k-coloring problem and on randomly generated binary CNs.

Given a graph G with n vertices and k-colors, the CN that encodes the k-coloring problem for G has n variables corresponding to the vertices of G. The domain of every variable is $\{1, \ldots, k\}$. Pairs of variables that correspond to adjacent vertices of G are connected by the inequality constraint.

We generated 3 sets of instances: the first with 60 and 6 colors, the second with 45 vertices and 8 colors and the third with 30 vertices and 10 colors. For every set of instances we tried densities from 10% to 90% by steps of 5%.

The results of comparison of 2FC and FC on the first set of instances are shown on Figures 2 and 3. In this set of instances the phase transition region

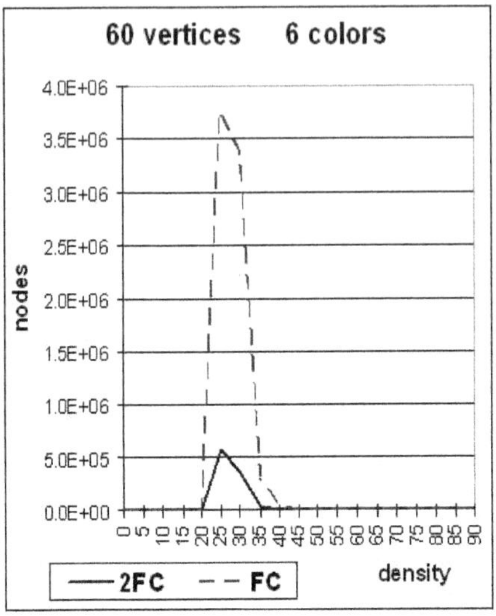

Fig. 2. 2FC vs. FC for graphs with 60 vertices and 6 colors (nodes visited)

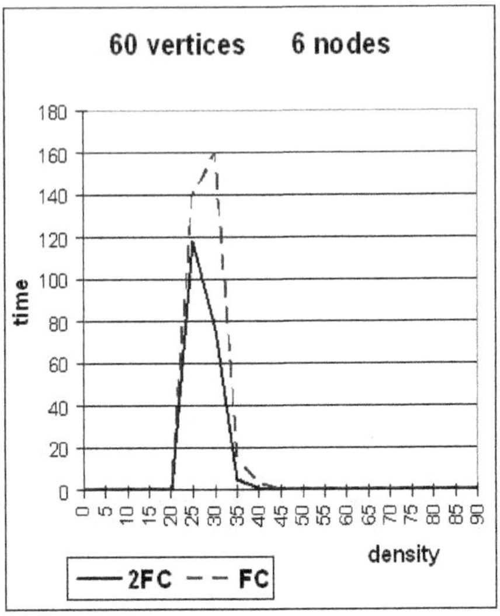

Fig. 3. 2FC vs. FC for graphs with 60 vertices and 6 colors (runtimes)

falls to the area of small density. Clearly, 2FC performs better than FC on this set of instances.

The results of comparison of 2FC and FC on the second set of instances are shown on Figures 4 and 5. In this experiment the graph that are most hard for coloring have an average density. Note that for denser graphs the rate of improvement of 2FC with respect to FC grows.

The results of comparison of 2FC and FC on the third set of instances are shown on Figures 6 and 7. In this experiments the phase transition region falls to the area of dense graphs. Note that here 2FC exhibits a larger factor of improvement as compared to the previous cases.

Comparing 2FC and FC on randomly generated CNs, we generated them using 4 parameters: the number of variables, the domain size, density, and tightness [6]. To generate a set of instances, we fixed the number of variables, the domain size, and the density and varied the tightness from 10% to 90% by steps of 5%.

In the first set of experiments, the generated CNs have 60 variables domains of size 10 and density 10%. Figures 8 and 9 compare the number of nodes visited and the runtimes, respectively. We can see that 2FC outperforms FC on this set of instances.

Unfortunately, on denser instances of randomly generated CNs, 2FC works worse than FC. Moreover, 2FC becomes worse and worse compared to FC as the underlying CN gets denser. To see this, consider the following two sets of sets of experiments (Figures 10, 11, 12, and 13). On the set of instances with density 0.2, 2FC continues to perform better in the number of nodes visited while spends more runtime. However, on the instances with density 0.8, it looks worse with respect to the both measures.

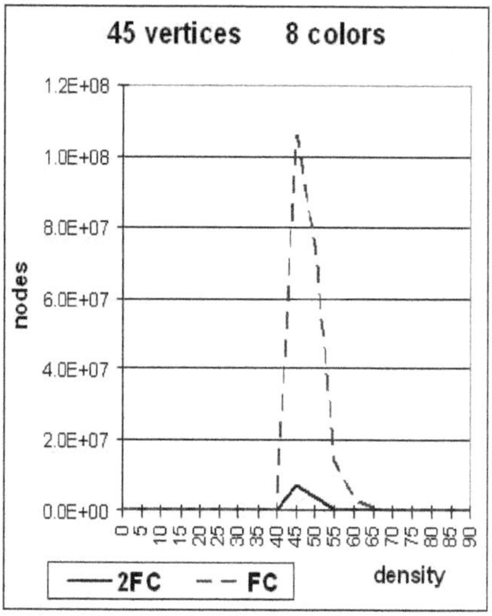

Fig. 4. 2FC vs. FC for graphs with 45 and 8 colors (nodes visited)

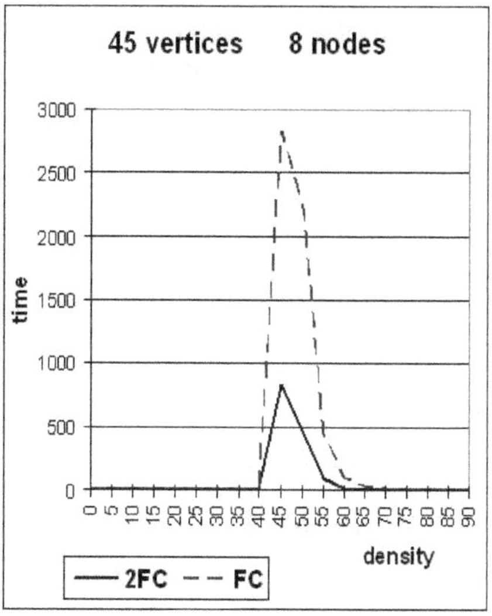

Fig. 5. 2FC vs. FC for graphs with 45 and 8 colors (runtimes)

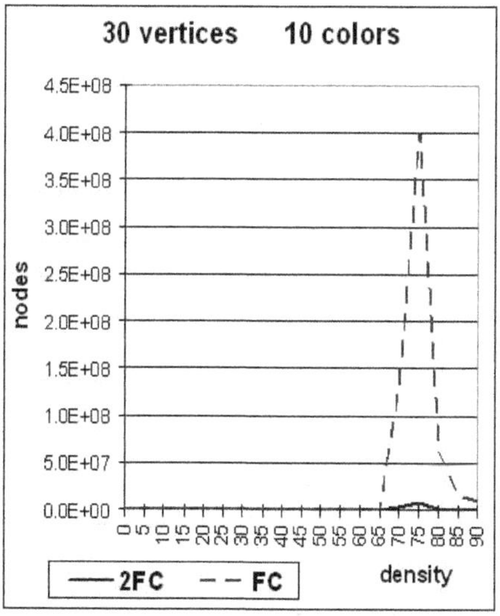

Fig. 6. 2FC vs. FC for graphs with 30 and 10 colors (nodes visited)

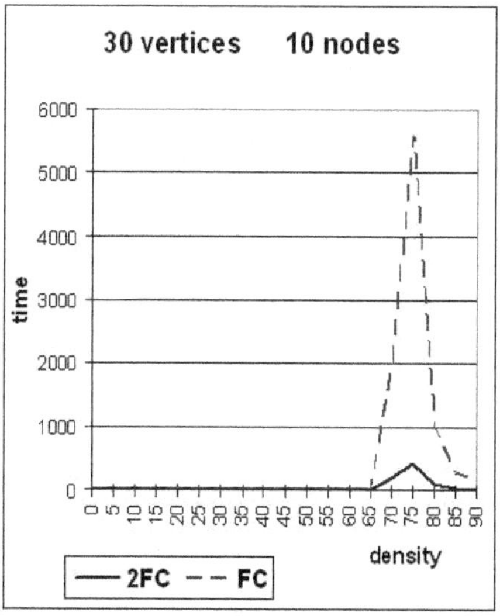

Fig. 7. 2FC vs. FC for graphs with 30 and 10 colors (runtimes)

Thus, according to our experiments, 2FC performs better than FC on graph coloring problems and non-dense instances of randomly generated CN, while works worse on denser random CNs.

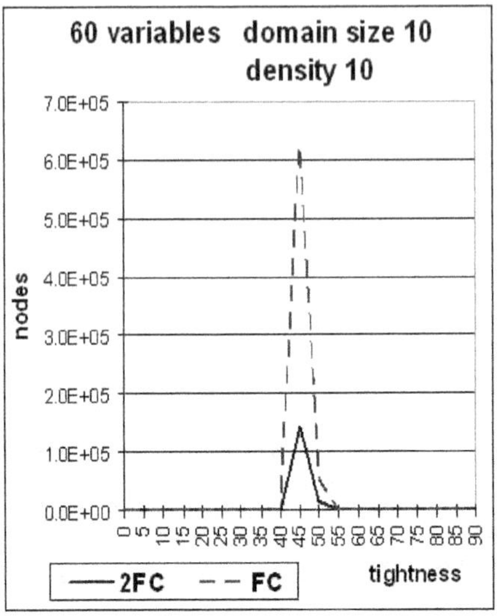

Fig. 8. 2FC vs. FC for CNs with 60 variables, domain size 10, and density 10 (nodes visited)

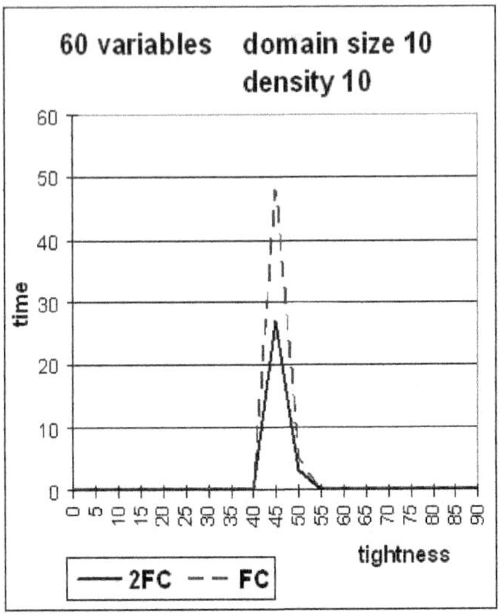

Fig. 9. 2FC vs. FC for CNs with 60 variables, domain size 10, and density 10 (runtimes)

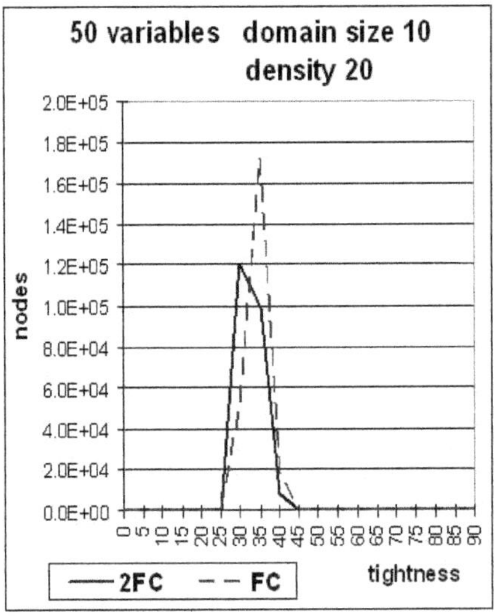

Fig. 10. 2FC vs. FC for CNs with 50 variables, domain size 10, and density 20 (nodes visited)

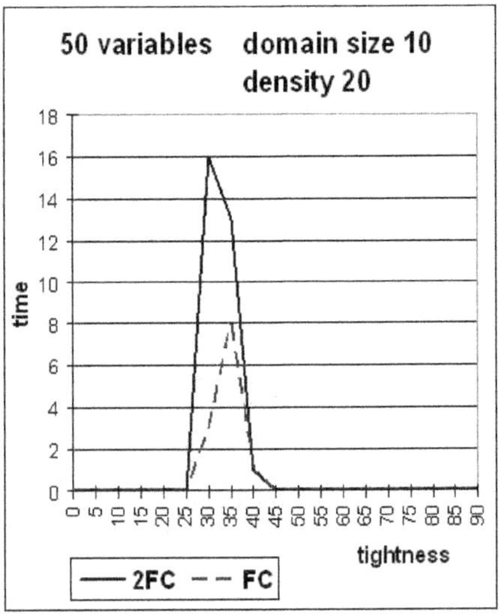

Fig. 11. 2FC vs. FC for CNs with 50 variables, domain size 10, and density 20 (runtimes)

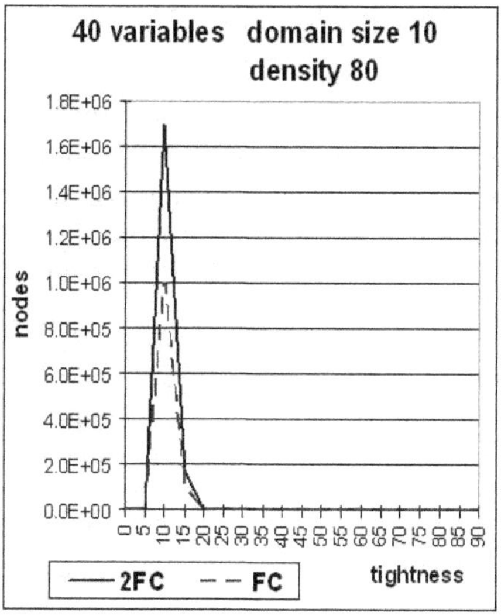

Fig. 12. 2FC vs. FC for CNs with 40 variables, domain size 10, and density 80 (nodes visited)

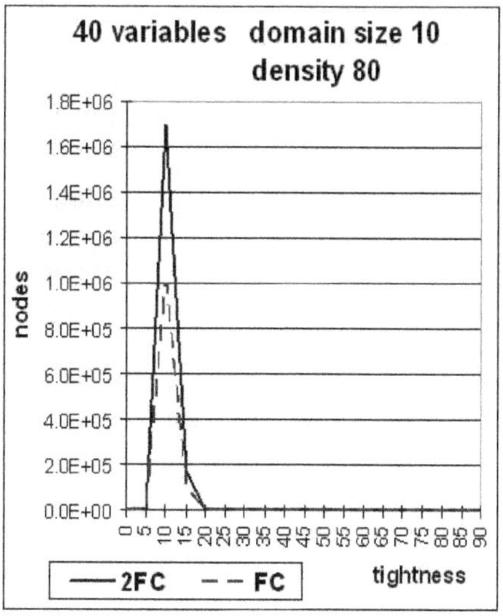

Fig. 13. 2FC vs. FC for CNs with 40 variables, domain size 10, and density 80 (runtimes)

6 Discussion

We introduced the 2FC algorithm which is based on the idea of assigning a variable with two values instead of one. In this section we discuss possible applications of the proposed approach and directions of further development.

According to our experimental results, 2FC performs very well on graph k-coloring problem. This result suggests the possibility of combining the proposed approach (of assigning a vertex with 2 colors) with branch-and-bound algorithms that find chromatic numbers of graphs (like [7]). The proposed approach could also be useful in the area of resource allocation problems because many of such problems, like timetabling [8], have binary constraint networks with inequality constraints.

On the other hand, 2FC is not very successful on random constraint networks. A natural way of improvement of its pruning ability is replacing FC by MAC, that is design of 2MAC. We expect that 2MAC would behave better with respect to MAC than 2FC does with respect to FC. This is because maintaining arc-consistency has a better ability than FC to utilize the conflicts that are added after every new assignment.

An interesting direction of further research is the application of the approach to CNs with non-binary constraints. Note that the application cannot be straightforward because solving a 2-CN with non-binary constraints is NP-complete in general (it can be shown by reduction from SAT). A possible way to recognize dead-ends early is maintaining the current extended partial solution S together with a solution T of the CN induced by S. Every time when S grows by assigning a new variable, T must grow also. Solving a 2-CN with non-binary constraints at every iteration of the algorithm could require too much time, therefore one has to develop heuristic methods of quick solving of such CNs.

2FC could also be useful in dynamic environments where solutions are frequently discarded because of updating of constraints. The set of values returned by 2FC can contain many solutions and they can be efficiently extracted. Therefore, there is a chance that once a single solution is discarded, another solution could be found instantly without applying search.

Finally, there is an intriguing connection of the proposed approach with the technique of bucket elimination [9]. In its simplest form, the principle of bucket elimination states that whenever there is an unassigned variable v conflicting with at most two other unassigned variables, variable v can be eliminated. To preserve consistency, conflicts must be added between the pairs of values that wipe out the current domain of v. Note that the described bucket elimination technique as well as assigning a variable with two values have the following common paradigm: *assign a variable v with a subset s of its domain such that every minimal consistent partial solution on the "future" variables that wipes s out has the size at most 2.* Bucket elimination is an "extremal" realization of the paradigm where a variable is assigned with the whole domain. Assigning a variable with only one value is another case of extremal realization. Then assigning a variable with two values can be considered as some "intermediate" case. Continuing the reasoning, we derive that there may be other "intermediate" realizations of the paradigm. For example, a more flexible version of bucket elimination can be considered, where a variable is assigned with a subset of its values that conflict with at most two unassigned variables.

References

1. Jeavons, P., Cohen, D., Cooper, M.: Constraints, consistency, and closure. Artificial Intelligence **101** (1998) 251–265
2. Eppstein, D.: Improved algorithms for 3-coloring, 3-edge coloring and constraint satisfaction. In: SODA-2001. (2001) 329–337
3. Angelsmark, O., Jonsson, P.: Improved algorithms for counting solutions in constraint satisfaction problems. In: CP 2003. (2003) 81–95
4. Dechter, R.: Constraint Processing. Morgan Kaufmann Publishers (2003)
5. Haralick, R.M., Elliott, G.: Increasing tree search efficiency for constraint satisfaction problems. Artificial Intelligence **14** (1980) 263–313
6. Prosser, P.: An empirical study of phase transition in binary constraint satisfaction problems. Artificial Intelligence **81** (1996) 81–109
7. Caramia, M., Dell'Olmo, P.: Constraint propagation in graph coloring. Journal of Heuristics **8** (2002) 83–107
8. Meisels, A., Schaerf, A.: Modelling and solving employee timetabling problems. Annals of Mathematics and Artificial Intelligence **39** (2003) 41–59
9. Dechter, R.: Bucket elimination: A unifying framework for reasoning. Artificial Intelligence **113** (1999) 41–85

Analysis of Heuristic Synergies

Richard J. Wallace

Cork Constraint Computation Centre and Department of Computer Science,
University College Cork, Cork, Ireland
r.wallace@4c.ucc.ie

Abstract. "Heuristic synergy" refers to improvements in search performance when the decisions made by two or more heuristics are combined. This paper considers combinations based on products and quotients, and a less familiar form of combination based on weighted sums of ratings from a set of base heuristics, some of which result in definite improvements in performance. Then, using recent results from a factor analytic study of heuristic performance, which had demonstrated two main effects of heuristics involving either buildup of contention or look-ahead-induced failure, it is shown that heuristic combinations are effective when they are able to balance these two actions. In addition to elucidating the basis for heuristic synergy (or lack thereof), this work suggests that the task of understanding heuristic search depends on the analysis of these two basic actions.

1 Introduction

Combining variable ordering heuristics that are based on different features sometimes results in better performance that can be obtained by either heuristic working in isolation. Perhaps the best-known instance of this is the domain/degree heuristic of [1]. Recently, further examples have been found based on weighted sums of rated selections produced by a set of heuristics [2].

As yet, we do not have a good understanding of the basis for such heuristic synergies. Nor can we predict in general which heuristics will synergise. In fact, until now there has been no proper study of this phenomena, and perhaps not even a proper recognition that it is a phenomenon. The present paper initiates a study of heuristic synergies. A secondary purpose is to test the weighted sum strategy in a setting that is independent of its original machine learning context.

The failure to consider this phenomenon stems in part from our inability to classify heuristic strategies beyond citing the problem features used by a heuristic. However, recent work has begun to shown how to delineate basic strategies, and with this work we can begin to understand how heuristics work in combination. Although the work is still in its early stages, it is already possible to predict which heuristics will synergise in combination and to understand to some extent why this occurs.

The analysis to be presented depends heavily on the factor analysis of heuristic performance, i.e. of the efficiency of search when a given heuristic is used to order the variables. This approach is based on inter-problem variation. If the action of two heuristics is due to a common strategy, then the pattern of variation should be similar. Using this method, it has been possible to show that, for certain simple problem classes, such

B. Hnich et al. (Eds.): CSCLP 2005, LNAI 3978, pp. 73–87, 2006.

variation can be ascribed to only two factors, which can in turn be interpreted as basic heuristic actions [3].

The next section describes the basic methodology. Section 3 gives results for heuristic combinations involving products and quotients. Section 4 gives results for weighted sums of heuristic ratings. Section 5 gives a brief overview of factor analysis as well as methodological details for the present work and gives the basic results of a factor analysis of variable ordering heuristics and their interpretation. Section 6 uses these results to predict successes and failures of heuristic combinations. Section 7 considers extensions using more advanced heuristics. Section 8 gives conclusions.

2 Description of Methods

The basic analyses in this paper used a set of well-known variable ordering heuristics that could be combined in various ways. These are listed below together with the abbreviations used in the rest of the paper.

- Minimum domain size (dom, dm). Choose a variable with the smallest current domain size.
- Maximum forward degree (fd). Choose a variable with the largest number of neighbors (variables whose nodes are adjacent to the chosen variable in the constraint graph) within the set of uninstantiated variables.
- Maximum backward degree (bkd). Choose the variable with largest number of neighbors in the set of instantiated variables.
- Maximum static degree (stdeg, dg). Choose a variable with the largest number neighbors (i.e. the variable of highest degree).

In most cases, ties were broken according to the lexical order of the variable labels. In such cases, max forward and max backward degree are both fixed-order heuristics, as is max static degree.

The initial tests were done with homogeneous random CSPs because these are easy to generate according to different parameter patterns. Problems were generated according to a probability-of-inclusion model for adding constraints, domain elements and constraint tuples, but where selection was repeated until the number of elements matched the expected value for the given probability. In all cases generation began with a spanning tree to ensure that the constraint graph was connected. Density as given in this paper was calculated as the proportion of additional edges added to the graph. Typically, there were 100 problems in a set, although similar results were found in some cases for sets of 500 problems. Problem parameters were chosen so that problems were in a critical complexity region of the parameter space.

Some further tests were based on geometric problems, which are random problems with small-world characteristics. Geometric problems are generated by choosing n points at random within the unit square to represent the n variables, and then connecting all pairs of variables whose points lie within a threshold distance. In this case, connectivity was ensured by checking for connected components, and if there were more than one, adding an edge between the two variables in different components separated by the shortest distance.

Unless otherwise noted, the tests in this paper were based on the MAC-3 algorithm. The basic measures of performance were, (i) nodes visited during search, (ii) constraint checks. In these experiments, both measures produced similar patterns of differences, so for brevity the results in this paper are restricted to search nodes.

Synergy was evaluated for two kinds of strategy. The first type of strategy was to take products and quotients of the basic heuristics, as is done in the well-known domain/degree heuristics. (For quotients and products involving backward degree, when this component was zero, a value of one was used instead.) The second was to combine evaluations of individual heuristics into weighted sums. This strategy was derived from one used in a contemporary learning system [2]; to my knowledge there has been no examination of its efficacy outside this context. In addition to being an alternative strategy for obtaining improved heuristics, this method is useful in the present context because it may allow more quantitative assessment of synergistic effects.

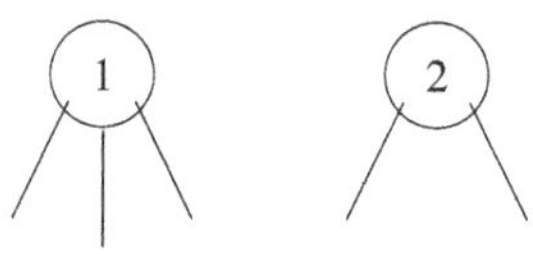

$\text{Domain}_1 = \{a, b, c\}$

$\text{Domain}_2 = \{x\}$

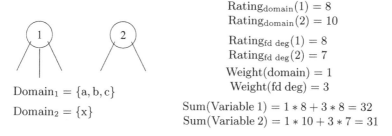

$$\text{Rating}_{\text{domain}}(1) = 8$$
$$\text{Rating}_{\text{domain}}(2) = 10$$
$$\text{Rating}_{\text{fd deg}}(1) = 8$$
$$\text{Rating}_{\text{fd deg}}(2) = 7$$
$$\text{Weight(domain)} = 1$$
$$\text{Weight(fd deg)} = 3$$
$$\text{Sum(Variable 1)} = 1 * 8 + 3 * 8 = 32$$
$$\text{Sum(Variable 2)} = 1 * 10 + 3 * 7 = 31$$

Fig. 1. Example of a weighted sum calculation for two variables (labeled 1 and 2) based on two heuristics, minimum domain size and maximum forward degree. Edges from nodes 1 and 2 represent adjacent uninstantiated neighbors. Variable 1 has a domain of size 3, Variable 2 of size 1.

Weighted sums were obtained by assigning each individual heuristic a weight, then at each choice point allowing all heuristics to rate the choices (variables) beginning with a score of 10 as the best rating, 9 for the next-best rating, 8 for the next, and so forth down to a minimum of 1. Thus, if the current domain sizes were 1, 2, 2, 3, 4, 4, 5, the corresponding ratings for min domain would be 10, 9, 9, 8, 7, 7, 6. The ratings were then combined for each choice by multiplying the rating for each heuristic by its weight and adding the products. The variable with the highest weighted sum was the one chosen (again, ties were broken lexically by choosing the variable with the smallest integer label).

An example of this process is shown in Figure 1. Here two variables (among others not shown) are rated by two heuristics, min domain and max forward degree. Min domain gives its highest rating to Variable 2 and a lower rating to Variable 1. Max forward degree gives a higher rating to Variable 1 than to 2. (Note that although the these latter ratings are not determined completely by the information in the figure, they must be one apart.) Under the assumption of a weight of 1 for min domain and a weight of 3 for max forward degree, the weighted sums for Variables 1 and 2 are 32 and 31, respectively; in this case, therefore, Variable 1 would be chosen over Variable 2.

3 Heuristic Combinations Based on Quotients and Products

The next two sections present a number of empirical results, some of which are fairly striking, that constitute a body of findings that must be accounted for by any explanation of heuristic synergies. At the same time, these results provide a number of hints about the nature of the variables that may underlie synergistic and non-synergistic effects.

Several examples of quotients and products based on the four simple heuristics described in the last section are presented in Table 1. Among them only two exhibit synergistic effects, and the only marked effect is produced by the well-known domain/forward degree heuristic. Interestingly, for this set of problems domain/static degree did not give better performance than static degree alone, in contrast to domain/forward degree.

Table 1. Results for Products and Quotients

simple heuristic	nodes	combination	nodes
dom	11,334	min dom/stdeg	2076
fd	2625	min dom/fd	**1621**
bkd	27,391	min dom/bkwd	15081
stdeg	2000	max fd/bkwd	2886
		max stdeg * fd	2417
		max bkwd * fd	**2447**

Mean nodes per problem. <50,10,0.184,0.32> problems.
Bold entries show results superior to either heuristic alone.

4 Heuristic Combinations Based on Weighted Sums

Table 2 gives results, in terms of nodes searched, for six "individual" heuristics and for combinations of these heuristics using the technique of weighted sums described in Section 2. For these tests, heuristics were given equal weights. These data include examples of heuristic synergy as well as non-synergy.

Note that in these tests the domain/degree quotients were used as components with respect to the weighted sums in addition to the four simple heuristics, and that this form of combination sometimes gave better results than the quotient alone. At the same time, such combinations were not superior to the best weighted sums based on the simpler heuristics.

There are a number of significant findings in this table:

- Some combinations do better, in terms of number of search nodes, than any heuristic used by itself. Some do even better than the best heuristic-quotient tested, which was min domain/forward-degree.
- Simply combining heuristics is not sufficient to obtain synergy; only certain combinations are effective.

- The effectiveness of heuristic combinations does not correlate well with the effectiveness of the individual components.
- The effectiveness of heuristic combinations is not related to the inclusion of any particular component in and of itself.
- The best results for combinations of two heuristics were as good as the best results for combinations of more than two heuristics.

Table 2. Selected Results for Weighted Sums

heuristic	nodes	combination	nodes	combination	nodes
dom	11,334	dm/dg+dm/fd	1800	dom+fd+bkwd	**1430**
dm/dg	2076	dm/fd+fd	**1304**	dom+bkwd+stdeg	1822
dm/fd	1621	dom+dm/fd	1890	fd+bkwd+stdeg	1991
fd	2625	dom+fd	**1317**		
bkd	27,391	fd+stdeg	2344	dom+dm/dg+fd+bkwd	1657
stdeg	2000	bkwd+stdeg	**1876**	dom+dm/dg+fd+stdeg	**1374**
				dom+dm/dg+bkwd+stdeg	1834
		dom+dm/dg+stdeg	1654		
		dom+fd+stdeg	**1374**	dom+dm/dg+fd+bkd+stdeg	**1470**

Mean nodes per problem. <50,10,0.184,0.32> problems. Bold entries show results that are better than any individual heuristic. In these tests component heuristics were given equal weights.

It is important to note in this connection that weighted sums gave better results than tie-breaking strategies based on the same heuristics. For comparison, here are results on the same set of problems with four tie-breaking strategies:

- min domain, ties broken by max forward degree: 3101
- min domain, ties broken by max static degree: 3155
- forward degree, ties broken by min domain: 2239
- static degree, ties broken by min domain: 1606

Naturally, tie-breaking does reduce the size of the search tree in comparison with the primary heuristic when used alone, but not as much as some heuristic combinations.

Another significant result is that, when combinations of *two* heuristics showed a high degree of synergy, equal weights gave better results than unequal weights, and in these cases performance deteriorated as a function of the difference in weights. This is shown in Table 3. In cases in which weight combinations did not synergise or synergised weakly in comparison with the best individual heuristic in the combination, unequal weights sometimes gave some improvement, although the effect was never marked. An additional finding is that when weights were unequal, there were sometimes marked asymmetries or biases in the effect of weighting one heuristic more than the other. Evidence of this can be seen in each of the three columns of data to the right in the table. In the other pair (dom+fd), the effects of weights were highly symmetric, so that the increase in search effort rose in concert with the degree of difference in the weights regardless of which heuristic was more highly weighted.

Table 3. Two-Heuristic Combinations with Different Weights

wt ratio	dom+fd	dom+stdeg	stdeg+bkwd	fd+stdeg
1:1	1317	1427	1876	2344
1:2	1433	**1420**	2471	2455
2:1	1405	1620	**1852**	**2235**
1:3	1652	1454	3054	2458
3:1	1651	1885	**1812**	**2223**
1:5	2033	1557	3960	2458
5:1	2368	2504	**1816**	**2223**

Notes. Mean nodes per problem. <50,10,0.184,0.32> problems. The weight ratio, read from left to right, corresponds to the weights given to each heuristic each combination, again reading from left to right. For ease of comparison, the results for equal weights are repeated in the first row of the table, where cases of synergy are underlined. Bold entries show results that are better than the 1:1 condition.

In contrast to the two-heuristic case, when three or more heuristics were used in combination, the best results were obtained when one of the three was weighted more heavily than the others. This is shown in Tables 4 and 5. An interesting feature of these results is that in each group, the best performance occurs when a particular heuristic is weighted more strongly than the others. For example, in Table 4, for the dom+stdeg+fd combination, all of the best results occurred when dom was weighted more highly than the other two heuristics. Similarly, for the second and third combinations, the best results occurred when stdeg was more highly weighted. In Table 5, all of the best results ($<$ 1400 nodes) occurred when fd was highly weighted, and all results that bettered the equal-weight condition involved weighting fd and/or stdeg more highly than the other heuristics. (Note also that in the one case where weighting one of these heuristics more strongly did not better the equal-weight condition [third line from bottom in Table 5], dom and d/deg were also weighted highly.)

The geometric problems had 50 variables, a distance parameter = 0.4 (giving an average density of around 0.3), $|d| = 10$, and tightness = 0.18. These were fairly easy for most, but not all, heuristics, with greater relative differences than those found with the homogeneous random problems. Nonethess, synergies could be readily obtained (Table 6). Thus, the effects generalise to at least some structured problems.

Since the main concern of this work is to explain heuristic performance, even if the methods described here are too expensive to be of practical use, it is of interest to understand why search is made more efficient - in terms of nodes (and constraint checks). In fact, since the effects shown in Tables 2-5 are rather modest, in these cases the decrease in search nodes is offset by the expense of calculating weights. In addition, calculating weighted sums has an inherently higher time complexity than simpler forms of heuristic assessment due to the sorting requirement. However, it is naturally of interest to see if the effects observed here will scale up. Some preliminary data on this point have been obtained for large 'easy' problems (<200,6,0.054,0.2>). For these problems min domain/forward degree gave a mean of 3886 search nodes, while the combination of five heuristics given in Table 2 gave a mean of 1293; in this case there was also a 50%

reduction in average time. Evidently, then, for some problems the effects can scale up, so if efficient means can be found for computing weighted sums (or even approximations), this technique may be of practical importance.

Table 4. Three Heuristics with Different Weights

wt ratio	dom+stdeg+fd	dom+stdeg+dm/dg	dom+stdeg+bkwd
1:1:1	1374	1654	1822
3:1:1	**1372**	1947	2229
1:3:1	1519	**1406**	**1510**
1:1:3	1717	1923	2847
3:3:1	**1348**	**1499**	**1548**
3:1:3	**1331**	2043	2952
1:3:3	1767	**1570**	**1791**

Mean nodes per problem. <50,10,0.184,0.32> problems. Other conventions as in Table 3.

Table 5. Five Heuristics with Different Weights

wt ratio					nodes
dom	stdeg	dm/dg	fd	bkwd	
1	1	1	1	1	1470
3	1	1	1	1	1635
1	3	1	1	1	**1409**
1	1	3	1	1	1649
1	1	1	3	1	**1332**
1	1	1	1	3	1741
3	3	1	1	1	**1448**
1	3	3	1	1	1481
1	1	3	3	1	**1401**
1	1	1	3	3	**1414**
3	1	1	3	1	**1343**
1	3	1	3	1	**1376**
3	3	3	1	1	1562
3	3	1	3	1	**1342**
3	1	3	1	3	1933

<50,10,0.184,0.32> problems. Other conventions as in Table 3.

5 Factor Analysis of Heuristic Performance

We turn now to the task of determining why search performance is sometimes improved (and sometimes worsened) by combining heuristics. To this end, a statistical technique called "factor analysis" was employed.

Factor analysis is a technique for determining whether a set of measurements can be accounted for by a smaller number of "factors". Strictly speaking, the notion of a factor is solely statistical and refers either to a repackaging of the original patterns of variation (variance) across individuals and measurements or to a set of linear relations that can account for the original statistical results. However, since variation must have causes, this technique if used carefully can yield considerable insight into the causes underlying the measurements obtained. In other words, the factors may be closely related to underlying variables that are sufficient to account for much of the variance.

Table 6. Results for Weighted Sums with Geometric Problems

		combinations			
heuristic	nodes	dom+fd		fd+stdeg	
		ratio	nodes	ratio	nodes
dom	11,222	1:1	**399**	1:1	570
dm/dg	368	1:3	**541**	1:3	554
dm/fd	372	3:1	**337**	3:1	586
fd	642	1:5	**552**	1:5	555
stdeg	550	5:1	**337**	5:1	592

Mean nodes per problem. 50-variable geometric problems.
Bold entries show synergies.

The strategy used here was to see, (i) if patterns of variation in search effort could be ascribed to a relatively few factors in the factor analysis, (ii) whether such factors could, in turn, be ascribed to any definable causal variables, (iii) whether such variables, if discovered, could serve to explain the patterns of synergy or non-synergy for heuristic combinations.

5.1 Resumé of Factor Analysis

The basic factor analysis model can be written as a set of linear relations of the form (taken from [4]):

$$z_j = a_{j1}F_1 + a_{j2}F_2 + \ldots + a_{jm}F_m + d_jU_j \quad (j = 1, 2, \ldots, n)$$

for the jth measure, or

$$z_{ij} = a_{j1}F_{i1} + a_{j2}F_{i2} + \ldots + a_{jm}F_{im} + d_jU_{ij} \quad (j = 1, 2, \ldots, n)$$

for the ith individual on the jth measure, where the F_i are *common factors*, i.e. factors that are common to some of the original measures, and U_j is a *unique factor* associated with measure j. Usually $m << n$. The coefficients a_{jk} are often referred to as "loadings". The square of the coefficient of U_j is referred to as the uniqueness, because this is the portion of the variance unique to measure j, and the coefficient itself is called the unique factor loading.

Factor analysis is based on a matrix of correlations, derived from a sample of n values for each measure. For example, if the measurements were scores on cognitive or personality tests, then the correlation between test i and test j would be based on scores from n individuals. In the present experiments, the individuals are individual problems, and each measurement is an efficiency measure, such as search nodes or constraint checks, for a given heuristic. A factor extraction process is applied, based on a standard method of approximation. The present work uses the method of maximum likelihood, which starts from a hypothesis of m common factors and determines maximum-likelihood estimates of them using the original correlation matrix [5].

Factor analysis methods such as the maximum likelihood method obtain factors that are uncorrelated with each other. In this case, each a_{jk} above is identical to the correlation coefficient holding between z_j and F_k [4].

Once obtained, the factors (which constitute a basis for a space of m dimensions) can be rotated according to various criteria. Here the varimax rotation was used; this method tries to eliminate negative loadings while producing maximal loadings on the smallest possible set of measures.

The interpretation of patterns of differences cannot assume that causal factors behave additively, only that patterns of variation can be derived from additive combinations. Factor analysis, therefore, can only identify common sources of variation whose interpretation requires further investigation.

5.2 Methodology

The software used in these analyses was System R, which was downloaded from

http://www.r-project.org.

In this package, the factanal function was used for the factor analysis.

As already noted, maximum likelihood methods require the number of factors as input. Since the number of significant factors was not known beforehand, various numbers of factors were tested, first, to determine at what point factor extraction ceased to account for any significant part of the variance, second, to determine which of these factors gave strong, reliable results. The first kind of test can be taken as setting an upper bound on the number of useful factors.

If there are other sources of variation than the ones emphasized here, since they are less important in their effects and less reliable across experiments, they are likely to be related to features of specific problem sets interacting with vagaries of the search process. In addition, the possible existence of further factors does not necessarily diminish the importance of the ones demonstrated here. (In other words, the explanatory process may have to be extended, but it will not need to backtrack if the arguments for the factors described here are cogent.)

5.3 Factor Patterns for CSP Heuristics and Their Interpretation

Table 7 shows selected results for an analysis based on 12 heuristics (described more fully in [3]). (The heuristics not included in the table were mainly diagnostic pseudo-heuristics: the FFx series of [6] and a variable ordering heuristic based on maximizing the summed "promise" across the values of a domain, derived from [7].) On the left are results from the basic experiment with the same set of random problems used in the present work. In this case, the analysis indicated that there were two major factors, but that min domain and max backward degree had idiosyncratic patterns of variation, reflected in their high uniqueness. Further experiments showed that the latter were due to random choices made at the top of the search tree; this occurs because for these heuristics there is no distinction among variables at the start of search. The results of one of these experiments are shown on the right hand side of the table. In this test, for each measurement the first three choices were in lexical order; thereafter, a particular heuristic was used. In this experiment, therefore, the effect of initial random selections was equalized. As a result, all heuristics had moderate to high loadings on two major factors, and the proportion of the total variance accounted for by these two factors was 0.95.

Table 7. Factor Analysis for CSP heuristics

heuristic	heuristic alone				3 lexical, heuristic			
	nodes	factor 1	factor 2	unique	nodes	factor 1	factor 2	unique
dom	11334	0.146	0.281	**0.900**	19587	**0.804**	0.565	0.034
fd	2625	0.443	**0.873**	0.042	9551	0.602	**0.796**	0.005
bkd	27391	0.107	0.224	**0.938**	37536	**0.708**	0.488	0.261
stdeg	2000	0.486	**0.835**	0.067	7980	0.648	**0.752**	0.015
dm/dg	2076	**0.913**	0.394	0.011	7712	**0.752**	0.652	0.010
dm/fd	1621	**0.909**	0.404	0.010	6473	**0.744**	0.660	0.011
dg*fd	2418	0.436	**0.897**	0.005	8567	0.626	**0.775**	0.008

Notes. <50,10,0.184,0.32> problems. Loadings ≥ 0.7 are shown in bold.

Various lines of evidence suggest the following interpretation of these factors (discussed at length in [3] [8]). One factor appears to be based on buildup of contention that results in eventual failure; heuristics such as min domain and backward degree load highly on it (when confounding variables are removed), as well as the FF series of [6]. The other factor appears to emphasize failure among future variables, so heuristics such as max forward degree and other look-ahead heuristics load highly on it. These have been tentatively designated as "contention" and "look-ahead" factors, respectively. It is of interest to note that both act as fail-first strategies, since the same factor pattern was found for problems with the same parameters that had no solutions. It is also important to bear in mind that the factor analysis guarantees that the factors are uncorrelated, which is a further argument for positing two independent actions underlying the different heuristics.

6 Factor Analysis Factors and Heuristic Synergies

6.1 Synergies with MAC

If we reconsider the results of Tables 1 and 2 in the light of this analysis, we see that successful weighted sums were composed of heuristics that load on each of the two major factors. This leads to a simple rule for predicting synergy or the lack of it: paired heuristics that load most heavily on separate factors will synergise, while pairs of heuristics that load most heavily on the same factor will not. This rule was verified in more extensive testing. For example, for weighted sums based on pairs of heuristics with equal weights, this rule was verified for all fifteen pairings of the original set of six heuristics (Table 8).

Table 8. Predicted and Actual Synergies for Equal-Weight Pairs

heuristics	first	second	compound
dom+fd	11,334	2625	**1317**
dom+bkwd	11,334	27,391	12,521
dom+stdg	11,334	2000	**1427**
dom+dm/dg	11,334	2076	2327
dom+dm/fd	11,334	1621	1890
fd+bkwd	2625	27,391	**1962**
fd+stdg	2625	2000	2344
fd+dm/dg	2625	2076	**1369**
fd+dm/fd	2625	1621	**1304**
bkwd+stdg	27,391	2000	**1876**
bkwd+dm/dg	27,391	2076	2436
bkwd+dm/fd	27,391	1621	1861
stdg+dm/dg	2000	2076	**1527**
stdg+dm/fd	2000	1621	**1386**
dm/dg+dm/fd	2076	1621	1800

Mean nodes per problem. <50,10,0.184,0.32> problems. Italicised entries are predicted synergy based on factor loadings. Bold entries show actual synergistic effects.

This rule is also consistent with the two cases of synergy among the products and quotients (cf. Table 2). However, for quotients there appears to be a further (reasonable) condition: that both the numerator and denominator favor selections consistent with those favored by the original heuristic. This consideration accounts for the failure to find synergy with the max forward degree/backward degree heuristic, although the components load most heavily on different factors. In this case, choosing according to this heuristic will favor variables with larger forward degrees, which accords with this component heuristic, but it will also favor variables with smaller backward degrees, which is counter to this component heuristic.

Evidence that the *balance* between the two factors is important can be found in Tables 3-5. This, in fact, seems to explain both the decline in quality for the two-heuristic combinations when the weights are made unequal (Table 3) and the distinguished heuristic phenomenon that was noted in the data shown in Table 4. In each case, the single heuristic that loaded on a different factor from the other two heuristics was the one that needed to be weighted more strongly. A similar phenomenon seems to be involved in the pattern of results shown in Table 5.

6.2 Synergies with FC

Striking instances of synergy can be obtained by using forward checking instead of MAC. For forward checking with random CSPs, it has been found that look-ahead heuristics show a marked fall-off in efficiency. Naturally, there is an increase in number of search nodes for all heuristics in comparison with the results for MAC, but while the increase is by an order of magnitude for the contention heuristics, it is by three to four orders of magnitude for the look-ahead heuristics, as shown in Table 9.

Table 9. Performance of Forward Checking

heuristic	nodes
min domain	212,389
min dom/stdeg	32,336
min dom/fwddeg	31,138
max forward degree	38,568,409
max static degree	2,450,958

Notes. Basic heuristics and selected quotients. Means for <50,10,0.184,0.32> problems.

Despite this drastic loss in efficiency for one class of heuristics, the rule of combination presented above continues to hold, as shown in Table 10. Thus, despite the fact that for these problems forward checking with max forward degree required more than 10^7 nodes on average, when this heuristic was combined with min domain, it sometimes produced an order-of-magnitude improvement with respect to the latter, which was the best individual heuristic in this combination. In this case synergy based on weighted sums of paired heuristics is most marked when the weights are unequal so as to favor the contention heuristic.

Table 10. Two-Heuristic Combinations with Forward Checking

wt ratio	dom+fd	dom+stdeg	dm/dg+fd
1:1	234,936	125,850	120,489
3:1	37,041	39,895	33,884
5:1	38,006	40,260	31,586
7:1	45,062	45,996	31,252

Notes. Mean nodes per problem. <50,10, 0.184,0.32> problems.

6.3 Assessment of Weighted-Sum Strategies in Terms of Heuristic Policies

A more detailed analysis of heuristic quality can be made by assessing heuristic performance in terms of adherence to optimal policies. In addition to the overall policy of minimizing effort, there are two basic sub-policies, depending on whether search is currently on a solution path or in an insoluble subtree. In the former case, the optimal policy is to maximize the likelihood of remaining on the solution path ("promise" policy); in the latter, the optimal policy is to find a refutation of the original mistake as quickly as possible ("fail-first" policy).

Although the two policies cannot be realized in practice (nor can the policy of finding a solution after a minimum number of search nodes), we can still measure adherence to these policies and thereby compare heuristics in these terms. For the promise policy, we have an absolute measure when probabilities can be reasonably assigned to alternative assignments, obtained by summing probability products at each level of search (described in [9]); for the fail-first policy, we can obtain a relative measure by averaging the sizes of all the insoluble subtrees (cf. [10]). The latter measure can be obtained for either the entire search tree or the part of the tree explored before finding the first solution. Although the promise measure necessarily involves the entire search tree, a rough measure can be obtained for the part of the tree explored by counting the number of "mistakes" (the number of times an insoluble subtree was entered).

For measures of overall efficiency we use, as before, the number of search nodes. We also include the number of failures, which has been suggested recently as an alternative measure of overall performance [11].

Table 11 gives data for promise and fail-first measures, together with measures of overall efficiency, and some descriptive measures of heuristic performance. This analysis involved max forward degree, min domain and the weighted sum of the two (with equal weights; cf. Table 2). These data indicate that this heuristic combination shows better adherence to both the fail-first and promise policies than the component heuristics acting alone.

The descriptive measures suggest that the heuristic combination tends to compromise on the beneficial effects of the two components, since the measures for the former always fall between those for the latter. This is particularly interesting in connection with the consistent superiority demonstrated in the quality measures.

7 Limits to Synergy?

Now that some understanding of heuristic combination has been obtained, an important question is whether this knowledge can be used to even greater effect than in the tests reported in earlier sections. Two kinds of strategies have been tried, using weighted sums. The first is based on the finding that if results for weighted sums are added to the factor analysis, they are usually found to load more heavily on one factor than the other. Hence, according to the rule for combining heuristics to produce synergies, it should be possible by appropriate weighting to combine a given weighted sum that loads most heavily on one factor with a basic heuristic (or weighted sum) that loads most heavily on the other. The second strategy was to combine more powerful heuristics that show differences in loadings, to see if synergistic effects can be obtained that are greater than those found by combining simpler heuristics.

Although heuristic combinations tend to load more heavily on one factor than another (in most cases on the contention factor), it was not possible to combine them with other heuristics to obtain greater synergy. This finding was, in fact, anticipated in the results shown in Tables 2-5.

The work with more advanced heuristics is still in its preliminary stages. To date, only one such combination has been tested that involved the min domain/weighted-degree heuristic of [12] and the min kappa heuristic of [13]. These were chosen for combination because for the 50-variable problems the former loaded more heavily on the contention factor while the latter was more heavily correlated with the look-ahead factor. When used individually, the mean nodes searched was 1575 for min kappa and

1517 for min domain/weighted-degree. Both are superior to the best single heuristic or quotient in the previous tests. When these were combined into a weighted sum, with equal weight for each heuristic, the mean nodes was 1309. Therefore, synergy did occur as predicted, but the result was no better than the best results in the earlier experiments.

Table 11. Policy-Adherence and Descriptive Measures for Heuristics and Weighted Sum

measure	max forward degree	min domain	dom+fd
	efficiency measures		
nodes	2625	11334	1317
failures	2060	5419	844
	promise measures		
prom	0.00037	0.00027	0.00060
no. mistakes	231.2	407.5	150.5
	fail-first measure		
mistake-tree size	139.5	844.9	102.2
	descriptive measures		
|d| of variable chosen	4.1	1.9	2.6
fwd-deg of variable chosen	9.7	7.2	9.1
fail-depth	5.4	12.0	6.8

Note. Means for <50,10,0.184,0.32> problems.

8 Conclusions

This paper presents a study of the effects of combining heuristics. It begins by presenting a collection of data showing significant cases of synergy, as well as striking patterns of synergistic and non-synergistic effects. Some of these effects are counter-intuitive, since the heuristics in a synergistic combination may result in mediocre or even dreadful performance when used alone. The work also shows that weighted sums are in fact quite good at improving search performance by reducing the amount of search; this must be because this strategy improves the quality of variable selection.

Some insight was gained into the basis for this improvement, using the recent discovery that there are two basic types of heuristic action: here labeled "contention" and "look-ahead" [3]. This, in turn, led to the formulation of a simple rule for predicting success on the basis of the factor loadings of component heuristics. The success of this rule suggests that heuristic combinations work to improve search performance by balancing the two basic actions. Conversely, when the two are not well-balanced, as in some of the cases in Tables 1-6, performance is not improved and can even deteriorate in comparison with the component heuristics. Preliminary analysis of the features of search based on effective combinations supports the idea these hypotheses.

This work raises a number of important questions to address in further research:

- How general are the present synergistic principles with respect to problem classes? (So far they seem quite general with respect to algorithms.)
- To what degree are more advanced heuristics managing to balance the two basic heuristic factors? Is this why they are effective?

- Are there other principles underlying improvements in heuristic performance, such as the degree to which alternative choices can be discriminated based on different amounts of information?
- How does the kind of balancing in evidence here serve to restrict search?

Acknowledgment. This work was supported by Science Foundation Ireland under Grant 00/PI.1/C075.

References

1. Bessière, C., Régin, J.C.: Mac and combined heuristics: Two reasons to forsake fc (and cbj?) on hard problems. In Freuder, E.C., ed.: Principles and Practice of Constraint Programming -CP'96. LNCS. No. 1118, Berlin, Springer (1996) 61–75
2. Epstein, S.L., Freuder, E.C., Wallace, R., Morozov, A., Samuels, B.: The adaptive constraint engine. In van Hentenryck, P., ed.: Principles and Practice of Constraint Programming - CP2002. LNCS. No. 2470, Berlin, Springer (2002) 525–540
3. Wallace, R.J.: Factor analytic studies of csp heuristics. In van Beek, P., ed.: Principles and Practice of Constraint Programming-CP'05. Number 3709 in Lecture Notes in Computer Science, Berlin, Springer (2005) 712–726
4. Harman, H.H.: Modern Factor Analysis. 2nd edn. University of Chicago, Chicago and London (1967)
5. Lawley, D.N., Maxwell, A.E.: Factor Analysis as a Statistical Method. 2nd edn. Butterworths, London (1971)
6. Smith, B.M., Grant, S.A.: Trying harder to fail first. In: Proc. Thirteenth European Conference on Artificial Intelligence-ECAI'98, John Wiley & Sons (1998) 249–253
7. Geelen, P.A.: Dual viewpoint heuristics for binary constraint satisfaction problems. In: Proc. Tenth European Conference on Artificial Intelligence-ECAI'92. (1992) 31–35
8. Wallace, R.J.: Csp heuristics categorized with factor analytic. In Creaney, N., ed.: Proc. Sixteenth Irish Conference on Artificial Intelligence and Cognitive Science, Coleraine, NI, University of Ulster (2005) 213–222
9. Beck, J.C., Prosser, P., Wallace, R.J.: Variable ordering heuristics show promise. In: Principles and Practice of Constraint Programming-CP'04. LNCS No. 3258. (2004) 711–715
10. Beck, J.C., Prosser, P., Wallace, R.J.: Trying again to fail-first. In: Recent Advances in Constraints. Papers from the 2004 ERCIM/CologNet Workshop-CSCLP 2004. LNAI No. 3419, Berlin, Springer (2005) 41–55
11. Bessière, C., Zanuttini, B., Fernández, C.: Measuring search trees. In: ECAI 2004 Workshop on Modelling and Solving Problems with Constraints. (2004) 31–40
12. Boussemart, F., Hemery, F., Lecoutre, C., Sais, L.: Boosting systematic search by weighting constraints. In: Proc. Sixteenth European Conference on Artificial Intelligence-ECAI'04. (2004) 146–150
13. Gent, I., MacIntyre, E., Prosser, P., Smith, B., Walsh, T.: An empirical study of dynamic variable ordering heuristics for the constraint satisfaction problem. In: Principles and Practice of Constraint Programming-CP'96. LNCS No. 1118. (1996) 179–193

Complexity Analysis of Heuristic CSP Search Algorithms

Igor Razgon

Computer Science Department, University College Cork, Ireland
i.razgon@cs.ucc.ie

Abstract. CSP search algorithms are exponential in the worst-case. A trivial upper bound on the time complexity of CSP search algorithms is $O^*(d^n)$, where n and d are the number of variables and the maximal domain size of the underlying CSP, respectively.

In this paper we show that a combination of heuristic methods of constraint solving can reduce the time complexity. In particular, we prove that the FC-CBJ algorithm combined with the fail-first variable ordering heuristic (FF) achieves time complexity of $O^*((d-1)^n)$, where n and d are the number of variables and the maximal domain size of the given CSP, respectively. Furthermore, we show that the combination is essential because neither FC-CBJ alone nor FC with FF achieve the above complexity. The proposed results are interesting because they establish connection between theoretical and practical approaches to CSP research.

1 Introduction

CSP search algorithms are exponential in the worst-case. An upper bound on the time complexity of CSP search algorithms is $O^*(d^n)$, where n and d are the number of variables and maximal domain size, respectively (we use O^* notation to suppress polynomial factors in the complexity expression). This upper bound is obtained by taking into account that a search algorithm assigns n variables and for every variable, the branching factor is at most d. Thus the $O^*(d^n)$ upper bound is not "tight". On the other hand, in the constraint satisfaction area there are many sophisticated pruning techniques. An interesting question is, whether a combination of heuristic pruning methods can reduce the time complexity.

In this paper we answer the question affirmatively. In particular, we show that the FC-CBJ algorithm [5] combined with the fail-first variable ordering heuristic (FF) [4] has the worst-case time complexity of $O^*((d-1)^n)$. Furthermore, we show that the use of both the conflict-directed backjumping and the FF are essential for reducing complexity by demonstrating that FC-CBJ with no specified ordering heuristic and FC with FF both have a complexity greater than $O^*((d-1)^n)$.

We do not claim that the combination of FC-CBJ with the FF achieve the best time complexity for constraint satisfaction problem. In fact, there are methods

B. Hnich et al. (Eds.): CSCLP 2005, LNAI 3978, pp. 88–99, 2006.

that solve CSP much more efficiently [3]. The main contribution of the present paper is providing evidence that the complexity of CSP solving can be improved by using heuristic methods that were designed for the purely "practical" purpose of improving the runtime of CSP solving on real-world instances.

The results proven in this paper also provide theoretical insight into the strength of "most constrained first" ordering heuristics studied in [2]. The fact that FF improves the complexity of FC-CBJ while leaves the complexity of FC unchanged indicates that the strength of an ordering heuristic depends on the underlying search algorithm.

The rest of the paper is organized as follows. Section 2 contains the relevant background. Section 3 is the central in the paper. In this section we prove that FC-CBJ with FF has worst-case complexity of $O^*((d-1)^n)$. In Section 4 we show that neither FC with the FF nor FC-CBJ do not achieve the above complexity. Section 5 concludes the paper.

2 Preliminaries

2.1 Notations and Terminology

The present paper considers only binary CSPs. A CSP Z consists of three components. The first component is a set of variables. Every variable has a domain of values. We denote a value val of a variable v by $\langle v, val \rangle$. The set of domains of variables comprises the second component of Z. The *constraint* between variables u and v is a subset of the Cartesian product of the domains of u and v. A pair of values $(\langle u, val_1 \rangle, \langle v, val_2 \rangle)$ is compatible if it belongs to the constraint between u and v. Otherwise the values are incompatible (*conflicting*). The set of all constraints comprises the third part of Z.

A set P of values of different variables is *consistent* (*satisfies* all the constraints) if all the values of P are mutually compatible. In this case, we call P a *partial solution* of Z. If we let $\langle u, val \rangle \in P$, we say that P *assigns* u. Accordingly, $\langle u, val \rangle$ is the *assignment* of u in P. Let V' be a subset of the set of variables assigned by P. We denote by $P(V')$ the subset of P that assigns V'. If P assigns all the variables, it is a *solution* of P. The task of a CSP search algorithm is to find a solution of Z or to report that no solution exists.

Generally, not every partial solution is a subset of a full solution. If a partial solution P is not a subset of any solution, it is called a *nogood*. Note that sometimes in the literature, the notion of nogood has a broader meaning in that it includes also a set of assignments with inner conflicts. In the present work a nogood is a specific case of a partial solution, that is, a consistent set of assignments.

2.2 The FC, FC-CBJ Algorithms, and FF Ordering Heuristic

Forward Checking algorithm (FC) [5] is a CSP search algorithm based on enumeration of partial solutions. It starts from the empty partial solution. In every iteration, FC selects an unassigned variable, assigns it with a value and appends to the current partial solution. The characteristic feature of FC is that whenever new assignment is added to the current partial solutions, the values of unassigned variables that are incompatible with the new assignment are temporarily removed from the domains of the variables. Therefore, when we consider some state that occurs during execution of FC, we frequently refer to the *current domain* of some variable v, having in mind the subset of values that were not removed from the domain of v.

If FC assigns all the variables of the underlying CSP, it returns a solution. However, during the iterative enlargement of the current partial solution, the current domain of some unassigned variable might be emptied. In this case, FC backtracks, that is, discards the last assignment of the current partial solution and replaces it by another assignment of the same variable. Note that when an assignment is discarded, all the values, removed because of incompatibility with the assignment, are restored in their current domains. It may also happen that FC cannot replace the discarded assignment by another one. In this case it backtracks again. Finally, it might happen that FC tries to backtrack, but the current partial solution is empty. In this case, FC reports insolubility.

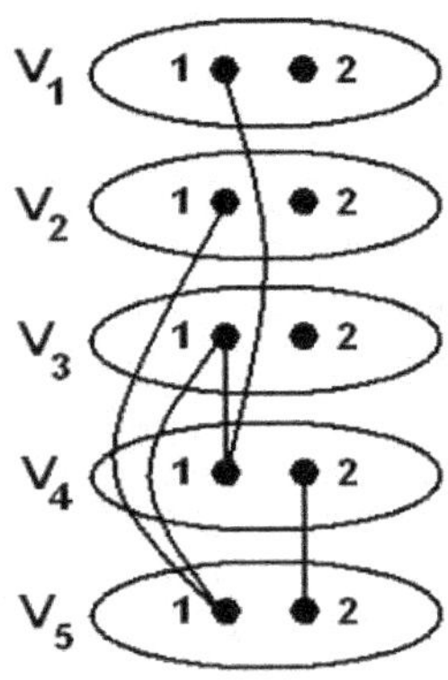

Fig. 1. CSP used for illustration of work of search algorithms

We demonstrate a possible scenario of execution of FC on the CSP shown in Figure 1, where ellipses represent variables, black circles represent values, arcs between values represent conflicts. FC starts from the empty current partial solution. Then $\langle v_1, 1\rangle$ is appended to the current partial solution and $\langle v_4, 1\rangle$ is removed because of incompatibility with $\langle v_1, 1\rangle$. The next assignment appended to the current partial solution is $\langle v_2, 1\rangle$; the assignment causes removal of $\langle v_5, 1\rangle$. The next appended assignment is $\langle v_3, 1\rangle$. Then FC adds to the current partial solution assignment $\langle v_4, 2\rangle$; as a result, $\langle v_5, 2\rangle$ is removed, the domain of v_5 is emptied and FC backtracks.

Performing backtrack, FC discards $\langle v_4, 2\rangle$ and removes it from the current domain of v_4. As well, $\langle v_5, 2\rangle$ is restored in the current domain of v_5. The backtracking empties the domain of v_4, hence FC backtracks again, discarding $\langle v_3, 1\rangle$

and restoring $\langle v_4, 2\rangle$. Note that $\langle v_4, 1\rangle$ is not restored because it was removed by incompatibility with $\langle v_1, 1\rangle$, which still belongs to the current partial solution Then $\langle v_3, 2\rangle$ is appended to the current partial solution. After that FC appends again $\langle v_4, 2\rangle$ which causes three consecutive backtracks discarding assignments $\langle v_4, 2\rangle$, $\langle v_3, 2\rangle$, and $\langle v_2, 1\rangle$. Then FC appends $\langle v_2, 2\rangle$ to the current partial solution. The assignment $\langle v_3, 1\rangle$ appended next is discarded after a number of iterations. After appending of assignments $\langle v_3, 2\rangle$, $\langle v_4, 1\rangle$ and $\langle v_5, 1\rangle$, FC obtains a full solution, which is returned.

States of a search algorithm. The execution of a CSP search algorithm can be represented as a sequence of atomic operations of updating of the current partial solution (addition or removal of assignments) accompanied by appropriate updating of the maintained data structures in order to preserve consistency. The information recorded in the data structures before the beginning of the execution or after performing an atomic operation constitutes a *state* of a search algorithm. Thus a sequence of states is another possible representation of a search algorithm. We use this representation in the present paper, in order to prove properties of the analyzed algorithms.

Forward Checking with Conflict-directed Backjumping (FC-CBJ) is a modification of FC that can backtrack more than 1 step backwards (backjump). The completeness of enumeration is preserved by maintaining *conflict sets* of variables. In a given state of FC-CBJ, the conflict set of a variable v, denoted by $conf(v)$, contains all variables whose assignments in the current partial solution are "culprit" for removing values from the current domain of v. In particular, if P is the current partial solution then every removed value $\langle v, val\rangle$ of v is incompatible with $P(conf(v))$ or $P(conf(v)) \cup \{\langle v, val\rangle\}$ is a nogood.

The detailed description of FC-CBJ is quite technical and long, hence we list only those features of the algorithm that are relevant to the theorems we are going to prove.

- Initially all conflict sets are empty.
- Whenever a value $\langle u, val\rangle$ is appended to the current partial solution and a value of an unassigned variable v is removed as a result of incompatibility with $\langle u, val\rangle$, u is added to $conf(v)$.
- Whenever the empty domain of a variable v causes backtrack, FC-CBJ backjumps to the last assigned variable u that appears in $conf(v)$ and discards the assignment of this variable. The assignments of variables that were appended to the current partial solution after the assignment of u are just canceled as if they were not performed at all (of course, with the restoring of values removed by these assignments). Note that removing an assignment of a variable from the current partial solution, FC-CBJ removes appearances of this variable from all conflict sets.
- Whenever the empty current domain of a variable v causes backtrack and the backtrack process discards the assignment of a variable u, $conf(u)$ is set to $conf(u) \cup conf(v) \setminus \{u\}$.

Assume that the CSP illustrated on Figure 1 is processed by FC-CBJ. In the beginning, the execution is similar to that of FC with the only difference that whenever new assignments are appended to the current partial solution the conflict sets of the corresponding variables are updated. In particular adding assignment $\langle v_1, 1\rangle$ causes adding v_1 to $conf(v_4)$, v_2 is added to $conf(v_5)$ as a result of appending of $\langle v_2, 1\rangle$. Note that the assignment $\langle v_3, 1\rangle$ does not cause updating of conflict sets. Finally the assignment $\langle v_4, 5\rangle$ causes adding v_4 to $conf(v_5)$. The first backtrack of FC-CBJ is caused by the empty domain of v_5. At the time of the backtrack, $conf(v_5) = \{v_2, v_4\}$, hence FC-CBJ jumps to v_4. Note that before the backtrack, $conf(v_4) = \{v_1\}$. After backtrack the set is updated to $\{v_1, v_2\}$ as a result of union with $conf(v_5)$ and removing of v_4. Also, v_4 is removed from $conf(v_5)$.

The second backtrack occurs because of emptying of the domain of v_4. Because the last variable in $conf(v_4)$ is v_2, FC-CBJ jumps over v_3 and discards the assignment of v_2. Thus FC-CBJ avoids processing of an unnecessary assignment $\langle v_3, 2\rangle$ performed by FC after the second backtrack.

CSP search algorithms do not specify explicitly the order of selection of variables to be assigned. This job is done by ordering heuristics. One of the simplest and the most successful ordering heuristics is called Fail-First (FF) [4]. Every time when a new variable must be assigned, FF selects a variable with the smallest size of the current domain. The time complexity of FF is linear in the number of unassigned variables. The implementation of FF requires maintaining array of domain sizes of variables which is updated dynamically when values are removed or restored. All what FF does is selection of the minimal element among the entries of the array that correspond to the domains of unassigned variables.

Consider the execution of FC with FF on the CSP of Figure 1, assuming that in case of existence of two or more variables with the smallest domain size, one is selected according to the lexicographic ordering.

Initially, the current domains of all the variables are of equal size, so v_1 is assigned with 1. After removing of $\langle v_4, 1\rangle$ as a result of the assignment, v_4 becomes the variable with the smallest domain size, so $\langle v_4, 2\rangle$, the only remaining value is appended to the current partial solution. The value $\langle v_5, 2\rangle$ is removed because of the incompatibility with $\langle v_4, 2\rangle$, hence v_5 becomes the variable with the smallest domain size and the assignment $\langle v_5, 1\rangle$ is added to the current partial solution. The values $\langle v_2, 1\rangle$ and $\langle v_3, 1\rangle$ are incompatible with $\langle v_5, 1\rangle$, hence they are removed from the current domain of v_2 and v_3. The next two iterations append to the current partial solution $\langle v_2, 2\rangle$ and $\langle v_3, 2\rangle$. The obtained full solution is returned after that.

The above example demonstrates the strength of FF, because it allows to avoid backtracks during processing of the given CSP.

2.3 Complexity of Backtrack Algorithms

All complete CSP search algorithms (those that return a solution if one exists or report insolubility otherwise) have exponential time-complexity. Discussing aspects related to the complexity of backtracking algorithms, we follow two agreements:

- We express the time-complexity (upper bound) by O^* notation [7], which suppresses the polynomial factor. For example, instead of $O(n^2 * 2^n)$, we write $O^*(2^n)$. Note, that for a constant $d > 1$ $O^*((d-1)^n)$ is smaller than $O^*(d^n)$ because $O^*(d^n) = O^*((d/d-1)^n * (d-1)^n)$, where $(d/(d-1))^n$ is a growing exponential function that cannot be suppressed by the O^* notation. On the other hand, given constants d and k, $O^*(d^{n+k})$ is the same as $O^*(d^n)$ because $O^*(d^{n+k}) = O^*(d^k * d^n)$, where d^k can be suppressed as a constant.
- We express the time complexity of a CSP search algorithm by the number of partial solutions generated by the algorithm. This is a valid representation because the time complexity can be represented as the number of partial solutions multiplied by a polynomial factor which is ignored by the O^* notation.

The worst-case complexity of FC and FC-CBJ when applied to a CSP with n variables and maximum domain size d is widely considered to be $O^*(d^n)$.

The Ω^*-notation is used to express the lower bound on the complexity of exponential algorithms. The constant and polynomial factors are suppressed analogously to the O^*-notation.

3 FC-CBJ Combined with FF Has $O^*((d-1)^n)$ Complexity

In this section we will show that the use of heuristic techniques can decrease the complexity of a search algorithm. In particular we prove that the FC-CBJ algorithm [5] combined with the FF heuristic [4] has a worst-case complexity of $O^*((d-1)^n)$, where n and d are the number of variables and the maximal domain size, respectively. During the proof, we extensively use the notion of maximal partial solution.

Definition 1. *Let P be a partial solution explored by a search algorithm during solving a CSP Z. Then P is maximal if it is not a subset of any other partial solution visited by the algorithm during solving Z.*

We now prove a theorem that states an upper bound on the number of maximal solutions explored by FC-CBJ with FF. The overall complexity of FC-CBJ with FF will follow from this result.

Theorem 1. *FC-CBJ with FF applied to a CSP Z with $n \geq 2$ variables and maximal domain size d explores at most $M(n) = d * \Sigma_{i=0}^{n-2}(d-1)^i$ maximal partial solutions.*

In order to prove the theorem, we need an additional lemma.

Lemma 1. *Let Z be a CSP with the maximal domain size d. Consider a state S of FC-CBJ that occurs during processing of Z. Let P be the current partial solution maintained by FC-CBJ in this state. Assume that in P is not empty and that the current domain size of every unassigned variable is d. Let Z' be a*

CSP created by the current domains of unassigned variables. Assume that Z' is insoluble. Then, after visiting state S, the execution of FC-CBJ is continued as follows: FC-CBJ detects insolubility of Z', immediately discards all the values of P, reports insolubility, and stops.

Proof. Considering that d is the maximum possible domain size, we infer that the current domains of the unassigned variables are the same as their initial domains. It follows that all values of the original domains of the unassigned variables are compatible with all values of P. Consequently, the conflict sets of all the unassigned variables are empty.

Observe that when processing Z', a variable assigned by P does not appear in any conflict set of a variable of Z'. This observation can be verified by induction on the sequence of events updating the conflict sets of Z'. Note that the observation holds *before* FC-CBJ starts to process Z', because all the conflict sets are empty (see the argumentation in the previous paragraph). Assuming that the observation holds for the first k events, let us consider the $k+1$-th one. Assume that v is the variable whose conflict set is updated. If this updating results in insertion of the currently assigned variable then the variable being inserted belongs to Z' which is not assigned by P. Otherwise, $conf(v)$ is united with the conflict set of another variable u of Z'. However, $conf(u)$ does not contain variables assigned by P by the induction assumption.

If Z' is insoluble, FC-CBJ will eventually discard P. This means that FC-CBJ will arrive at a state in which the current domain of a variable v of Z' is empty and $conf(v)$ does not contain any variable of Z'. On the other hand, $conf(v)$ will not contain any variable assigned by P. That is, the conflict set of v will be empty. Consequently, FC-CBJ will jump "over" all the assigned variables, report insolubility of Z, and stop. ∎

Now we are ready to prove Theorem 1.

Proof of Theorem 1. We prove the theorem by induction on n. For the basic case assume that $n = 2$. Let v_1 and v_2 be the variables of Z and assume that v_1 is assigned first. Consider the situation that occurs when v_1 is assigned with a value $\langle v_1, val\rangle$. If the value is compatible with at least one value in the domain of v_2, FC-CBJ returns a solution. Otherwise, it instantiates $\langle v_1, val\rangle$ with another value of v_1 or reports insolubility if all values of v_1 have been explored. Thus, every value of v_1 participates in at most one partial solution. Keeping in mind that there are at most d such values, we get that at most d partial solutions are explored. Observe that $M(2) = d$. That is, the theorem holds for $n = 2$.

Assume that $n > 2$ and that the theorem holds for all CSPs having less than n variables. We consider two possible scenarios of execution of FC-CBJ.

According to the first scenario whenever the current partial solution is not empty (at least one variable has been already instantiated), FC-CBJ combined with FF selects for instantiation a variable with the current domain size smaller than d. Then FC-CBJ explores a search tree in which at most d edges leave the root node and at most $d-1$ edges leave any other node.

Note that when FC-CBJ has assigned all the variables but one, it does not execute branching on the last variable. If the domain of the last variable is not empty, FC-CBJ takes any available value and returns a full solution. Otherwise, it backtracks. It follows that in the search tree explored by FC-CBJ only the first $n-1$ levels can contain nodes with two or more leaving edges. The branching factor on the first level is d, but the branching factor of a node at any other of $n-2$ remaining levels is $d-1$. Consequently, the number of leaves of the search tree is at most $d*(d-1)^{n-2}$. Taking into account that the leaves of the search tree correspond to the maximal partial solutions, we see that in the considered case, FC-CBJ explores at most $d*(d-1)^{n-2} \leq M(n)$ maximal partial solutions. Thus, the theorem holds in the case of the first scenario.

If the first scenario does not occur then FC-CBJ, having at least one variable instantiated, selects for assignment a variable with the current domain size d. Consider the first time when such a selection occurs and denote by P the current partial solution maintained by FC-CBJ in the considered state. Denote by Z' the CSP created by the current domains of variables that are no assigned by P. Proceeding the execution, FC-CBJ solves Z'. If Z' is soluble then FC-CBJ finds a solution of Z', returns its union with P, and stops.

The case when Z' is insoluble is **the main point in the proof of the theorem**. Note that FC-CBJ uses FF. If a variable with the current domain size d is selected, the current domain sizes of the other unassigned variables are at least d. On the other hand, d is the maximal possible domain size, hence the current domain sizes of the other variables are exactly d. By Lemma 1, FC-CBJ stops after detecting insolubility of Z'. (Note that both FC-CBJ and FF contributed to the validity of this claim. The contribution of FF is ensuring that the current domains of all the unassigned variables are exactly d. The contribution of FC-CBJ is explained in the proof of Lemma 1. Note also that Lemma 1 has been proven for the general case of FC-CBJ, hence it holds, in particular, for FC-CBJ combined with FF.)

Thus we have shown that whenever FC-CBJ selects a variable with the current domain size d given that the current partial solution is non-empty, the algorithm always stops when the solving of Z' is finished.

The number of maximal partial solutions visited by FC-CBJ in this case equals the number of maximal partial solutions explored before visiting P plus the number of maximal partial solution explored after visiting P.

Recall that we consider the first time during the execution when a variable with the current domain size d is selected given that the current partial solution is not empty. Therefore, before arriving to the considered state, FC-CBJ explores at most $d*(d-1)^{n-2}$ maximal partial solutions, according to the argumentation provided for the first scenario.

All maximal partial solutions explored after visiting P are visited during solving of Z'. Therefore every maximal partial solution P_1 visited after exploring of P can be represented as $P_1 = P \cup P_2$, where P_2 is a maximal partial solution of Z' (non-maximality of P_2 contradicts maximality of P_1). Thus the number of maximal partial solutions explored after visiting of P equals the number of maximal partial solutions explored by FC-CBJ during solving of Z'.

Considering that P is not empty, it follows that Z' contains at most $n-1$ variables. By the induction assumption, FC-CBJ explores at most $M(n-1)$ of maximal partial solutions during solving of Z'. Thus the overall number of maximal partial solutions is at most $d*(d-1)^{n-2}+M(n-1)=M(n)$, what completes the proof for the second scenario. ■

Corollary 1. *FC-CBJ with FF explores $O^*((d-1)^n)$ maximal partial solutions.*

Proof. By definition of $M(n)$, $M(n) \leq dn(d-1)^{n-2} = O^*((d-1)^n)$. ■

We have shown that the number of maximal partial solutions explored by FC-CBJ with FF is bounded by $O^*((d-1)^n)$. Clearly, every partial solution is a subset of some maximal partial solution. On the other hand, every maximal partial solution serves as a subset of at most n partial solutions. Indeed, every partial solution generated by FC-CBJ corresponds to a node of the search tree explored by FC-CBJ. Note that subsets of the given partial solution P correspond to the ancestors of P in the search tree. Taking into account that every path from the root to a leaf in the search tree has a length of at most n, we infer that P cannot have more than n ancestors. Consequently, the number of partial solutions explored by FC-CBJ is at most the number of maximal partial solutions multiplied by n. Thus we have proved the following theorem.

Theorem 2. *The complexity of FC-CBJ with the fail-first ordering heuristic is $O^*((d-1)^n)$.*

To understand the strength of the theorem, consider the following corollary.

Corollary 2. *FC-CBJ with FF efficiently solves any CSP with at most two values in every domain.*

Proof. If a CSP contains at most two values in every domain then $d = 2$. Substituting $d = 2$ to the statement of Theorem 2, we get that FC-CBJ with FF solves such a CSP in $O^*(1^n)$ with is a polynomial according to the definition of O^* notation. ■

The collection of CSPs with at most 2 values in every domain is a well-known polynomially-solvable CSP class. According to Corollary 2, FC-CBJ recognizes CSPs from this class without any additional "domain-dependent" procedures.

4 Both FC with FF and FC-CBJ Have a Complexity Greater Than $O^*((d-1)^n)$

It may seem that a combination of FC-CBJ with FF is far too complex to achieve the purpose of reducing complexity. We will show that this is not so. In particular, we will show that both FC (without CBJ) with FF and FC-CBJ alone have a complexity greater than $O^*((d-1)^n)$.

Let us start by the analyzing of the complexity of FC with FF. We prove that for every n there is a CSP Z with $n+1$ variables and d values in every domain (d is an arbitrary number) such that in order to solve Z, the algorithm generates at least d^n partial solutions. Let $v_1, \dots, v_{n+1}$ be the variables of the considered CSP. Every value of v_n conflicts with every value of v_{n+1}. There are no other conflicts in the CSP. This CSP is illustrated in Figure 2.

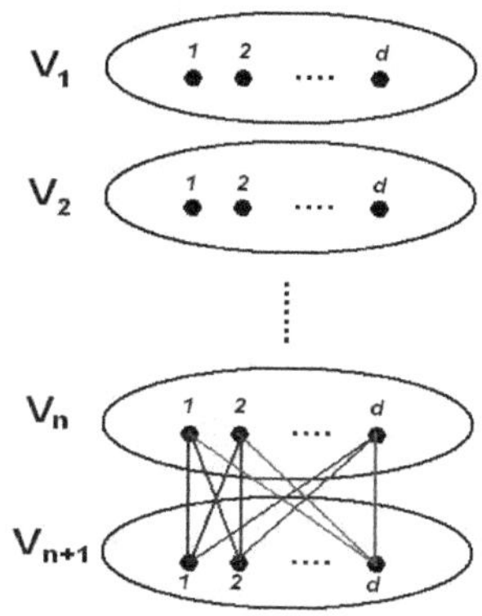

Fig. 2. A hard CSP for FC with FF

We assume that if during the search there are two or more variables with the smallest current domain size, FC with FF will select the first of them according to lexicographic ordering. This is a valid assumption, because we are going to refute the claim that FC with FF has a better complexity than $O^*(d^n)$. It is implied by the claim that if there are two or more variables with the smallest current domain size, these variables can be ordered arbitrarily. Therefore, to refute the claim, it is sufficient to show that FC combined with FF and a *particular* ordering in the case of existence of two or more variables with the smallest domain size has a complexity greater than $O^*((d-1)^n)$.

Observe that the source of insolubility of Z is that v_n and v_{n+1} have no pair of compatible values. However, FC with the heuristic described above will not be able to recognize the insolubility source, because it will assign first v_1, then v_2, and so on. Note that to refute Z, the algorithm will have to explore all the partial solutions assigning variables $v_1, \dots, v_n$. Clearly, there are at least d^n such partial solutions. Denoting $n+1$ by m we obtain that for every m there is a CSP with m variables such that FC with FF explores at least d^{m-1} partial solutions solving this CSP. That is, the complexity of FC with FF is $\Omega^*(d^{m-1}) = \Omega^*(1/d * d^m) = \Omega^*(d^m)$ as claimed.

Let us now analyze the complexity of FC-CBJ. Note that if some CSP search algorithm has a complexity of $O^*((d-1)^n)$ then for *any* value of d, the algorithm explores $O^*((d-1)^n)$ partial solutions. Consequently, to prove that an algorithm has a greater complexity, it is enough to show that the above does not happen for at least one d. This is the way we show that FC-CBJ alone has a greater complexity than $O^*((d-1)^n)$. Note that we are free to choose an ordering heuristic for FC-CBJ because FC-CBJ does not specify any particular ordering heuristic.

Let Z be a CSP with $n+1$ variables $v_1, \ldots v_{n+1}$. The domain of each variable contains n values, say, $val_1, \ldots, val_n$. The only conflicts of Z are found between the values of v_{n+1} and the values of other variables. In particular, a value $\langle v_{n+1}, val_i \rangle$ conflicts with all the values of variable v_i. The CSP is illustrated in Figure 3. We assume that FC-CBJ orders variables lexicographically.

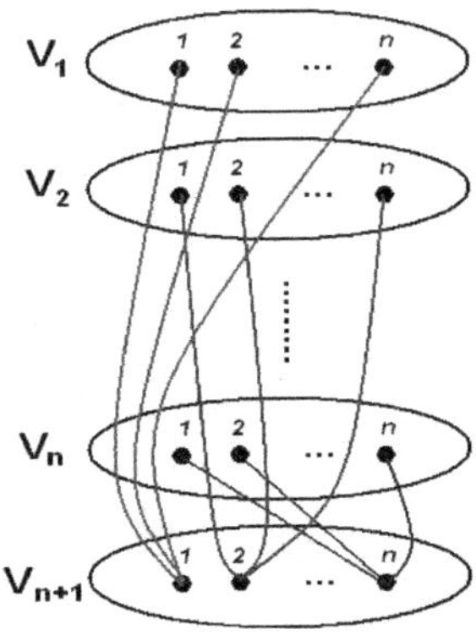

Fig. 3. A hard CSP for FC-CBJ

The source of insolubility of Z is that every value of v_{n+1} conflicts with the domain of some variable from $v_1, \ldots, v_n$. However, FC-CBJ is unable to recognize the source of insolubility because it assigns v_{n+1} last, according to the specified ordering heuristic. Observe that all maximal partial solutions generated by FC-CBJ are of the form $\{\langle v_1, val_{i_1}, \rangle, \ldots, \langle v_n, val_{i_n} \rangle\}$, because no assignment to a proper subset of $\{v_1, \ldots, v_n\}$ can discard all the values of v_{n+1}. Clearly, there are n^n partial solutions of the above form and we shall show that FC-CBJ explores all of them, which proves that for any given n, there is d for which there is a class of CSPs that cannot be solved by FC-CBJ in $O^*((d-1)^n)$.

To show that FC-CBJ explores all the partial solutions of the form $\{\langle v_1, val_{i_1}, \rangle, \ldots, \langle v_n, val_{i_n} \rangle\}$, it is sufficient to show that FC-CBJ never backjumps more than 1 step backwards when applied to Z. First, we show that FC-CBJ never backjumps when explores a maximal partial solution. Actually, an assignment of every v_i conflicts only with $\langle v_{n+1}, val_i \rangle$. That is, every assignment of a maximal partial solution conflicts with the unique value of v_{n+1}. This means that when the current domain of v_{n+1} is emptied, all the variables of $\{v_1, \ldots, v_n\}$ appear in $conf(v_{n+1})$. Therefore, after discarding the assignment of v_n, the set $\{v_1, \ldots, v_n\} \setminus \{v_n\}$ is added to the conflict set of v_n. Further, when the domain of v_n is emptied, FC-CBJ has no choice but to backtrack to v_{n-1}.

Tracing further the execution of FC-CBJ, we observe that whenever an assignment of v_i is discarded, the set $\{v_1, \ldots, v_{i-1}\}$ is added to $conf(v_i)$. Hence, when the current domain of v_i is emptied, FC-CBJ backtracks to v_{i-1}. This argumentation shows that FC-CBJ applied to Z with lexicographic ordering heuristic never backjumps and thus explores at least n^n partial solutions.

5 Conclusion

In this paper we presented complexity analysis of a few heuristic algorithm for solving of CSPs. In particular, we proved that FC-CBJ combined with FF has time-complexity of $O^*((d-1)^n)$. We have also demonstrated that the above combination of techniques is necessary is order to reduce complexity. In particular, we have proven that FC with FF as well as FC-CBJ without an ordering heuristic both have a complexity greater than $O^*((d-1)^n)$.

The results presented can be further generalized. Note that the only property of FF used in the proof of Theorem 1 is that FF *does not* select a variable with the largest current domain. Consequently, the result of Theorem 1 can be generalized for a combination of FC-CBJ with any heuristic that has the above property. Note also that FC-CBJ can be replaced by another intelligent backtracking algorithm like MAC-CBJ [6] or CCFC- [1].

References

1. Fahiem Bacchus. Extending forward checking. In *Principles and Practice of Constraint Programming*, pages 35–51, 2000.
2. C. Beck, P. Prosser, and R. Wallace. Trying again to fail-first. In *CSCLP 2004*, pages 41–55, 2004.
3. D. Eppstein. Improved algorithms for 3-coloring, 3-edge coloring and constraint satisfaction. In *SODA-2001*, pages 329–337, 2001.
4. R. M. Haralick and G.L. Elliott. Increasing tree search efficiency for constraint satisfaction problems. *Artificial Intelligence*, 14:263–313, 1980.
5. P. Prosser. Hybrid algorithms for the constraint satisfaction problem. *Computational Intelligence*, 9:268–299, 1993.
6. P. Prosser. MAC-CBJ: maintaining arc consistency with conflict-directed backjumping. Technical Report Research Report/95/177, Dept. of Computer Science, University of Strathclyde, 1995.
7. G. Woeginger. Exact algorithms for np-hard problems: A survey. In *Combinatorial Optimization: "Eureka, you shrink", LNCS 2570*, pages 185–207, 2003.

A Type System for CHR

Emmanuel Coquery[1,2] and François Fages[1]

[1] INRIA Rocquencourt, Projet Contraintes,
BP 105, F-78153 Le Chesnay, France
[2] LIRIS, Université Claude Bernard Lyon 1, Btiment Nautibus,
8, boulevard Niels Bohr 69622 Villeurbanne cedex France

Abstract. We propose a generic type system for the *Constraint Handling Rules* (CHR), a rewriting rule language for implementing constraint solvers. CHR being a high-level extension of a host language, such as Prolog or Java, this type system is parameterized by the type system of the host language. We show the consistency of the type system for CHR w.r.t. its operational semantics. We also study the case when the host language is a constraint logic programming language, typed with the prescriptive type system we developed in previous work. In particular, we show the consistency of the resulting type system w.r.t. the extended execution model CLP+CHR. This system is implemented through an extension of our type checker TCLP for constraint logic languages. We report on experimental results about the type-checking of twelve CHR solvers and programs, including TCLP itself.

1 Introduction

The language of *Constraint Handling Rules* (CHR) of T. Frühwirth [1] is a successful rule-based language for implementing constraint solvers in a wide variety of domains. It is an extension of a host language, such as Prolog [2], Java [3] or Haskell [4], allowing the introduction of new constraints in a declarative way. CHR is used to handle user-defined constraints while the host language deals with other computations using *native* constraints. CHR is a committed-choice language of guarded rules that rewrite constraints into simpler ones until they are in solved forms. One peculiarity of CHR is that it allows multiple heads in rules.

Typed languages have numerous advantages from the point of view of program development, such as the static detection of programming errors or program composition errors, and the documentation of the code by types. CHR has already been used for the typing of programming languages, either for solving subtyping constraints [5, 6] or for handling overloading in functional languages [7] and constraint logic languages [8, 6]. There has been however not much work on the typing of CHR itself. In [4], Chin, Sulzmann and Wang propose a monomorphic type system for the embedding of CHR into Haskell.

In this article, we propose a generic type system for CHR inspired by the TCLP type system for constraint logic programs [9]. CHR being an extension of a host language, this system is parameterized by the type system of the

B. Hnich et al. (Eds.): CSCLP 2005, LNAI 3978, pp. 100–117, 2006.

host language. We will make three assumptions on the type system of the host language:

- Typing judgments of the form $\Gamma \vdash t : \tau$ are considered, where τ is a type associated to the expression t in a typing environment Γ. Moreover *well-typed* constraints in a typing environment Γ are defined by a derivation system for typing judgments.
- The constraint $t_1 = t_2$ is well-typed in the environment Γ if there exists a type τ such as $\Gamma \vdash t_1 : \tau$ and $\Gamma \vdash t_2 : \tau$.
- If a conjunct c of native constraints is well-typed in an environment Γ and is equivalent to a conjunct d, then d is also well-typed in Γ.

Using these assumptions, we show the consistency of the type system for CHR w.r.t. its operational semantics. This is expressed by a subject reduction theorem which establishes that if a program is well-typed then all the derived goals from a well-typed goal are well-typed.

We also study the instantiation of this type system with the TCLP type system for constraint logic programs [9]. We show a subject reduction theorem for the CLP+CHR execution model [1] in which it is possible to extend the definition of constraints by clauses. This result is interesting because constraint logic programming is a very natural framework for using CHR constraint solvers. A type system for CLP+CHR allows us to type-check, on the one hand, CHR constraint solvers together with the CLP programs that use them, and, on the other hand, complex constraint solvers written with a combination of CHR rules using CLP predicates, and CLP clauses posting CHR constraints.

The rest of the paper is organized as follows. Section 2 recalls the syntax and operational semantics of CHR, including the CLP+CHR execution model. Section 3 presents the type system and section 4 presents its instantiation with the type system for CLP. Section 5 presents some experimental results on the typing of some CHR solvers, using the implementation of the system in TCLP [10]. Finally, we conclude in section 6.

2 Preliminaries on CHR

Here, we recall the syntax and semantics of CHR, as given in [1]. We distinguish the user-defined *CHR constraints* from the *native constraints* of the host language, which represent auxiliary computations that take place during the application of a CHR rule. We assume that native constraints are handled by a predefined solver of the host language. We also assume that native constraints include the equality constraint $=/2$ and the constraint *true*. Expressions[1] of the host language are noted s, t and constraints are noted $c(t_1, \ldots, t_n)$. We note $\mathcal{X}$ the domain of native constraints, and $\mathcal{CT}$ its (possibly incomplete) first-order logic theory.

[1] When the host language is a CLP dialect, as in section 4, the expressions are simply the CLP terms.

2.1 Syntax

Definition 1. *A CHR rule is either:*

- *a* simplification *rule of the form:*
  $H_1, \ldots, H_i$ `<=>` $G_1, \ldots, G_j \mid B_1, \ldots, B_k$
- *a* propagation *rule of the form:*
  $H_1, \ldots, H_i$ `==>` $G_1, \ldots, G_j \mid B_1, \ldots, B_k$
- *or a* simpagation *rule of the form:*
  $H_1, \ldots, H_l \setminus H_{l+1}, \ldots, H_i$ `<=>` $G_1, \ldots, G_j \mid B_1, \ldots, B_k$

with $i > 0$, $j \geq 0$, $k \geq 0$, $l > 0$ and $H_1, \ldots, H_i$ is a nonempty sequence of CHR constraints, the guard $G_1, \ldots, G_j$ being a sequence of native constraints and the body $B_1, \ldots, B_k$ being a sequence of CHR and native constraints.

A CHR program is a finite sequence of CHR rules.

The constraint *true* is used to represent empty sequences. The empty guard can be omitted, together with the | symbol. The notation *name*@*R* gives a name to a CHR rule *R*.

Informally, a simplification rule replaces the constraints of the head by the constraints of the body if its guard is implied by the constraint store. A propagation rule adds the constraints of the body while keeping the constraints of the head in the store. A simpagation rule is a mix of the two preceding kind of rules: the constraints $H_{l+1}, \ldots, H_i$ are replaced by the body, while the constraints $H_1, \ldots, H_l$ are kept.

For the sake of simplicity, and because the distinction of propagation and simpagation rules are not needed for typing purposes, we will consider that a propagation or a simpagation rule of the form

$$H_1, \ldots, H_l \setminus H_{l+1}, \ldots, H_i \texttt{ <=> } G_1, \ldots, G_j \mid B_1, \ldots, B_k$$

is just an abbreviation for the simplification rule

$$H_1, \ldots, H_i \texttt{ <=> } G_1, \ldots, G_j \mid H_1, \ldots, H_l, B_1, \ldots, B_k.$$

where $H_1, \ldots, H_l$ are explicitely removed and put back into the store.

Example 1. The following CHR program, taken from [1], defines a solver for a general ordering constraint `=<`.

```
reflexivity  @ X=<Y <=> X=Y | true.
antisymetry  @ X=<Y , Y=<X <=> X=Y.
transitivity @ X=<Y , Y=<Z ==> X=<Z.
identity     @ X=<Y \ X=<Y <=> true.
```

The rule `reflexivity` eliminates the `=<` constraints when its two arguments are equal. Rule `antisymmetry` simplifies a double inequality into an equality. The rule `transitivity` adds constraints corresponding to the transitive closure of `=<`. Finally, `identity` eliminates redundant `=<` constraints.

2.2 Operational Semantics

The operational semantics of CHR is expressed by a transition system, noted $\longmapsto$, over states which are triples $\langle F, E, D\rangle$, where F is a goal, that is a multiset of native and CHR constraints, E is a CHR constraint store and D is a native constraint store. A state is thus a conjunction of CHR and native constraints.

In the following definition, the equality is extended to constraints by morphism, that is $c(t_1, \ldots, t_n) = c(t'_1, \ldots, t'_n)$ if $t_1 = t'_1 \wedge \ldots \wedge t_n = t'_n$. The conjunction notation $\wedge$ is used to express the matching of a constraint in a multiset, The equality is also extended to conjunctions of constraints: $H_1 \wedge \ldots \wedge H_n = H'_1 \wedge \ldots \wedge H'_n$ if $H_1 = H'_1 \wedge \ldots \wedge H_n = H'_n$.

Definition 2. *Let P be a CHR program. The transition relation $\longmapsto$ is given by the following rules, where the variables appearing in triples stand for conjunctions of constraints and $\bar{x}$ represents the set of variables appearing in the head H.*

Solve
$\langle C \wedge F, E, D\rangle \longmapsto \langle F, E, D'\rangle$
if C is a native constraint and $CT \models (C \wedge D) \Leftrightarrow D'$.

Introduce
$\langle H \wedge F, E, D\rangle \longmapsto \langle F, H \wedge E, D\rangle$
if H is a CHR constraint.

Simplify
$\langle F, H' \wedge E, D\rangle \longmapsto \langle B \wedge F, E, H = H' \wedge D\rangle$
if (H `<=>` $G \mid B$) is in P renamed with fresh variables, and $CT \models D \Rightarrow \exists\bar{x}(H = H' \wedge G)$.

Propagate
$\langle F, H' \wedge E, D\rangle \longmapsto \langle B \wedge F, H' \wedge E, H = H' \wedge D\rangle$
if (H `==>` $G \mid B$) is in P renamed with fresh variables, and $CT \models D \Rightarrow \exists\bar{x}(H = H' \wedge G)$.

The **Solve** transition corresponds to a transition of the native constraint solver. The **Introduce** transition simply transfers a CHR constraint from the goal to the CHR constraint store The **Simplify** transition correspond to the application of CHR simplification. The **Propagate** transition is indicated for the sake of clarity, although it is treated as an abbreviation for a simplification rule in the rest of the paper. The condition for applying these rules is that the head of the rule can be instantiated such that the guard and the matching condition of the head are implied by the current native constraint store. The body of the rule is then added to the current goal and, when applying a **Simplify** transition, the constraints matching the head are removed from the constraint store.

Definition 3. *An* initial state *consists in a goal F and two empty constraint stores: $\langle F, true, true\rangle$. A* final state *is either of the form $\langle F, E, false\rangle$ (*failure*), or of the form $\langle true, E, D\rangle$ where D is satisfiable (*success*).*

The following example illustrates the execution of a CHR program.

Example 2. Let us consider the solver given in example 1 together with the initial state $\langle \texttt{X=<Y} \wedge \texttt{Y=<Z} \wedge \texttt{Z=<X}, \mathit{true}, \mathit{true}\rangle$. One possible execution is:

$\langle \texttt{Z=<X}, \texttt{X=<Y} \wedge \texttt{Y=<Z}, \mathit{true}\rangle$	(**Introduce** ×2)
$\langle \texttt{X=<Z} \wedge \texttt{Z=<X}, \texttt{X=<Y} \wedge \texttt{Y=<Z}, \mathit{true}\rangle$	(**Propagate** `transitivity`)
$\langle \mathit{true}, \texttt{X=<Z} \wedge \texttt{Z=<X} \wedge \texttt{X=<Y} \wedge \texttt{Y=<Z}, \mathit{true}\rangle$	(**Introduce** ×2)
$\langle \texttt{X=Z}, \texttt{X=<Y} \wedge \texttt{Y=<Z}, \mathit{true}\rangle$	(**Simplify** `antisymmetry`)
$\langle \mathit{true}, \texttt{X=<Y} \wedge \texttt{Y=<Z}, \texttt{X=Z}\rangle$	(**Solve**)
$\langle \texttt{X=Y}, \mathit{true}, \texttt{X=Z}\rangle$	(**Simplify** `antisymmetry`)
$\langle \mathit{true}, \mathit{true}, \texttt{X=Y} \wedge \texttt{X=Z}\rangle$	(**Solve**)

One can remark that in this operational semantics, once a propagation rule can be applied, it can be applied infinitely often, which leads to a trivial case of non termination. In the preceding example, one could have applied the **`transitivity`** rule instead of the **`antisymmetry`** rule, thus reintroducing the constraint $\texttt{X=<Z}$ that was eliminated at the fourth step. In [11], Abdennadher gives refined operational semantics that are more faithful to the actual implementation of CHR. In particular the previous behavior is avoided by restricting the application of a rule only once on the same constraints. The subject reduction theorems given in the following sections express that given a well-typed program, a transition occurring from a well-typed state leads to a well-typed state. It is worth noting that they thus hold also in these more realistic semantics.

2.3 CLP+CHR

When the host language is a constraint logic programming language of the class $CLP(\mathcal{X})$ [12], it is possible to tightly integrate CHR to the host language. To this end, Frühwirth [1] proposed to extend CHR with the construct *label_with* used to define CHR constraints by CLP clauses. We recall here the syntax and operational semantics of this extension. We note $\mathcal{S}_F$ (resp. $\mathcal{S}_P$) the set of function (resp. predicate) symbols, given with their arity, and $\mathcal{V}$ the set of variables. An *atom* is either a native constraint, a CHR constraint or of the form $p(t_1, \ldots, t_n)$, where p/n is a program predicate symbol.

Definition 4. *A* labeling declaration *for a CHR constraint H is an expression of the form:*

$$\mathit{label\_with}\ H\ \mathit{if}\ G_1, \ldots, G_j$$

where $G_1 \ldots, G_j$ is a conjunction of native constraints.
Clauses are of the form:

$$H\ \texttt{:-}\ B_1, \ldots, B_n$$

where H an atom corresponding either to a predicate or to a CHR constraint but not to a native constraint, and $B_1, \ldots, B_k$ is a sequence of atoms.

The declaration *label_with* $c(t_1,\ldots,t_n)$ *if* $G_1,\ldots,G_j$ expresses that if the guard $G_1,\ldots,G_j$ is implied by the constraint store, then $c(t_1,\ldots,t_n)$ is non deterministically replaced by the body of one of the clauses for c/n. The following definition gives formal semantics to *label_with* declarations and to predicate calls.

Definition 5. *The relation transition between CHR states is extended by the two following rules:*

Unfold
$\langle H' \wedge F, E, D\rangle \longmapsto \langle B \wedge F, E, H = H' \wedge D\rangle$
if $(H$:- $B)$ *is in* P *renamed with fresh variables,*
and H *is not a CHR constraint.*

Label
$\langle F, H' \wedge E, D\rangle \longmapsto \langle B \wedge F, E, H = H' \wedge D\rangle$
if $(H$:- $B)$ *and (label_with* H'' *if* $G)$ *are in* P *renamed with fresh variables,*
and $\mathcal{CT} \models D \Rightarrow \exists \bar{x}(H' = H'' \wedge G)$

The **Unfold** transition is close to the CSLD resolution rule [12]. The difference is that, under CSLD resolution, the constraints in the body of the resolving clause are added to the native constraint store and the resulting store, i.e. $H = H' \wedge D \wedge C$, must be satisfiable, which is not demanded here. The CLP clauses for CHR constraints can only be used in a **Label** transition, requiring that the guards declared using *label_with* are implied by the current native constraint store.

3 Type System

3.1 Assumptions About the Type System of the Host Language

Since CHR is an extension of a host language, the type system we propose is parameterized by the type system, noted $\vdash_N$, of the host language. We will make the following assumptions on $\vdash_N$.

We suppose that $\vdash_N$ is based on a type algebra, the set of types being noted $\mathcal{T}$. Types are noted using the letter τ. Typing environments, noted Γ, associate types to program variables. Given an expression t and a typing environment Γ, $\vdash_N$ is used to deduce typing judgments of the form $\Gamma \vdash_N t : \tau$. Similarly, $\vdash_N$ is used to deduce *well-typed* constraints in a typing environment Γ, a conjunction $C_1 \wedge \ldots \wedge C_n$ of native constraints being well-typed in Γ if for each $i \in \{1,\ldots,n\}$, C_i is well-typed in Γ. We note $\Gamma \vdash_N C\ Atom$, the fact that C is well-typed in the typing environment Γ. We also assume that the equality constraint $s = t$ between s and t is well-typed in Γ if there exists a type τ such that $\Gamma \vdash_N s : \tau$ and $\Gamma \vdash_N t : \tau$.

We assume that the union of type environments over disjoint sets of variables can be formed with an operation noted $\uplus$ such that if $\Gamma \vdash_N t : \tau$ then $\Gamma \uplus \Gamma' \vdash_N t : \tau$ for any typing environment Γ' disjoint from Γ.

We also assume that if a conjunction of native constraints C is well-typed in a typing environment Γ and $\mathcal{CT} \models C \Leftrightarrow D$, then there exists a typing environment

Γ', such that the conjunction of constraints D is well-typed in $\Gamma \uplus \Gamma'$. This condition, needed for theorem 1, expresses that **Solve** transitions performed by the native constraint solver do not produce ill-typed constraint stores from well-typed ones.

3.2 Type System for CHR

The type system we propose for CHR defines a notion of well-typedness for CHR rules. To each CHR constraint symbol c/n is associated a set of types $types(c/n)$, each type being of the form $\tau_1 \times \ldots \times \tau_n$. This set of types is assumed to be fixed, for example using some declarations provided by the programmer. This framework allows the use of parametric polymorphism [13]. A parametric type scheme $\forall \alpha_1 \ldots \alpha_k.\ \tau_1 \times \ldots \times \tau_n$ is represented by the set of all its possible instantiations. For example, declaring that $types(\texttt{append}/3) = \{list(\tau) \times list(\tau) \times list(\tau) \mid \tau \in \mathcal{T}\}$ allows one to give the type $\forall \alpha.\ list(\alpha) \times list(\alpha) \times list(\alpha)$ to the constraint `append/3`.

Table 1. Type system for CHR

(*Native*) $$\frac{\Gamma \vdash_N C\ Atom}{\Gamma \vdash C\ Atom}$$ if C is a native constraint

(*CHR Atom*) $$\frac{\Gamma \vdash_N t_1 : \tau_1 \quad \ldots \quad \Gamma \vdash_N t_n : \tau_n}{\Gamma \vdash c(t_1, \ldots, t_n)\ Atom}$$ if c/n a CHR constraint and if $\tau_1 \times \ldots \times \tau_n \in types(c/n)$

(*Goal*) $$\frac{\Gamma \vdash B_1\ Atom \quad \ldots \quad \Gamma \vdash B_n\ Atom}{\Gamma \vdash B_1, \ldots, B_n\ Goal}$$

(*CHR Head*) $$\frac{\Gamma \vdash_N t_1 : \tau_1 \quad \ldots \quad \Gamma \vdash_N t_n : \tau_n}{\Gamma \vdash c(t_1, \ldots, t_n)\ Head_{\tau_1 \times \ldots \times \tau_n}}$$ if c/n a CHR constraint and if $\tau_1 \times \ldots \times \tau_n \in types(c/n)$

(*MultiHead*) $$\frac{\Gamma \vdash H_1\ Head_{\sigma_1} \quad \ldots \quad \Gamma \vdash H_i\ Head_{\sigma_i}}{\Gamma \vdash H_1, \ldots, H_i\ MHead_{\sigma_1, \ldots, \sigma_i}}$$

(*Simpl CHR*) $$\frac{\forall \bar{\sigma} \in \bar{S}, \exists \Gamma_{\bar{\sigma}} \quad \begin{array}{l} \Gamma_{\bar{\sigma}} \vdash H_1, \ldots, H_n\ MHead_{\bar{\sigma}} \\ \Gamma_{\bar{\sigma}} \vdash G_1, \ldots, G_r\ Goal \\ \Gamma_{\bar{\sigma}} \vdash B_1, \ldots, B_q\ Goal \end{array}}{\vdash H_1, \ldots, H_n \texttt{ <=> } G_1, \ldots, G_r \mid B_1, \ldots, B_q\ Rule}$$

where $\bar{\sigma} = (\sigma_1, \ldots, \sigma_n)$, $\bar{S} = S_1 \times \ldots \times S_n$ and for all $i \in \{1, \ldots, n\}$, $H_i = c_i(t_1^i, \ldots, t_{m_i}^i)$ and $S_i = types(c_i/m_i)$

The rules of the type system for CHR are given in table 1, where σ's represent types of CHR constraints and S's represent sets of such types. A CHR constraint H is *well-typed* in Γ if the judgment $\Gamma \vdash H\ Atom$ can be derived from the typing rule. Terms or expressions appearing as arguments of the constraints are typed using the type system $\vdash_N$ for the host language.

The typing rules resemble the rules of Chin, Sulzmann and Wang [4], but add the possibility for a CHR constraint to have more than one type, and abstract from the type system of the host language.

The rules (*CHR Head*) and (*MultiHead*), differ from (*CHR Atom*) and (*Goal*) in that they add an annotation for keeping track of the type used for typing each head. The rule (*Simpl CHR*) requires, for each combination $\sigma_1, \ldots, \sigma_n$ of the types of the different occurrences of the CHR constraints of the head of the CHR rule, that the head, the guard and the body of the CHR rule are well-typed in some typing environment $\Gamma_{\sigma_1,\ldots,\sigma_n}$. As shown in section 4.3, in the case of parametric polymorphism, this can be ensured by renaming the type scheme of each occurrence of CHR constraints in the head with distinct variables, which can be seen as applying the principle of *definitional genericity* [14] to the typing of CHR constraints. In the context of logic programming, this principle establishes that the type of the head of a clause must be equivalent to, up to renaming but not an instance of, the declared type of the predicate.

The following lemma expresses that the well-typedness of goals is preserved by extension of the environment:

Lemma 1. *Let G be a goal and Γ a typing environment such that $\Gamma \vdash G$ Goal. Let Γ' be a typing environment such that $\Gamma \uplus \Gamma'$ is defined. Then $\Gamma \uplus \Gamma' \vdash G$ Goal.*

Proof. By induction on the derivation and by using the assumption that if $\Gamma \vdash_N t : \tau$ then $\Gamma \uplus \Gamma' \vdash_N t : \tau$.

The consistency of the type system w.r.t. the operational semantics of CHR is given by the following subject reduction theorem, which expresses that the well-typedness of goals is preserved by transitions:

Theorem 1. *Let P be a well-typed CHR program. Let $\langle F, E, D\rangle$ and $\langle F', E', D'\rangle$ be two states such that $\langle F, E, D\rangle \longmapsto \langle F', E', D'\rangle$. If there exists a typing environment Γ such that $\Gamma \vdash F, E, D$ Goal, then there exists a typing environment Γ' such that $\Gamma' \vdash F', E', D'$ Goal. Moreover, if the transition rule contains a guard G then $\Gamma' \vdash G$ Goal.*

Proof. By case on the transition.

Solve. By hypothesis, $\Gamma \vdash D$ *Goal* and $\Gamma \vdash C$ *Atom*. Since $\mathcal{CT} \models (C \wedge D) \Leftrightarrow D'$, and by assumption on $\vdash_N$, there exists a typing environment Γ'' such that $\Gamma \uplus \Gamma'' \vdash_N D'$ *Goal*. By posing $\Gamma' = \Gamma \uplus \Gamma''$ and by lemma 1, we obtain $\Gamma' \vdash F, E$ *Goal*, thus $\Gamma' \vdash F, E, D'$ *Goal*.

Introduce. This transition only moves a constraint from the goal to the CHR constraint store, thus the resulting state is also well-typed in Γ.

Simplify. Let $H = c_1(t^1_1, \ldots, t^1_{m_1}) \wedge \ldots \wedge c_n(t^n_1, \ldots, t^n_{m_n})$. Moreover, for some $E = H' \wedge E''$, with $\mathcal{CT} \models D \Rightarrow H' = H$. This means $H' = c_1(s^1_1, \ldots, s^1_{m_1}) \wedge \ldots \wedge c_n(s^n_1, \ldots, s^n_{m_n})$. Since H' is well typed in Γ, for each $i \in \{1, \ldots, n\}$, there exists $\sigma_i \in types(c_i/m_i)$ such that $\sigma_i = \tau^i_1 \times \ldots \times \tau^i_{m_i}$ and, for each $j \in \{1, \ldots, m_i\}$, $\Gamma \vdash_N s^i_j : \tau^i_j$.

Since the rule (H `<=>` $G \mid B$) is well-typed, there exists a typing environment $\Gamma'' = \Gamma_{\sigma_1,\ldots,\sigma_n}$ such that $\Gamma'' \vdash H_1, \ldots, H_n \; MHead_{\sigma_1,\ldots,\sigma_n}$, $\Gamma'' \vdash G \; Goal$ and $\Gamma'' \vdash B \; Goal$.

By lemma 1, and by posing $\Gamma' = \Gamma \uplus \Gamma''$, we obtain $\Gamma' \vdash F, E, D \; Goal$ and $\Gamma' \vdash G, B \; Goal$. It remains to prove that $H = H'$ is well-typed in Γ'. We have for each $i \in \{1, \ldots, n\}$, for each $j \in \{1, \ldots, m_i\}$, $\Gamma' \vdash_N s^i_j : \tau^i_j$. Since $\Gamma'' \vdash H \; MHead_{\sigma_1,\ldots,\sigma_n}$, then for each $i \in \{1, \ldots, n\}$, $\Gamma'' \vdash H_i \; Head_{\sigma_i}$. Thus for each $j \in \{1, \ldots, m_i\}$, $\Gamma'' \vdash_N t^i_j : \tau^i_j$. Thus $\Gamma' \vdash_N t^i_j = s^i_j \; Atom$. Thus, we obtain $\Gamma' \vdash B, F, E, H = H', D \; Goal$ and $\Gamma' \vdash H = H', G \; Goal$.

The following example shows the necessity of considering all possible combinations of types when typing a CHR rule with multiple heads.

Example 3. Let us assume that the constraint `=<` has the type scheme $\forall \alpha. \alpha \times \alpha$. Let us consider the polymorphic type $list(\alpha)$ for lists and the types *int* and *string*. We assume that the empty list `[]` has type $\forall \alpha.\; list(\alpha)$, that the list constructor has type $\forall \alpha.\; \alpha \times list(\alpha) \to list(\alpha)$, and that $list(int)$ and $list(string)$ are incompatible[2]. Then the `transitivity` rule is not well-typed:

```
X=<Y, Y=<Z  ==> X=<Z
```

For example, one might consider the type $list(int) \times list(int)$ for the first occurrence of `=<`/2 and the type $list(string) \times list(string)$ for the second one, in which case the head is not well-typed because `Y` can not have both types $list(int)$ and $list(string)$.

The transitivity rule above can produce an ill-typed state from a well-typed one. The state $\langle true,$ `["a"] =< []` $\wedge$ `[] =< [1]`$, true\rangle$ is well-typed. However the rule would add `X = ["a"]` $\wedge$ `Z = [1]` $\wedge$ `X =< Z` to the current goal. This subgoal is not well-typed because, when typing `X =< Z`, the type chosen for `=<`/2 must be compatible both with $list(string)$ and $list(int)$. In other words it is possible to end up with an inequality constraint between two terms with incompatible types, while the type of inequality explicitly state that they should have the same type, which can lead to unexpected errors during the execution of the program.

4 Integration with CLP

In this section we are interested in the particular case where the host language is a constraint logic language, typed using the prescriptive type system TCLP [9]. This system combines parametric polymorphism, subtyping and overloading to obtain the flexibility that is needed for typing CLP programs that are originally untyped. In particular, subtyping is used for typing the simultaneous use of different constraint domains: for instance, the relation $boolean \leq int$ allows one to see booleans as integers, and thus to type check constraints combining boolean

[2] For example, this is the case if we consider the native constraint domain to be the Herbrand universe typed with the Mycroft-O'Keefe type system [13] without overloading.

variables with integer variables (such as in a sum of boolean variables). Subtyping is also used for the typing of programs using meta-programming techniques: the relation $list(\alpha) \leq term$ allows one to see homogeneous lists as terms and to apply decomposition predicates to them, such as `functor/3`, `arg/3` or `=../2`.

In [9], the type system of TCLP is proved consistent w.r.t. the CSLD execution model [12], which is an abstract model of execution proceeding by constraint accumulation. In particular, the transformations that can be made by the constraint solver are not considered. In the following, we assume that the solver for native constraints only performs simplifications that preserve well-typedness, according to the assumptions of section 3.1. This can be obtained either by using a typed execution model, as proposed in [9], or, in the case of the equality constraint, by using modes to fix the dataflow [15].

First, we present the type algebra used in the system, then we recall the typing rules for CLP, together with a typing rule for the labeling declaration *label_with*. The resulting system is proven consistent w.r.t. the CLP+CHR execution model.

4.1 Type Structure

We consider a partial order $(\mathcal{K}, \leq_{\mathcal{K}})$ of *type constructors*, given with their arity. The set $\mathcal{T}$ of types is the set of finite or infinite types built on $\mathcal{K}$.

Subtyping Relation. The use of subtyping for meta-programming purposes requires to consider relations like $list(\alpha) \leq term$. This form of non-structural non-homogeneous subtyping links different constructors of different arities. Such subtyping relations require to express the correspondence between the different arguments of type constructors. For example, by writing $k_1(\alpha, \beta) \leq k_2(\beta)$, we specify that types built with k_1 are subtypes of those built with k_2, provided that the second argument of k_1 is a subtype of the argument of k_2, the first argument of k_1 being forgotten in the subtyping relation. One way to express the correspondence is to use a formalism of labels, as proposed by Pottier [16]. In this formalism, a label is associated to each argument of type constructors, the correspondence being expressed by the fact that two arguments of type constructors have the same label. The subtyping order $\leq$ is built from the order $\leq_{\mathcal{K}}$ on type constructors and from the labels. A formal description of the type structure is given in [5], where the structures of types and type constructors are quasi-lattices, i.e. partial orders in which two elements have a least upper (resp. greatest lower) bound if and only if they have an upper (resp. lower) bound.

Subtyping Constraints. Let $\mathcal{W}$ be a set of *type variables*, or *parameters*, noted $\alpha, \beta, \ldots$. We note $\mathcal{T}_{\mathcal{W}}$ the set of types built on $\mathcal{K} \cup \mathcal{W}$.

Definition 6. *A* subtyping constraint *is of the form* $\tau_1 \leq \tau_2$, *where* $\tau_1, \tau_2 \in \mathcal{T}_{\mathcal{W}}$ *are finite types. A substitution* $\rho : \mathcal{W} \to \mathcal{T}$ satisfies *the constraint* $\tau_1 \leq \tau_2$, *noted* $\rho \models \tau_1 \leq \tau_2$, *if* $\rho(\tau_1) \leq \rho(\tau_2)$. *The subtyping constraint* $\tau_1 \leq \tau_2$ *is* satisfiable *if there exists a substitution* ρ *such that* $\rho \models \tau_1 \leq \tau_2$.

In [5], sufficient conditions on $(\mathcal{K}, \leq_{\mathcal{K}})$ are given for the decidability of the satisfiability of subtyping constraints in quasi-lattices, this problem is shown to be NP-complete, and a practical algorithm (used in section 5) is given for computing explicit solutions.

4.2 Type System for CLP+CHR

In order to support the overloading of CLP function and predicate symbols, we assume that a set $types(f/n)$ of type schemes of the form $\forall\bar{\alpha}.\tau_1 \times \ldots \times \tau_n \rightarrow \tau$ is associated to each function symbol f/n (resp. predicate symbol p/n), where $\bar{\alpha}$ is the set of parameters occurring in types $\tau_1, \ldots, \tau_n, \tau$. These sets of types are supposed to be fixed, for example using declarations provided by the programmer. We also assume that the type of the constraint $= /2$ is the type scheme $\forall\alpha.\alpha \times \alpha$. For the sake of simplicity, the quantification $\forall\bar{\alpha}$ will be omitted in type schemes, each occurrence of a type scheme being renamed with fresh parameters.

A typing environment is a partial mapping $\Gamma : \mathcal{V} \mapsto \mathcal{T}_{\mathcal{W}}$, also noted $\{X_1 : \tau_1, \ldots, X_n : \tau_n\}$. The operation $\uplus$ on typing environments is defined as disjoint union, that is $(\Gamma_1 \uplus \Gamma_2)(X) = \Gamma_1(X)$ if $X \in dom(\Gamma_1)$, $(\Gamma_1 \uplus \Gamma_2)(X) = \Gamma_2(X)$ if $X \in dom(\Gamma_2)$, and $(\Gamma_1 \uplus \Gamma_2)(X)$ is undefined otherwise.

Table 2. Type system for CLP and *label_with*

$$(Var)\ \frac{X : \tau \in \Gamma}{\Gamma \vdash X : \tau} \qquad (Sub)\ \frac{\Gamma \vdash t : \tau \quad \tau \leq \tau'}{\Gamma \vdash t : \tau'}$$

$$(Func)\ \frac{\Gamma \vdash t_1 : \tau_1\rho \quad \ldots \quad \Gamma \vdash t_n : \tau_n\rho}{\Gamma \vdash f(t_1, \ldots, t_n) : \tau\rho} \quad \begin{array}{r}\rho \text{ is a type substitution} \\ \tau_1 \times \ldots \tau_n \rightarrow \tau \in types(f/n)\end{array}$$

$$(Atom)\ \frac{\Gamma \vdash t_1 : \tau_1\rho \quad \ldots \quad \Gamma \vdash t_n : \tau_n\rho}{\Gamma \vdash p(t_1, \ldots, t_n)\ Atom} \quad \begin{array}{r}\rho \text{ is a type substitution} \\ \tau_1 \times \ldots \tau_n \in types(p/n)\end{array}$$

$$(Head)\ \frac{\Gamma \vdash t_1 : \tau_1\rho \quad \ldots \quad \Gamma \vdash t_n : \tau_n\rho}{\Gamma \vdash p(t_1, \ldots, t_n)\ Head_{\tau_1 \times \ldots \times \tau_n}} \quad \begin{array}{r}\rho \text{ is a type renaming} \\ \tau_1 \times \ldots \tau_n \in types(p/n)\end{array}$$

$$(Clause)\ \frac{\forall\sigma \in types(p/n) \quad \begin{array}{c}\Gamma_\sigma \vdash p(t_1, \ldots, t_n)\ Head_\sigma \\ \Gamma_\sigma \vdash B_1\ Atom \quad \ldots \quad \Gamma_\sigma \vdash B_k\ Atom\end{array}}{\vdash p(t_1, \ldots, t_n)\ \text{:-}\ B_1, \ldots, B_k\ Clause}$$

$$(Label\ with)\ \frac{\Gamma \vdash H\ Atom \quad \Gamma \vdash G\ Goal}{\vdash label\_with\ H\ if\ G\ Label\_with}$$

Table 2 gives the typing rules for CLP, together with the typing rule for the declaration *label_with*. The typing rules for CLP resemble the rules of Mycroft and O'Keefe [13] with the addition of subtyping and overloading. A predicate call $p(t_1, \ldots, t_n)$ (resp. a native constraint) is *well-typed* in a typing environment

Γ if $\Gamma \vdash p(t_1,\ldots,t_n)$ *Atom* can be derived from the rules. A clause H :- B is *well-typed* if $\vdash H$:- B *Clause* can be derived from the rules. A labeling declaration *label_with H if G* is well-typed if $\vdash$ *label_with H if G Label_with* can be derived. The (*Sub*) rule gives the semantics of subtyping by expressing that if a term t has type τ, then it has all types that are greater than τ.

The set of rules of tables 1 and 2 define the type system for CLP+CHR. A CLP+CHR program is well-typed if all its CHR rules, all its clauses and all its labeling declarations are well-typed.

The distinction between rules (*Atom*) and (*Head*) expresses the principle of *definitional genericity* [14], which establishes that the type of the head of a clause must be equivalent to, up to renaming but not an instance of, the declared type of the predicate. The rule (*Clause*) imposes that a clause must be well-typed for all possible types of the defined predicate, in a typing environment Γ_σ that depends on the considered type σ. This can be seen as a condition similar to definitional genericity for overloading. These two conditions are useful for the following subject reduction theorem which expresses the consistency of the type system with reference to the operational semantics of CLP+CHR.

Theorem 2. *Let us consider a well-typed CHR+CLP program. Let* $\langle F, E, D\rangle$ *and* $\langle F', E', D'\rangle$ *be two states and* Γ *be a typing environment such that* $\Gamma \vdash F, E, D$ *Goal. If* $\langle F, E, D\rangle \longmapsto \langle F', E', D'\rangle$*, then there exists a typing environment* Γ' *such that* $\Gamma' \vdash F', E', D'$ *Goal. Moreover, if the transition rules contain a guard* G *then* $\Gamma' \vdash G$ *Goal.*

The proof of theorem 2 is preceded by a lemma which expresses that in a derivation apart from (*Head*) or (*Clause*), the types can be arbitrarily instantiated.

Lemma 2. *For any typing environment* Γ*, for any judgment* R *different from Head or Clause and any type substitution* ρ*, if* $\Gamma \vdash R$ *then* $\Gamma\rho \vdash R\rho$*.*

Proof. By induction on the derivation.

Proof (of theorem 2). One can check that the assumptions of section 3.1 are correct for the the system of table 2. Moreover, an atom corresponding to a predicate call and an atom corresponding to a native constraint are typed in the same way. Therefore, by theorem 1, if the transition is one of **Solve**, **Introduce** or **Simplify**, then there exists a typing environment Γ' such that $\Gamma' \vdash F', E', D'$ *Goal* and $\Gamma' \vdash G$ *Goal* in case of need.

Let us consider the **Unfold** transition. We can assume, without loss of generality, that $H' = p(s)$ and $H = p(t)$. Since $\Gamma \vdash p(s)$ *Atom*, there exists a type scheme $\tau \in types(p)$ and a substitution ρ such that $\Gamma \vdash s : \tau\rho$. Since the program is well-typed, $\vdash H$:- B *Clause*, thus there exists a typing environment Γ_τ such that $\Gamma_\tau \vdash B$ *Goal* and $\Gamma_\tau \vdash p(t)$ *Head*$_\tau$, that is $\Gamma_\tau \vdash t : \tau\rho_r$ where ρ_r is a renaming of τ. By posing $\rho' = \rho_r^{-1}\rho$, and by lemma 2, we obtain $\Gamma_\tau\rho' \vdash t : \tau\rho$ and $\Gamma_\tau\rho' \vdash B$ *Goal*. By posing $\Gamma' = \Gamma_\tau\rho' \uplus \Gamma$, we obtain $\Gamma' \vdash t = s$ *Atom*. Thus $\Gamma' \vdash B, F, E, s = t, D$ *Goal*.

Let us finally consider the case of a **Label** transition. Similarly to the case of the **Unfold** transition, there exists a typing environment Γ', such that $\Gamma' \vdash$

$B, F, E, t = s, D$. Since H' is a CHR constraint, τ does not contain any parameter, that is ρ'' is the identity substitution. We have $H'' = p(u)$ for some term u. Since $\vdash$ *label_with* H'' *if* G *Label_with*, there exists a typing environment Γ_{lw} such that $\Gamma_{lw} \vdash G$ *Goal* and $\Gamma_{lw} \vdash H''$ *Atom*, that is $\Gamma_{lw} \vdash u : \tau$. By posing $\Gamma'' = \Gamma' \uplus \Gamma_{lw}$, we obtain $\Gamma'' \vdash s = u$ *Atom*, $\Gamma'' \vdash B, F, E, s = t, D$ and $\Gamma'' \vdash G$ *Goal*, and thus $\Gamma'' \vdash s = u, G$ *Goal*.

4.3 Typing of Polymorphic CHR Constraints

In this section, we show how to type check CHR constraints in the presence of parametric polymorphism. The set $types(c/n)$ of the types of the constraint c/n is restricted to a finite set of type schemes of the form $\forall \bar{\alpha}.\ \tau_1 \times \ldots \times \tau_n$. This does not mean that $types(c/n)$ itself is finite, as a type scheme represent an infinite set of types. More precisely, we assume a finite set $types_p(c/n)$ of type schemes and define $types(c/n) = \{\tau_1\rho \times \ldots \times \tau_n\rho \mid \forall \bar{\alpha}.\ \tau_1 \times \ldots \times \tau_n \in types_p(c/n) \text{ and } \rho : \bar{\alpha} \to \mathcal{T}\}$.

Table 3. Typing rules for polymorphic CHR constraints

$$(\mathit{CHR\ Atom}_p)\ \frac{\Gamma \vdash t_1 : \tau_1\rho \quad \ldots \quad \Gamma \vdash t_n : \tau_n\rho}{\Gamma \vdash c(\tau_1, \ldots \tau_n)\ \mathit{Atom}} \quad \begin{array}{r}\rho \text{ is a type substitution} \\ \forall \bar{\alpha}.\ \tau_1 \times \ldots \times \tau_n \in types_p(c/n)\end{array}$$

$$(\mathit{CHR\ Head}_p)\ \frac{\Gamma \vdash t_1 : \tau_1\rho \quad \ldots \quad \Gamma \vdash t_n : \tau_n\rho}{\Gamma \vdash c(\tau_1, \ldots \tau_n)\ \mathit{Head}_{\tau_1 \times \ldots \times \tau_n, \rho}} \quad \begin{array}{r}\rho \text{ is a type renaming} \\ \forall \bar{\alpha}.\ \tau_1 \times \ldots \times \tau_n \in types_p(c/n)\end{array}$$

$$(\mathit{MultiHead}_p)\ \frac{\begin{array}{c}\forall i \in \{1, \ldots, n\}\ \Gamma \vdash H_i\ \mathit{Head}_{\sigma_i, \rho_i} \\ \forall\, 1 \leq i < j \leq n\ \mathit{codom}(\rho_i) \cap \mathit{codom}(\rho_j) = \emptyset\end{array}}{\Gamma \vdash H_1, \ldots, H_n\ \mathit{MHead}_{\sigma_1, \ldots, \sigma_n}}$$

A type system that deals directly with parametric polymorphism can be obtained by replacing rules (*CHR Atom*), (*CHR Head*) and (*MultiHead*) by their counterparts given in table 3 and by replacing $types(c_i/m_i)$ by $types_p(c_i/m_i)$ in rule (*Simpl CHR*). The resulting type system is noted $\vdash_p$. The following proposition expresses the equivalence of the two type systems:

Proposition 1. *A CHR rule (resp. goal) is well-typed in* $\vdash$ *if and only if it is well-typed in* $\vdash_p$.

Proof. First we show the proposition for atoms, which extends straightforwardly to goals. Let us assume that $\Gamma \vdash c(t_1, \ldots, t_n)$ *Atom*. Then there exists $\tau_1 \times \ldots \times \tau_n \in types(c/n)$ such that for each $i \in \{1, \ldots, n\}$, $\Gamma \vdash t_i : \tau_i$. By definition, there exists a type substitution ρ and a type scheme $\forall \bar{\alpha}.\ \tau'_1 \times \ldots \times \tau'_n \in types_p(c/n)$ such that for each $i \in \{1, \ldots, n\}$, $\tau_i = \tau'_i\rho$. Therefore, $\Gamma \vdash_p c(t_1, \ldots, t_n)$ *Atom*. On the other hand, if $\Gamma \vdash_p c(t_1, \ldots, t_n)$ *Atom*, then there exists $\forall \bar{\alpha}.\ \tau'_1 \times \ldots \times \tau'_n \in types_p(c/n)$ and ρ such that for each $i \in \{1, \ldots, n\}$, $\Gamma \vdash t_i : \tau'_i\rho$. Since $\tau_1\rho \times \ldots \tau_n\rho \in types(c/n)$, we obtain $\Gamma \vdash c(t_1, \ldots, t_n)$ *Atom*.

Now we show that if a rule is well-typed in $\vdash_p$, then it is well-typed in $\vdash$. Similarly to lemma 2, if $\Gamma \vdash_p t : \tau$ (resp. $\Gamma \vdash_p A$ *Atom*), then $\Gamma\rho \vdash_p t : \tau\rho$ (resp.

$\Gamma\rho \vdash_p A\ Atom$). We pose, for each $i \in \{1,\ldots,n\}$, $H_i = c_i(t^i_1,\ldots,t^i_{m_i})$. Let us consider $(\sigma_1 \times \ldots \times \sigma_n) \in types(c_1/m_1) \times \ldots \times (c_n/m_n)$. For each $i \in \{1,\ldots,n\}$ there exists ρ'_i and $\sigma'_i \in types_p(c_i/n_i)$ such that $\sigma_i = \sigma'_i\rho'_i$. By rules (*Simpl CHR*) and (*MultiHead*$_p$), there exists a typing environment Γ_p and some type renamings $\rho_1,\ldots,\rho_n$, with distinct codomains, such that, for each $i \in \{1,\ldots,n\}$, $\Gamma \vdash_p H_i\ Head_{\sigma'_i,\rho_i}$. Since all ρ_i's have distinct codomains, we can define $\rho_p = \bigcup_{i=1}^n \rho^1_i\rho'_i$. Thus, for each $i \in \{1,\ldots,n\}$, $\Gamma_p\rho_p H_i\ Head_{\sigma'_i\rho_i\rho_i^{-1}\rho'_i}$. Thus $\Gamma_p\rho_p \vdash H_1,\ldots,H_n\ MHead_{\sigma_1,\ldots,\sigma_n}$. Moreover $\Gamma_p\rho_p \vdash_p G_1,\ldots,G_r,B_1,\ldots,B_q\ Goal$, thus $\Gamma_p\rho_p \vdash G_1,\ldots,G_r,B_1,\ldots,B_q\ Goal$. As this holds for any $(\sigma_1 \times \ldots \times \sigma_n) \in types(c_1/m_1) \times \ldots \times (c_n/m_n)$, we deduce that the rule is well-typed in $\vdash$.

Finally, we show that if a rule is well-typed in $\vdash$, then it is well-typed in $\vdash_p$. Let $(\sigma_1,\ldots,\sigma_n) \in types_p(c_1/m_1) \times \ldots \times types_p(c_n/m_n)$. Let $\rho_1,\ldots\rho_n$ be type renamings of $\sigma_1,\ldots,\sigma_n$ with distinct codomains. For each $i \in \{1,\ldots,n\}$, by definition of $types(c_i/m_i)$, $\sigma_i\rho_i \in types(c_i/m_i)$. Thus there exists Γ such that $\Gamma \vdash H_1,\ldots,H_n\ MHead_{\sigma_1\rho_1,\ldots,\sigma_n\rho_n}$ and $\Gamma \vdash G_1,\ldots,G_r,B_1,\ldots,B_q\ Goal$. Thus we have $\Gamma \vdash_p G_1,\ldots,G_r,B_1,\ldots,B_q\ Goal$. It remains to show that $\Gamma \vdash_p H_1,\ldots,H_n\ MHead_{\sigma_1,\ldots,\sigma_n}$ Since $\Gamma \vdash H_1,\ldots,H_n\ MHead_{\sigma_1\rho_1,\ldots,\sigma_n\rho_n}$, then for each $i \in \{1,\ldots,n\}$, $\Gamma \vdash H_i MHead_{\sigma_i\rho_i}$ and thus, similarly to the case of atoms, $\Gamma \vdash_p H_i MHead_{\sigma_i,\rho_i}$. Thus we deduce $\Gamma \vdash_p H_1,\ldots,H_n\ MHead_{\sigma_1,\ldots,\sigma_n}$.

5 Experimental Results

The type system for CLP+CHR has been implemented as an extension of the TCLP software [10], which is a type checker for constraint logic programming. Furthermore, a type inference algorithm makes it possible to infer types for variables and for program predicates automatically. In a lattice of types with top element *term* however, the type *term* $\times \ldots \times$ *term* is always a possible type for predicates. For this reason, a heuristic type inference algorithm is used, providing a more informative type and often the expected type [9, 6]. This algorithm can also be used to infer the type of CHR constraints that are not declared by the user.

TCLP uses several solvers written in CHR. The main solver is the one for subtyping constraints. We also use a CHR solver to handle overloading of function and predicate symbols during type checking. Some other small CHR solvers are also used for handling typing environments and preliminary computations on the structure of type constructors. Hence, the possibility to type check CHR programs makes it possible that TCLP type checks its own source code.

The following example shows the typical kind of errors detected by TCLP:

Example 4. The following solver handles counters. The constraint `cpt/2` associates the name of the counter to its value, and has type *atom* $\times$ *int*.[3] The constraint `val/2` also has type *atom* $\times$ *int* and constraints `incr/1` and `init/1` have type *atom*.

[3] The type *atom* corresponds to Prolog atoms, that is symbols of arity 0, and not to the logical atoms.

```
init(C) <=> cpt(C,0).
cpt(C,V) \ val(C,X) <=> X=V.
incr(C), cpt(V,C) <=> V1 is V+1, cpt(C,V1).
```

The type checker produces the following message:

```
! Error in "count.pl", line 3 :
  Incompatible types for C : atom and int
```

It is in fact an argument inversion: in the head of the last rule, the arguments of the constraint `cpt` were inverted.

The following example shows the result of type inference on a small solver:

Example 5. The following solver, taken from [17], computes the greatest common divisor of two numbers.

```
gcd(0) <=> true.
gcd(N) \ gcd(M) <=>
   N=<M | L is M mod N, gcd(L).
```

The type checker infers the following type:

```
:- typeof gcd(int) is chr_constraint.
```

that is `gcd` has type *int*.

Performance. The speed of the type checker has been evaluated on ten CHR solvers taken from [17], on the solver for subtyping constraints, on the solver for overloading in TCLP, as well as on the complete TCLP source code. These tests were run on a 2 Ghz Pentium IV with 512 Mo of RAM, using the Sicstus Prolog implementation of TCLP for which the working memory space is limited to 256 Mo. The results are presented in table 4.

Table 4. Performance

			Type check		Type inference	
Program	# lines	# rules	CHR	Total	CHR	Total
gcd	10	2	0.03 s	0.03 s	0.04 s	0.04 s
varleq	30	4	0.04 s	0.26 s	0.07 s	0.43 s
bool	173	78	1.32 s	2.13 s	4.63 s	5.96 s
listdom	73	13	0.78 s	1.45 s	1.77 s	2.75 s
interval	145	24	3.41 s	3.5 s	8.93 s (99.58 s)	9.03 s (99.69 s)
domain	266	84	4.30 s	6.42 s	5.35 s (183.92 s)	7.75 s (186.94 s)
fourier-gauss	328	30	1.98 s	5.88 s	6.01 s (19.04 s)	16.16 s (30.42 s)
arc	47	2	0.14 s	0.81 s	0.23 s	1.09 s
allenComp	495	490	17.48 s	17.51 s	NA	NA
subtyping	595	57	4.52 s	6.22 s	9.96 s (319.66 s)	15.28 s (322.64 s)
overloading	465	10	0.43 s	3.99 s	1.10 s	8.01 s
TCLP	4594	82	5.22 s	53.97 s	26.61 s (416.08 s)	96.09 s (518.39 s)

The first column indicates the CLP+CHR program. The second column indicates the number of lines of codes in the program and the third one indicates the number of CHR rules in the program. Next, in column "Type check", the type checking times are given with type inference for variables, but without type inference for predicates or CHR constraints. Finally, the column "Type inference" indicates the times for inferring types to predicates and constraints. The typing times for CHR rules are given in columns "CHR", while the typing times for the whole CLP+CHR programs are given in the column "Total". The times given between parenthesis are obtained without breaking connected components as explained in the following.

The type checking times without type inference for predicates and constraints show that the type checker is usable in practice. For example, it takes less than 18 s to check the 490 rules of the `allenComp` solver, or less than 54 s to check about 4600 lines of code constituting the source of TCLP.

In presence of subtyping, type inference needs 71 times more CPU time than type checking. In the case of `allenComp`, type inference even fails by lack of memory due to the restriction to 256 Mo. This is due to the fact that, when inferring the type of a constraint, the type checker must consider at the same time all the rules and clauses in a same connected component of the call graph, while type checking can be done rule by rule. CHR solvers often use large connected components however. One reason for this difficulty is that a few constraints used as data structures, appear in the head of numerous rules, thus creating large connected components. For example, the solver for subtyping constraints has a connected component of 54 predicates and CHR constraints. Such connected components thus require to deal with a very large number of subtyping constraints and overloaded symbols at once. Moreover, algorithms for solving subtyping constraints and overloading are potentially exponential [8, 5]. From this point of view, the performance of type inference are quite satisfactory.

It is possible to reduce type inference type by breaking such connected components. This can be done by providing the type of the constraints that are used as data structures. This technique appears to be very efficient, reducing the time for type inference in `domain` from 184 s to 5.3 s, just by giving the type of one constraint. When no time is given between parenthesis, it means that the solver was already well stratified and thus didn't need the type for some CHR constraint to be given. Moreover, type inference can be used the first time a solver is written, the inferred types being used afterwards as declarations during the rest of the development of the solver.

6 Conclusion

We have presented a type system for the *Constraint Handling Rules* CHR language [1], parameterized by the type system of the host language. In the particular case of constraint logic programming, its combination with the prescriptive type system TCLP [9] for CLP languages has been presented. Under the assumption that the well-typedness of native constraints is preserved by logical equivalence, the type system has been proved consistent w.r.t. the operational semantics of CHR and CLP+CHR respectively.

The type system for CLP+CHR is implemented as an extension of the TCLP software [10]. The reported experimental results on ten CHR solvers plus TCLP itself show that the system is already usable and useful.

As for future work, we plan to get some practical experience from the users of the system, in particular for the development of complex modular [18] and/or collaborative CHR solvers. It would also be interesting to study the instantiation of the type system with the one of Java in the framework of the JACK toolkit implementation of CHR [3] and as well as with the Haskell implementation [4].

References

1. Frühwirth, T.: Theory and practice of constraint handling rules. Journal of Logic Programming, Special Issue on Constraint Logic Programming **37** (1998) 95–138
2. Holzbaur, C., Frühwirth, T.: A Prolog Constraint Handling Rules compiler and runtime system. Special Issue Journal of Applied Artificial Intelligence on Constraint Handling Rules **14** (2000)
3. Abdennadher, S., Krämer, E., Saft, M., Schmauss, M.: JACK: A Java Constraint Kit. In: Electronic Notes in Theoretical Computer Science. Volume 64. Elsevier (2000)
4. Chin, W.N., Sulzmann, M., Wang, M.: A type-safe embedding of constraint handling rules into Haskell. Technical report, National University of Singapore (2003) `http://www.comp.nus.edu.sg/~sulzmann/chr/hchr/hchr-tr.ps`.
5. Coquery, E., Fages, F.: Subtyping constraints in quasi-lattices. In Pandya, P., Radhakrishnan, J., eds.: Proceedings of the 23rd conference on foundations of software technology and theoretical computer science, FSTTCS'2003. Lecture Notes in Computer Science, Mumbai, India, Springer-Verlag (2003)
6. Coquery, E.: Typage et programmation en logique avec contraintes. PhD thesis, Université Paris 6 - Pierre et Marie Curie (2004)
7. Stuckey, P.J., Sulzmann, M.: A theory of overloading. In Peyton-Jones, S., ed.: Proceedings of the International Conference on Functional Programming, ACM Press (2002) 167–178
8. Coquery, E., Fages, F.: Tclp: overloading, subtyping and parametric polymorphism made practical for constraint logic programming. Technical Report RR-4926, INRIA Rocquencourt (2002)
9. Fages, F., Coquery, E.: Typing constraint logic programs. Journal of Theory and Practice of Logic Programming **1** (2001) 751–777
10. Coquery, E.: TCLP (2003) `http//contraintes.inria.fr/~coquery/tclp/`.
11. Abdennadher, S.: Operational semantics and confluence of constraint propagation rules. In: Proceedings of CP'1997, 3rd International Conference on Principles and Practice of Constraint Programming. Volume 1330 of Lecture Notes in Computer Science., Linz, Springer-Verlag (1997) 252–266
12. Jaffar, J., Lassez, J.L.: Constraint logic programming. In: Proceedings of the 14th ACM Symposium on Principles of Programming Languages, Munich, Germany, ACM (1987) 111–119
13. Mycroft, A., O'Keefe, R.: A polymorphic type system for Prolog. Artificial Intelligence **23** (1984) 295–307

14. Lakshman, T., Reddy, U.: Typed Prolog: A semantic reconstruction of the Mycroft-O'Keefe type system. In Saraswat, V., Ueda, K., eds.: Proceedings of the 1991 International Symposium on Logic Programming, MIT Press (1991) 202–217
15. Smaus, J.G., Fages, F., Deransart, P.: Using modes to ensure subject reduction for typed logic programs with subtyping. In: Proceedings of FSTTCS '2000. Number 1974 in Lecture Notes in Computer Science, Springer-Verlag (2000)
16. Pottier, F.: A versatile constraint-based type inference system. Nordic Journal of Computing **7** (2000) 312–347
17. Frühwirth, T., Schrijvers, T.: (CHR web page) `http//www.cs.kuleuven.ac.be/~dtai/projects/CHR/`.
18. Haemmerlé, R., Fages, F.: Closures are needed for closed module systems. Technical Report RR-5575, INRIA (2005)

Views and Iterators for Generic Constraint Implementations

Christian Schulte[1] and Guido Tack[2]

[1] ICT, KTH - Royal Institute of Technology, Sweden
schulte@imit.kth.se
[2] PS Lab, Saarland University, Saarbrücken, Germany
tack@ps.uni-sb.de

Abstract. This paper introduces an architecture for generic constraint implementations based on variable views and range iterators. Views allow, for example, to scale, translate, and negate variables. The paper shows how to make constraint implementations generic and how to reuse a single generic implementation with different views for different constraints. A wide range of applications of views exemplifies their usefulness and their potential for simplifying constraint implementations. We introduce domain operations compatible with views based on range iterators. The paper evaluates the applicability of the approach as well as different implementation techniques for the presented architecture.

1 Introduction

A challenging aspect in developing and extending a constraint programming system is implementing a *comprehensive* set of constraints. Ideally, a system should provide simple, expressive, and efficient abstractions that ease development and reuse of constraint implementations.

This paper contributes a new architecture based on variable views and range iterators. The architecture comprises an additional level of abstraction to decouple variable implementations from constraint implementations, the propagators. Propagators compute generically with variable views instead of variables.

A view of a variable presents an adaptor that performs transformations while accessing the variable it abstracts over. Views support operations like scaling, translation, and negation of variables. Views also abstract over the underlying data structure used for storing the variable domain. That way, cross-domain views can for example enable propagators for finite set constraints to operate on finite domain variables.

This simple layer of abstraction allows one propagator to be instantiated multiple times, with different views. For example, a simple generic propagator for linear equality $\sum_{i=1}^{k} x_i = c$ can be used with a scale-view $x_i = a_i \cdot y_i$ to obtain an implementation of $\sum_{i=1}^{k} a_i \cdot y_i = c$. Or a negated Boolean view can be used to derive an implementation of Boolean disjunction from a propagator for conjunction. As a final example, a cross-domain view of a finite domain variable as a singleton set, together with a subset propagator, yields a propagator for $x \in s$. Variable views thus assist in implementing propagators on a higher level of abstraction.

Range iterators support powerful and efficient domain operations on variables and variable views. The operations can access and modify multiple values of a variable

B. Hnich et al. (Eds.): CSCLP 2005, LNAI 3978, pp. 118–132, 2006.

domain simultaneously. Range iterators are efficient as they help avoiding temporary data structures. They simplify propagators by serving as adaptors between variables and propagator data structures.

The architecture is carefully separated from its implementation. Two different implementation approaches are presented and evaluated. An implementation using parametric polymorphism (such as templates in C++) is shown to not incur any runtime cost. The architecture can be used for arbitrary constraint programming systems and has been fully implemented in Gecode [2].

Plan of the paper. The next section presents a model for finite domain constraint programming systems. Sect. 3 introduces variable views and exemplifies their use. Sect. 4 presents Boolean views of finite domain variables and discusses pairs of symmetric propagators. Sect. 5 introduces iterator-based domain operations that are applied to views in the following section. Variable views for set constraints are discussed in Sect. 7. In Sect. 8 implementation approaches for views and iterators are presented, followed by their evaluation in Sect. 9. The last section concludes and discusses future work.

2 Constraint Programming Systems

This section introduces the model for finite domain constraint programming systems considered in this paper and relates it to existing systems.

Variables and propagators. Finite domain constraint programming systems offer services to support constraint propagation and search. In this paper we are only concerned with variables used for constraint propagation. We assume that a constraint is implemented by a *propagator*. A propagator maintains a collection of variables and performs constraint propagation by executing operations on them. In the following we consider finite domain variables and propagators. A finite domain variable x has an associated *domain* $\mathrm{dom}(x)$ being a subset of some finite subset of the integers.

Propagators do not manipulate variable domains directly but use operations provided by the variable. These operations return information about the domain or update the domain. In addition, they handle failure (the domain becomes empty) and control propagation.

Value operations. A *value operation* on a variable involves a single integer as result or argument. We assume that a variable x with $D = \mathrm{dom}(x)$ provides the following value operations: $x.\mathtt{getmin}()$ returns $\min D$, $x.\mathtt{getmax}()$ returns $\max D$, $x.\mathtt{adjmin}(n)$ updates $\mathrm{dom}(x)$ to $\{m \in D \mid m \geq n\}$, $x.\mathtt{adjmax}(n)$ updates $\mathrm{dom}(x)$ to $\{m \in D \mid m \leq n\}$, and $x.\mathtt{excval}(n)$ updates $\mathrm{dom}(x)$ to $\{m \in D \mid m \neq n\}$. These operations are typical for finite domain constraint programming systems like Choco [6], ILOG Solver [9, 11, 4], Eclipse [1], Mozart [8], and Sicstus [5]. Some systems provide additional operations such as for assigning values.

Domain operations. A *domain operation* supports simultaneous access or update of multiple values of a variable domain. In many systems this is provided by supporting an abstract set-datatype for variable domains, as for example in Choco [6], Eclipse [1], Mozart [8], and Sicstus [5]. ILOG Solver [9, 11, 4] only allows access by iterating over the values of a variable domain.

Range sequences. Range notation $[n \mathrel{..} m]$ is used for the set of integers $\{l \in \mathbb{Z} \mid n \leq l \leq m\}$. A *range sequence* $\mathrm{ranges}(I)$ for a finite integer set $I \subseteq \mathbb{Z}$ is the shortest sequence $s = \langle [n_1 \mathrel{..} m_1], \ldots, [n_k \mathrel{..} m_k] \rangle$ such that I is covered ($\mathrm{set}(s) = I$, where $\mathrm{set}(s)$ is defined as $\bigcup_{i=1}^{k} [n_i \mathrel{..} m_i]$) and the ranges are ordered by their smallest elements ($n_i \leq n_{i+1}$ for $1 \leq i < k$). The above range sequence is also written as $\langle [n_i \mathrel{..} m_i] \rangle_{i=1}^{k}$. Clearly, a range sequence is unique, none of its ranges is empty, and $m_i + 1 < n_{i+1}$ for $1 \leq i < k$.

3 Variable Views with Value Operations

This section introduces variable views with value operations. The full design with domain operations and a discussion of their properties follows in Sect. 6.

Example 1 (Smart n-Queens). Consider the well-known finite domain constraint model for n-Queens using three alldifferent constraints: each queen is represented by a variable x_i ($0 \leq i < n$) with domain $\{0, \ldots, n-1\}$. The constraints state that the values of all x_i, the values of all $x_i - i$, and the values of all $x_i + i$ must be pairwise different for $0 \leq i < n$.

If the used constraint programming system lacks versions of alldifferent supporting that the values of $x_i + c_i$ are different, the user must resort to using additional variables y_i and constraints $y_i = x_i + c_i$ and the single constraint that the y_i are different. This approach is clearly not very efficient: it triples the number of variables and requires additional $2n$ binary constraints.

Systems with this extension of alldifferent must implement two very similar versions of the same propagator. This is tedious and increases the amount of code that requires maintenance. In the following we make propagators *generic*: the same propagator can be reused for several variants.

To make a propagator generic, all its operations on variables are replaced by operations on variable views. A *variable view* (view for short) implements the same operations as a variable. A view stores a reference to a variable. Invoking an operation on the view executes the appropriate operation on the view's variable. Multiple variants of a propagator can be obtained by instantiating the single generic propagator with multiple different variable views.

Offset-views. For an *offset-view* $v = \mathrm{voffset}(x, c)$ for a variable x and an integer c, performing an operation on v results in performing an operation on $x + c$. The operations on the offset-view are:

$$
\begin{array}{ll}
v.\texttt{getmin}() := x.\texttt{getmin}() + c & v.\texttt{getmax}() := x.\texttt{getmax}() + c \\
v.\texttt{adjmin}(n) := x.\texttt{adjmin}(n - c) & v.\texttt{adjmax}(n) := x.\texttt{adjmax}(n - c) \\
v.\texttt{excval}(n) := x.\texttt{excval}(n - c) &
\end{array}
$$

To obtain both alldifferent propagators required by Example 1, also an *identity-view* is needed. An operation on an identity-view $\mathrm{vid}(x)$ for a variable x performs the same operation on x. That is, identity-views turn variables into views to comply with propagators now computing with views. In an implementation language that supports subtyping, variables can themselves be regarded as views, eliminating the need for identity views.

Obtaining the two variants of alldifferent is straightforward: the propagator is made generic with respect to which view it uses. Using the propagator with both an identity-view and an offset-view yields the required propagators.

Offset-views can also be used to obtain propagators for strict inequalities from propagators for the non-strict constraints. For instance, $x < y$ can be implemented as $x \leq \text{voffset}(y, -1)$.

Sect. 8 discusses how views can be implemented whereas this section focuses on the architecture only. However, to give some intuition, in C++ for example, propagators can be made generic by implementing them as templates with the used view as template argument. Instantiating the generic propagator then amounts to instantiating the corresponding template with a particular view.

Views are orthogonal to the propagator. In the above example, offset-views can be used for any implementation of alldifferent using value operations. This includes the naive version propagating when variables become assigned or the bounds-consistent version [10].

Scale-views. In the above example, views allow to reuse the same propagator for variants of a constraint, avoiding duplication of code and effort. In the following, views can also simplify the implementation of propagators.

Example 2 (Linear inequalities). A common constraint is linear inequality $\sum_{i=1}^{n} a_i \cdot x_i \leq c$ (equality and disequality is similar) with integers a_i and c and variables x_i. In the following we restrict the a_i to be positive.

A typical bounds-propagator executes for $1 \leq j \leq n$:

$$x_j.\texttt{adjmax}(\lceil (c - l_j)/a_j \rceil) \quad \text{with} \quad l_j = \textstyle\sum_{i=1, i \neq j}^{n} a_i \cdot x_i.\texttt{getmin}()$$

Quite often, models feature the special case $a_i = 1$ for $1 \leq i \leq n$. For this case, it is sufficient to execute for $1 \leq j \leq n$:

$$x_j.\texttt{adjmax}(c - l_j) \quad \text{with} \quad l_j = \textstyle\sum_{i=1, i \neq j}^{n} x_i.\texttt{getmin}()$$

As this case is common, a system should optimize it. An optimized version requires less space (no a_i required) and less time (no multiplication, division, and rounding). But, a more interesting question is: can one just implement the simple propagator and get the full version by using views?

With scale-views, the simple implementation can be used in both cases. A *scale-view* $v = \text{vscale}(a, x)$ for a positive integer $a > 0$ and a variable x defines operations for $a \cdot x$:

$$\begin{array}{ll}
v.\texttt{getmin}() := a \cdot x.\texttt{getmin}() & v.\texttt{getmax}() := a \cdot x.\texttt{getmax}() \\
v.\texttt{adjmin}(n) := x.\texttt{adjmin}(\lceil n/a \rceil) & v.\texttt{adjmax}(n) := x.\texttt{adjmax}(\lfloor n/a \rfloor) \\
v.\texttt{excval}(n) := \textbf{if } n \bmod a = 0 \textbf{ then } x.\texttt{excval}(n/a) &
\end{array}$$

From the simpler implementation the special case (identity-views) and the general case (scale-views) can be obtained. Multiplication, division, and rounding is separated from actually propagating the inequality constraint. Views hence support separation of concerns and can simplify the implementation of propagators. In particular, multiplication, division, and rounding need to be implemented only once for the scale-view: any generic propagator can use scale-views.

Minus-views. Another common optimization is to implement binary and ternary variants of commonly used constraints. This optimization reduces the overhead with respect to both time and memory as no array is needed.

Example 3 (Binary linear inequality). Consider a propagator for $v_1 + v_2 \leq c$ with views v_1 and v_2 propagating as described in Example 2. With scale-views $v_1 = \text{vscale}(a_1, x_1)$ and $v_2 = \text{vscale}(a_2, x_2)$ the propagator also implements $a_1 \cdot x_1 + a_2 \cdot x_2 \leq c$ provided that $a_1, a_2 > 0$. However, $x_1 - x_2 \leq c$ cannot be obtained with scale-views. Even if scale-views allowed negative constants, it would be inefficient to multiply, divide, and round to just achieve negation.

A *minus-view* $v = \text{vminus}(x)$ for a variable x provides operations such that v behaves as $-x$. Its operations reflect that the smallest possible value for x is the largest possible value for $-x$ and vice versa:

$$v.\texttt{getmin}() := -x.\texttt{getmax}() \qquad v.\texttt{getmax}() := -x.\texttt{getmin}()$$
$$v.\texttt{adjmin}(n) := x.\texttt{adjmax}(-n) \qquad v.\texttt{adjmax}(n) := x.\texttt{adjmin}(-n)$$
$$v.\texttt{excval}(n) := x.\texttt{excval}(-n)$$

With minus-views, $x_1 - x_2 \leq c$ can be obtained from an implementation of $v_1 + v_2 \leq c$ with $v_1 = \text{vid}(x_1)$ and $v_2 = \text{vminus}(x_2)$. With an offset-view it is actually sufficient to implement $v_1 + v_2 \leq 0$. Then $x_1 + x_2 \leq c$ can be implemented by an identity-view $\text{vid}(x_1)$ for v_1 and an offset-view $\text{voffset}(x_2, -c)$ for v_2. But again, given just $v_1 + v_2 \leq 0$, an implementation for $x_1 - x_2 \leq c$ with $c \neq 0$ cannot be obtained.

Minus-views implement the inverse for finite domain variables, thus all propagators that are symmetric with respect to the sign of their arguments can take advantage of minus views. An example for a pair of symmetric propagators on finite domain variables is minimum and maximum: $\max(x_1, \ldots, x_n)$ can be obtained from a the minimum propagator with $\min(\text{vminus}(x_1), \ldots, \text{vminus}(x_n))$. We will come back to inverse views in the sections about Boolean and set constraints.

Derived views. It is unnecessarily restrictive to define views in terms of variables. The actual requirement for a view is that its variable provides the same operations. It is straightforward to make views generic themselves: views can be defined in terms of other views. The only exception are identity-views as they serve the very purpose of casting a variable into a view. Views such as offset, scale, and minus are called *derived views*: they are derived from some other view.

With derived views being defined in terms of views, the first step to use a derived view is to turn a variable into a view by an identity-view. For example, a minus-view v for the variable x is obtained from a minus-view and an identity-view: $v = \text{vminus}(\text{vid}(x))$.

Example 4 (Binary linear inequality reconsidered). Using offset-views, minus-views, and scale-views, all possible variants of binary linear inequalities can now be obtained from a propagator for $v_1 + v_2 \leq 0$. For example, $a \cdot x_1 - x_2 \leq c$ with $a > 0$ can be obtained with $v_1 = \text{vscale}(a, \text{vid}(x_1))$ and $v_2 = \text{vminus}(\text{voffset}(\text{vid}(x_2), c))$ or $v_2 = \text{voffset}(\text{vminus}(\text{vid}(x_2)), -c)$.

Scale-views reconsidered. The coefficient of a scale-view is restricted to be positive. Allowing arbitrary non-zero constants a in a scale-view $s = \text{vscale}(a, x)$ requires to take the signedness of a into account. This can be seen for the following two operations (the others are similar):

s.`getmin()` $:=$ **if** $a < 0$ **then** $a \cdot x$.`getmax()` **else** $a \cdot x$.`getmin()`
s.`adjmax`(n) $:=$ **if** $a < 0$ **then** x.`adjmin`$(\lfloor n/a \rfloor)$ **else** x.`adjmax`$(\lfloor n/a \rfloor)$

This extension might be inefficient. Consider Example 2: inside the loop implementing propagation on all views, the decision whether the coefficient in question is positive or negative must be made. For modern computers, conditionals — in particular in tight loops — can reduce performance considerably. A more efficient way is to restrict scale-views to positive coefficients and use an additional minus-view for cases where negative coefficients are required.

Example 5 (Linear inequalities reconsidered). An efficient way to implement a propagator for linear inequality distinguishes positive and negative variables as in $\sum_{i=1}^{n} x_i + \sum_{i=1}^{m} -y_i \leq c$.

The propagator is simple: it consists of two parts, one for the x_i and one for the y_i. Both parts share the same implementation used with different views. To propagate to the x_i, identity-views are used. To propagate to the y_i, minus-views are used. Arbitrary coefficients are obtained from scale-views as shown above.

The example shows that it can be useful to make parts of a propagator generic and reuse these parts with different views. Puget presents in [10] an algorithm for the bounds-consistent alldifferent. The paper presents only an algorithm for adjusting the upper bounds of the variables x_i and states that the lower bounds can be adjusted by using the same algorithm on variables y_i where $y_i = -x_i$. With views, this technique for simplifying the presentation of an algorithm readily carries over to its implementation: the implementation can be reused together with minus-views.

Constant-views. Derived views exploit that views do not need to be implemented in terms of variables. This can be taken to the extreme in that a view has no access at all to a variable. A constant-view $v = \text{vcon}(c)$ for an integer c provides operations such that v behaves as a variable x being equal to c:

v.`getmin()` $:= c$ v.`getmax()` $:= c$
v.`adjmin`(n) $:=$ **if** $n > c$ **then fail** v.`adjmax`(n) $:=$ **if** $n < c$ **then fail**
v.`excval`(n) $:=$ **if** $n = c$ **then fail**

Example 6 (Ternary linear inequalities). Another optimization for linear constraints are ternary variants. Given a propagator for $v_1 + v_2 + v_3 \leq c$ and using a constant-view vcon(0) for one of the views v_i, all binary variants as discussed earlier can be obtained.

In summary, for linear inequalities (this carries over to linear equalities and disequalities), views support many optimized special cases from just two implementations (the general n-ary case and the ternary case). These implementations are simple as they do not need to consider coefficients.

4 Boolean Views

Constraints on 0/1 variables are a special case of finite domain constraints. However, specialized propagators can take advantage of the more precise knowledge about the domain.

A *Boolean-view* of a finite domain variable extends the variable's interface with operations for testing its value (x.`zero`(), x.`one`(), x.`none`()) and assigning the variable (x.`assign_one`(), x.`assign_zero`()). Propagators specialized for Boolean-views, such as equality ($b_1 = b_2$), conjunction ($(b_1 \wedge b_2) \Leftrightarrow b_3$), and equivalence ($(b_1 = b_2) \Leftrightarrow b_3$), can be implemented in a straightforward way using this interface.

Symmetric Boolean propagators. The inverse of a Boolean is its logical negation, implemented by a *negated Boolean-view*. The operations for a negated Boolean-view $v = \text{vneg}(x)$ are straightforward:

v.`zero`()	$:=x$.`one`()	v.`one`()	$:=x$.`zero`()
v.`none`()	$:=x$.`none`()		
v.`assign_one`()	$:=x$.`assign_zero`()	v.`assign_zero`()	$:=x$.`assign_one`()

Example 7 (Ternary disjunction). Boolean disjunction $(x \vee y) \Leftrightarrow z$ can be implemented as $(\neg x \wedge \neg y) \Leftrightarrow \neg z$. This translates directly to an instance of the Boolean conjunction propagator. Similarly, other Boolean propagators such as exclusive or and implication can be derived.

5 Domain Operations and Range Iterators

Today's constraint programming systems support domain operations either only for access or by means of an explicitly represented abstract datatype. In this paper, we propose domain operations based on range iterators. These operations are shown to be simple, expressive, and efficient. Additionally, range iterators are essential for views as presented in Sect. 6.

Range iterators. A *range iterator* r for a range sequence $s = \langle [n_i \,..\, m_i] \rangle_{i=1}^{k}$ allows to iterate over s: each of the $[n_i \,..\, m_i]$ can be obtained in sequential order but only one at a time. A range iterator r provides the following operations: r.`done`() tests whether all ranges have been iterated, r.`next`() moves to the next range, and r.`min`() and r.`max`() return the minimum and maximum value for the current range. By $\text{set}(r)$ we refer to the set defined by an iterator r (which must coincide with $\text{set}(s)$).

A possible implementation of a range iterator r for s maintains an index i_r which is initially $i_r = 1$, the operations can then be defined as:

$$r.\texttt{done}() := i_r > k \qquad r.\texttt{next}() := (i_r \leftarrow i_r + 1)$$
$$r.\texttt{min}() := n_{i_r} \qquad r.\texttt{max}() := m_{i_r}$$

A range iterator hides its implementation. Iteration can be by position as above, but it can also be by traversing a list. The latter is particularly interesting if variable domains are implemented as lists of ranges themselves.

Iterators are consumed by iteration. Hence, if the same sequence needs to be iterated twice, a fresh iterator is needed. If iteration is cheap, a reset-operation for an iterator can be provided so that multiple iterations are supported by the same iterator. For more expensive iterators, a solution is discussed later.

Domain operations. Variables are extended with operations to access and modify their domains with range iterators. For a variable x, the operation $x.\texttt{getdom}()$ returns a range iterator for $\text{ranges}(\text{dom}(x))$. For a range iterator r the operation $x.\texttt{setdom}(r)$ updates $\text{dom}(x)$ to $\text{set}(r)$ provided that $\text{set}(r) \subseteq \text{dom}(x)$. The responsibility for ensuring that $\text{set}(r) \subseteq \text{dom}(x)$ is left to the programmer and hence requires careful consideration. Later richer (and safe) domain operations are introduced. The operation $x.\texttt{setdom}(r)$ is *generic* with respect to r: any range iterator can be used.

Domain operations can offer a substantial improvement over value operations, if many values need to be removed from a variable domain simultaneously. Assume a typical implementation of a variable domain D which organizes $\text{ranges}(D) = \langle [n_i \mathinner{..} m_i] \rangle_{i=1}^{k}$ as a linked-list. Removing a single element from D takes $O(k)$ time and might increase the length of the linked-list by one (introducing an additional hole). Hence, in the worst case, removing l elements takes $O(l(k+l))$ time. With domain operations based on iterators, removal takes $O(k+l)$ time, as the update can be implemented as one linear pass over the linked list.

Range iterators serve as simplistic abstract datatype to describe finite sets of integers. However, they provide some essential advantages over an explicit set representation. First, any range iterator regardless of its implementation can be used to update the domain of a variable. This turns out to allow for simple, efficient, and expressive updates of variable domains. Second, no costly memory management is required to maintain a range iterator as it provides access to only one range at a time. Third, iterators are essential in providing domain operations on variable views as will be discussed in Sect. 6.

Intersection iterators. Let us consider intersection as an example for computing with range iterators. Intersection is computed by an intersection iterator $r = \text{iinter}(a, b)$, taking two range iterators a and b as input where $\text{set}(r) = \text{set}(a) \cap \text{set}(b)$. The intersection iterator maintains integers n and m for storing the smallest and largest value of its current range. When initialized, the operation $r.\texttt{next}()$ is executed once. The operations are shown in Figure 1.

The **repeat**-loop iterates a and b until their ranges overlap. The tests whether a or b are done ensure that no operation is performed on a done iterator. The remainder computes the resulting range and prepares for computing a next range.

The iterators a and b can be arbitrary iterators (again, the intersection iterator is *generic*), so it is easy to obtain an iterator that computes the intersection of three iterators by using two intersection iterators. Intersection is but one example for a generic

$r.\texttt{done}() := a.\texttt{done}() \vee b.\texttt{done}()$
$r.\texttt{min}() := \quad n$
$r.\texttt{max}() := \quad m$
$r.\texttt{next}() :=$ **if** $a.\texttt{done}() \vee b.\texttt{done}()$ **then return**
repeat
  while $\neg a.\texttt{done}() \wedge (a.\texttt{max}() < b.\texttt{min}())$ **do** $a.\texttt{next}()$
  if $a.\texttt{done}()$ **then return**
  while $\neg b.\texttt{done}() \wedge (b.\texttt{max}() < a.\texttt{min}())$ **do** $b.\texttt{next}()$
  if $b.\texttt{done}()$ **then return**
until $a.\texttt{max}() \geq b.\texttt{min}()$
$n \leftarrow \max(a.\texttt{min}(), b.\texttt{min}())$; $m \leftarrow \min(a.\texttt{max}(), b.\texttt{max}())$
if $a.\texttt{max}() < b.\texttt{max}()$ **then** $a.\texttt{next}()$ **else** $b.\texttt{next}()$

Fig. 1. Operations of an intersection iterator

iterator, other useful iterators are for example: iunion(a,b) for iterating the union of a and b, iminus(a,b) for iterating the set difference of a and b, and icompl(a) for iterating the complement of a with respect to some fixed universe.

Example 8 (Propagating equality). Consider a propagator that implements domain-consistent equality: $x = y$ (assuming that x and y are variables, views are discussed later). The propagator can be implemented as follows: get range iterators for x and y by $rx = x.\texttt{getdom}()$ and $ry = y.\texttt{getdom}()$, create an intersection iterator $ri = \text{iinter}(rx, ry)$, update one of the variable domains by $x.\texttt{setdom}(ri)$, and copy the domain from x to y by $y.\texttt{setdom}(x.\texttt{getdom}())$.

Cache-iterators. The above example suggests that for some propagators it is better to actually create an intermediate representation of the range sequence computed by an iterator. The intermediate representation can be reused as often as needed. This is achieved by a *cache-iterator*: it takes an arbitrary range iterator as input, iterates it completely, and stores the obtained ranges in an array. Its actual operations then use the array. The cache-iterator also implements a reset operation as discussed above. By this, the possibly costly input iterator is used only once, while the cache-iterator can be used as often as needed.

Richer domain operations. With the help of iterators, richer domain operations are effortless. For a variable x and a range iterator r, the operation $x.\texttt{adjdom}(r)$ replaces $\text{dom}(x)$ by $\text{dom}(x) \cap \text{set}(r)$, whereas $x.\texttt{excdom}(r)$ replaces $\text{dom}(x)$ by $\text{dom}(x) \setminus \text{set}(r)$:

$$x.\texttt{adjdom}(r) := x.\texttt{setdom}(\text{iinter}(x.\texttt{getdom}(), r))$$
$$x.\texttt{excdom}(r) := x.\texttt{setdom}(\text{iminus}(x.\texttt{getdom}(), r))$$

Value versus range iterators. Another design choice is to base domain operations on value iterators: iterate values rather than ranges of a set. This is not efficient: a value sequence is considerably longer than a range sequence (in particular for the common case of a singleton range sequence).

For implementing propagators, however, it can be simpler to iterate values. This can be achieved by a range-to-value iterator. A value iterator v has the operations $v.\texttt{done}()$,

v.`next`(), and v.`val`() to access the current value. A range-to-value iterator takes a range iterator as input and returns a value iterator iterating the values of the range sequence. The inverse is a value-to-range iterator: it takes as input a value iterator and returns the corresponding range iterator.

Iterators as adaptors. Global constraints are typically implemented by a propagator computing over some involved data structure, such as for example a variable-value graph for domain-consistent alldifferent [12]. After propagation, the new variable domains must be transferred from the data structure to the variables. This can be achieved by using a range or value iterator as adaptor. The adaptor operates on the data structure and iterates the range or value sequence for a particular variable. The iterator then can be passed to the appropriate domain operation.

6 Variable Views with Domain Operations

This section discusses domain operations for variable views using iterators.

Identity and constant views. Domain operations for identity-views and constant-views are straightforward. The domain operations for an identity-view $v = \mathrm{vid}(x)$ use the domain operations on x: $v.\mathtt{getdom}() := x.\mathtt{getdom}()$ and $v.\mathtt{setdom}(r) := x.\mathtt{setdom}(r)$. For a constant-view $v = \mathrm{vcon}(c)$, the operation $v.\mathtt{getdom}()$ returns an iterator for the singleton range sequence $\langle [c \mathinner{..} c] \rangle$. The operation $v.\mathtt{setdom}(r)$ just checks whether the range sequence of r is empty.

Derived views. Domain operations for an offset-view $\mathrm{voffset}(v, c)$ are provided by an offset-iterator. The operations of an offset-iterator o for a range iterator r and an integer c (created by $\mathrm{ioffset}(r, c)$) are as follows:

$$\begin{array}{ll} o.\mathtt{min}() \;\; := r.\mathtt{min}() + c & \quad o.\mathtt{max}() \;\; := r.\mathtt{max}() + c \\ o.\mathtt{done}() := r.\mathtt{done}() & \quad o.\mathtt{next}() := r.\mathtt{next}() \end{array}$$

The domain operations for an offset view $v = \mathrm{voffset}(x, c)$ are as follows:

$$v.\mathtt{getdom}() := \mathrm{ioffset}(x.\mathtt{getdom}(), c) \qquad v.\mathtt{setdom}(r) := x.\mathtt{setdom}(\mathrm{ioffset}(r, -c))$$

For minus-views we just give the range sequence as iteration is obvious. For a given range sequence $\langle [n_i \mathinner{..} m_i] \rangle_{i=1}^{k}$, the negative sequence is obtained by reversal and sign change as $\langle [-m_{k-i+1} \mathinner{..} -n_{k-i+1}] \rangle_{i=1}^{k}$. The same iterator for this sequence can be used both for `setdom` and `getdom` operations. Note that the iterator is quite complicated as it changes direction of the range sequence, possible implementations are discussed in Sect. 8.

Assume a scale-view $s = \mathrm{vscale}(a, v)$ with $a > 0$ and $\langle [n_i \mathinner{..} m_i] \rangle_{i=1}^{k}$ being a range sequence for v. If $a = 1$, the range sequence remains unchanged. Otherwise, the corresponding range sequence for s is $\langle \{a \cdot n_1\}, \{a \cdot (n_1 + 1)\}, \ldots, \{a \cdot m_1\}, \ldots, \{a \cdot n_k\}, \{a \cdot (n_k + 1)\}, \ldots, \{a \cdot m_k\} \rangle$.

Assume that $\langle [n_i \mathinner{..} m_i] \rangle_{i=1}^{k}$ is a range sequence for s. Then for $1 \le i \le k$ the ranges $[\lceil n_i / a \rceil \mathinner{..} \lfloor m_i / a \rfloor]$ correspond to the required variable domain for v, however they do not necessarily form a range sequence as the ranges might be empty, overlapping, or adjacent. Iterating the range sequence is simple by skipping empty ranges and conjoining overlapping or adjacent ranges.

Consistency. An important issue is how views affect the consistency of a propagator. Let us first consider all views except scale-views. These views compute bijections on the values as well as on the ranges of a domain D. A bounds (domain) consistent propagator for a constraint C with variables $x_1, \ldots, x_n$ establishes bounds (domain) consistency for the constraint C with all the variables replaced by $v_k(x_k)$ (if v_k computes the view of x_k).

Scale-views only compute bijections on values: a range does not remain a range after multiplication. This implies that bounds consistent propagators do not establish bounds consistency on scale-views. Consider for example a bounds consistent propagator for alldifferent. With $x, y, z \in \{1, 2\}$, alldifferent$(4x, 4y, 4z)$ cannot detect failure, while alldifferent(x, y, z) can. Note that this is not a limitation of our approach but a property of multiplication.

7 Views for Set Constraints

Views and iterators readily carry over to other constraint domains. This section shows how to apply them to finite sets.

Finite sets. Most systems approximate the domain of a finite set variable by a greatest lower and least upper bound [3]: $\mathrm{dom}(x) = (\mathrm{glb}(x), \mathrm{lub}(x))$. The fundamental operations are similar to domain operations on finite domain variables: x.`getglb`() returns $\mathrm{glb}(x)$, x.`getlub`() returns $\mathrm{lub}(x)$, x.`adjglb`(D) updates $\mathrm{dom}(x)$ to $(\mathrm{glb}(x) \cup D, \mathrm{lub}(x))$, and x.`adjlub`(D) updates $\mathrm{dom}(x)$ to $(\mathrm{glb}(x), \mathrm{lub}(x) \cap D)$.

All these operations take sets as arguments or return them. As the abstract datatype we use for representing sets is an iterator, iterators play the central role here. In fact, range iterators provide exactly the operations that set propagators need: union, intersection, and complement. Most propagators thus do not require temporary data structures.

As for finite domain variables, set propagators now operate on set views. The obvious views for set variables are the identity view and constant-views – like the empty set, the universe, or some arbitrary set. Constant-views again help derive binary propagators from ternary ones. For example, $s_1 \cap s_2 = s_3$ implements set disjointness if s_3 is the constant empty set.

Symmetric set constraints. The inverse of a set variable is its complement. A *complement view* $v = \mathrm{vcompl}(x)$ of a set view x can be easily derived using the iterators already introduced:

v.`getglb`() := icompl(x.`getlub`())	v.`getlub`() := icompl(x.`getglb`())
v.`adjglb`(D) := x.`adjlub`(icompl(D))	v.`adjlub`(D) := x.`adjglb`(icompl(D))

The propagators for symmetric constraints over Boolean views readily carry over to sets: $x_1 = x_2 \cup x_3$ can be implemented as $\mathrm{vcompl}(x_1) = \mathrm{vcompl}(x_2) \cap \mathrm{vcompl}(x_3)$, and $s_1 = s_2 \setminus s_3$ is equivalent to $s_1 = s_2 \cap \mathrm{vcompl}(s_3)$.

Cross-domain views. With finite domain and set constraints in a single system, cross-domain views come into play. The most obvious cross-domain view is a finite domain variable viewed as singleton set. Using generic propagators, this immediately leads to domain-connecting constraints.

Cross-domain views can support more than one implementation for the same variable type. Set variables, for example, can be implemented with lower and upper bounds or with their full domain using ROBDDs [7]. A cross-domain view allows lower/upper bound propagators to operate on ROBDD-based sets, reusing propagators for which no efficient BDD representation exists.

Finite domain constraints from set propagators. Singleton-views can also be used to derive pure finite domain constraints from set propagators. For example, the constraint $\text{same}([x_1,\ldots,x_n],[y_1,\ldots,y_m])$ states that the two sequences of finite domain variables take the same values. Using singleton views, $\bigcup_{i=1}^{n}\{x_i\} = \bigcup_{j=1}^{m}\{y_j\}$ yields an implementation for this constraint. If $m = n$, and all variables must take different values, a disjoint union can be used instead.

8 Implementation

The presented architecture can be implemented as an orthogonal layer of abstraction for any constraint programming system. This section presents the fundamental mechanisms necessary for iterators and views.

Polymorphism. The implementation of generic propagators, views, and iterators requires *polymorphism*: propagators operate on different views, domain operations and iterators on different iterators. Both subtype polymorphism (through inheritance in Java, inheritance and virtual methods in C++) and parametric polymorphism (through templates in C++, generics in Java, polymorphic functions in ML or Haskell) can be used.

In C++, parametric polymorphism through templates is resolved at compile-time, and the generated code is monomorphic. This enables the compiler to perform aggressive optimizations, in particular inlining. The hope is that the additional layer of abstraction can be optimized away entirely. Some ML compilers also apply monomorphization, so similar results could be achieved. Java generics are compiled into casts and virtual method calls, any optimization is left to the just-in-time compiler.

Achieving high efficiency in C++ with templates sacrifices expressiveness. Instantiation can *only* happen at compile-time. Hence, either C++ must be used for modeling, or all potentially required propagator variants must be provided by explicit instantiation. The *choice* which propagator to use can however be made at runtime: for linear equations, for instance, we can test if all coefficients are units, or all are positive, and post the respective optimized propagators. In Gecode, we currently only use template-based polymorphism.

For the instantiation of templates as well as for inlining, the code that is instantiated or inlined must be available at compile time of the code that uses it. This is why most of the actual code in Gecode resides in C++ header files, slowing down compilation of the system. On the interface level however, no templates are used, such that the header files needed for *using* the library are reasonably small.

System requirements. Variable views and range iterators can be added as an orthogonal extension to existing systems. While value operations are not critical as discussed in Sect. 2, depending on which domain operations a system provides, efficiency can differ. In the worst case, domain operations need to be translated into value operations. This would decrease efficiency considerably, however intermediate computations on range iterators would still be carried out efficiently.

A particularly challenging aspect is reversal of range sequences required for the minus-iterator. One approach to implement reversal is to extend all iterators such that they can iterate both backwards and forwards. Another approach is similar to a cache-iterator: store the ranges generated from the input iterator in an array and iterate in reverse order from the array. In Gecode, we have chosen so far the latter approach due to its simplicity. We are going to explore also the former approach: as variable domains in Gecode are provided as doubly-linked lists, iteration in both directions can be provided efficiently.

9 Analysis and Evaluation

This section analyzes the impact different implementations of iterators and views have on efficiency. Two aspects are evaluated: compile-time polymorphism versus run-time polymorphism, and iterators versus temporary data structures.

The experiments use the Gecode C++ (version 1.0.0) constraint programming library [2]. All tests were carried out on a Intel Pentium IV with 2.8GHz and 1GB of RAM, using Linux and the GNU C++ compiler, version 3.4.3. Runtimes are the average of 20 runs, with a coefficient of deviation less than 2% for all benchmarks. Gecode is competitive in efficiency with state-of-the art systems, a comparison is available on the Gecode web pages [2].

The *optimized* column in Table 1 gives the time in milliseconds of the optimized system, the other columns are relative to *optimized*. The examples used are standard benchmarks, the first group using only finite domain constraints, the second group using mainly set constraints.

Code inspection. A thorough inspection of the code generated by the GNU C++ compiler and the Microsoft Visual C++ compiler shows that they actually perform the optimizations we consider essential. Operations on both views and iterators are inlined entirely and thus implemented in the most efficient way. The abstractions do not impose a runtime penalty (compared to a system without views and iterators).

Templates versus virtual methods. As the previous section suggested, in C++, compile-time polymorphism using templates is far more efficient than virtual method calls. To evaluate this, we changed the basic operations of finite domain views such that they cannot be inlined. The required changes are rather involved, so we did not try the same for iterators and set views. An implementation based on virtual methods will typically exhibit an even higher overhead. Table 1 shows the results in column *no-inline*. Function calls that are not inlined cause a runtime overhead between 29% and 58%.

Temporary data structures. One important claim is that iterators are advantageous because they avoid temporary data structures. Table 1 shows in column *temporary* that

Table 1. Runtime comparison

Benchmark	*optimized*	*no-inline*	*temporary*
	time in ms	*relative %*	
Alpha	122.85	141.30	103.70
Donald	0.64	155.60	114.70
Golomb 10 (bound)	1 260.50	158.20	101.10
Golomb 10 (domain)	2 064.00	129.70	100.00
Magic Sequence 500	192.38	129.80	101.40
Magic Square 6	0.88	133.40	105.20
Partition 32	6 930,00	135.50	101.40
Photo	143.15	131.30	99.60
Queens 100	1.90	132.20	99.30
Crew	3.38	—	191.10
Golf 8-4-9	498.00	—	271.40
Hamming 20-3-32	1 496.00	—	200.70
Steiner 9	124.08	—	191.00

computing temporary data structures has limited impact (about 3%) on finite domain variables, but considerable impact for set constraints (up to 171% overhead). Temporary data structures have been emulated by wrapping all iterators in a cache-iterator as described in Sect. 5.

Applicability. Deriving several instances from a single propagator implementation significantly reduces the overall amount of code that needs to be written. In Gecode, 31 finite domain propagators are instantiated from 12 generic propagators, 9 Boolean propagators from 4 generic propagators, and 22 set propagators from 9 generic propagators. The generic propagators make up approximately 3800 lines of sources code, saving approximately 4800 lines of code to be written, tested, and maintained.

Obviously, views and iterators are no silver bullet. The mechanism only yields efficient propagators if the compiler can generate the code that would otherwise have been hand-written. If, for example, set complement views are used extensively, the overhead compared to a hand-written propagator can become prohibitive.

10 Conclusion and Future Work

The paper has introduced an architecture decoupling propagators from variables based on views and range iterators. We have argued how to make propagators generic, simpler, and reusable with views for different constraints. We have introduced range iterators as abstractions for efficient domain operations compatible with views. The architecture has been shown to be applicable to many finite domain and finite set constraints. Using parametric polymorphism for views and iterators leads to an efficient implementation that incurs no runtime cost.

Future Work. An obvious route for future work is to explore richer variable views. Possible candidates are sums and products of variables going beyond a single variable per view: the challenge here will be to provide efficient range iterators.

This paper explores views only for implementation purposes. A related question is whether views can also be useful for modeling or for automatic transformation of models.

Acknowledgements. Christian Schulte is partially funded by the Swedish Research Council (VR) under grant 621-2004-4953. Guido Tack is partially funded by DAAD travel grant D/05/26003. Thanks to Patrick Pekczynski for help with the benchmarks, and to Mikael Lagerkvist for helpful comments. We thank the anonymous reviewers, of this paper and of a previous version, for their constructive comments.

References

1. Pascal Brisset, Hani El Sakkout, Thom Frühwirth, Warwick Harvey, Micha Meier, Stefano Novello, Thierry Le Provost, Joachim Schimpf, and Mark Wallace. ECLiPSe Constraint Library Manual 5.8. User manual, IC Parc, London, UK, February 2005.
2. Gecode: Generic constraint development environment, 2005. Available as an open-source library from `www.gecode.org`.
3. Carmen Gervet. Interval propagation to reason about sets: Definition and implementation of a practical language. *Constraints*, 1(3):191–244, 1997.
4. ILOG S.A. *ILOG Solver 5.0: Reference Manual.* Gentilly, France, August 2000.
5. Intelligent Systems Laboratory. SICStus Prolog user's manual, 3.12.1. Technical report, Swedish Institute of Computer Science, Box 1263, 164 29 Kista, Sweden, April 2005.
6. François Laburthe. CHOCO: implementing a CP kernel. In Nicolas Beldiceanu, Warwick Harvey, Martin Henz, François Laburthe, Eric Monfroy, Tobias Müller, Laurent Perron, and Christian Schulte, editors, *Proceedings of TRICS: Techniques foR Implementing Constraint programming Systems, a post-conference workshop of CP 2000*, number TRA9/00, pages 71–85, 55 Science Drive 2, Singapore 117599, September 2000.
7. Vitaly Lagoon and Peter J. Stuckey. Set domain propagation using ROBDDs. In Mark Wallace, editor, *Tenth International Conference on Principles and Practice of Constraint Programming*, volume 3258 of *Lecture Notes in Computer Science*, pages 347–361, Toronto, Canada, September 2004. Springer-Verlag.
8. Tobias Müller. *Constraint Propagation in Mozart.* Doctoral dissertation, Universität des Saarlandes, Fakultät für Mathematik und Informatik, Fachrichtung Informatik, Im Stadtwald, 66041 Saarbrücken, Germany, 2001.
9. Jean-François Puget. A C++ implementation of CLP. In *Proceedings of the Second Singapore International Conference on Intelligent Systems (SPICIS)*, pages B256–B261, Singapore, November 1994.
10. Jean-François Puget. A fast algorithm for the bound consistency of alldiff constraints. In *Proceedings of the 15th National Conference on Artificial Intelligence (AAAI-98)*, pages 359–366, Madison, WI, USA, July 1998. AAAI Press/The MIT Press.
11. Jean-François Puget and Michel Leconte. Beyond the glass box: Constraints as objects. In John Lloyd, editor, *Proceedings of the International Symposium on Logic Programming*, pages 513–527, Portland, OR, USA, December 1995. The MIT Press.
12. Jean-Charles Régin. A filtering algorithm for constraints of difference in CSPs. In *Proceedings of the Twelfth National Conference on Artificial Intelligence*, pages 362–367, Seattle, WA, USA, 1994. AAAI Press.

A Hybrid Benders' Decomposition Method for Solving Stochastic Constraint Programs with Linear Recourse

S. Armagan Tarim[1] and Ian Miguel[2]

[1] University College Cork, Cork Constraint Computation Centre, Cork, Ireland
at@4c.ucc.ie
http://www-users.cs.york.ac.uk/~at/
[2] University of St.Andrews, School of Computer Science, St.Andrews, Scotland
ianm@dcs.st-and.ac.uk
http://www-users.cs.york.ac.uk/~ianm/

Abstract. We adopt Benders' decomposition algorithm to solve scenario-based Stochastic Constraint Programs (SCPs) with linear recourse. Rather than attempting to solve SCPs via a monolithic model, we show that one can iteratively solve a collection of smaller sub-problems and arrive at a solution to the entire problem. In this approach, decision variables corresponding to the initial stage and linear recourse actions are grouped into two sub-problems. The sub-problem corresponding to the recourse action further decomposes into independent problems, each of which is a representation of a single scenario. Our computational experience on stochastic versions of the well-known template design and warehouse location problems shows that, for linear recourse SCPs, Benders' decomposition algorithm provides a very efficient solution method.

1 Introduction

Stochastic constraint programming (*SCP*, see [12, 15]) extends constraint programming to deal with both *decision* variables, which can be set by the decision-maker, and *stochastic* variables, which follow some discrete probability distribution function. This framework is designed to model a wide variety of decision problems involving uncertainty and probability. Examples include nurse rostering given an uncertain workload and constructing a balanced bond portfolio.

Tarim *et al.* [15] provide a semantics for stochastic constraint programs based on *scenarios*, where a scenario is a possible set of values for the stochastic variables. Based on this semantics, they compile stochastic constraint programs down into conventional (non-stochastic) constraint programs. The advantage of this compilation is that existing constraint solvers can be used without modification. However, the number of scenarios grows exponentially with the number of decision stages, where each stage consists of a set of decision variables and a set of stochastic variables whose combined assignments determine the structure of the next stage. Tarim *et al.* propose a number of scenario reduction algorithms to reduce the scenario tree considered. These algorithms determine a subset of

B. Hnich et al. (Eds.): CSCLP 2005, LNAI 3978, pp. 133–148, 2006.

scenarios and a redistribution of probabilities relative to the preserved scenarios. Generally, however, this approach yields sub-optimal solutions.

This paper presents Benders' decomposition (*BD*) algorithm as an optimisation method for stochastic constraint programs with linear recourse (*SCPwLR*). *SCPwLR* constitutes an important subgroup of stochastic constraint programs. In this type of SCP the initial stage decisions involve discrete variables, whereas the following recourse actions comprise only continuous decision variables. A typical example of *SCPwLR* is the Warehouse Location Problem (WLP) (see [10], [11] and [13]) with stochastic demand. In Section 5, the capacitated version of the WLP with stochastic demand is addressed, along with a stochastic version of the Template Design problem [14], and the computational performance of Benders' algorithm is investigated.

The paper is organised as follows. Section 2 provides background, including an overview of Benders decomposition. Section 3 introduces the linear recourse stochastic constraint programs and an application of BD to such programs. Section 4 gives an illustrative example of BD applied to *SCPwLR* by means of the classical news vendor problem. In the following section, the computational efficiency of BD is investigated. Section 6 concludes the paper and points out important future work.

2 Background

This section gives the necessary background detail in stochastic constraint programming and Benders decomposition. We begin with the former.

2.1 Stochastic Constraint Programming

A stochastic constraint satisfaction problem [12] consists of a 6-tuple $\langle \mathcal{X}, \mathcal{S}, \mathcal{D}, \mathcal{P}, \mathcal{C}, \theta \rangle$. $\mathcal{X}$ is a set of decision variables, and $\mathcal{S}$ is a set of stochastic variables. $\mathcal{D}$ is a function mapping each element of $\mathcal{X}$ and each element of $\mathcal{S}$ to a domain of potential values. A decision variable $x \in \mathcal{X}$ is *assigned* a value from its domain. $\mathcal{P}$ is a function mapping each element of $\mathcal{S}$ to a probability distribution for its associated domain. $\mathcal{C}$ is a set of constraints, where a constraint $c \in \mathcal{C}$ on variables $x_i, \ldots, x_j$ specifies a subset of the Cartesian product $\mathcal{D}(x_i) \times \ldots \times \mathcal{D}(x_j)$ indicating mutually-compatible variable assignments. The subset of $\mathcal{C}$ that constrain at least one variable in $\mathcal{S}$ are *chance* constraints. θ is a function mapping each chance constraint to the interval [0,1], indicating the fraction of scenarios in which the constraint must be satisfied. Note that a chance constraint with a threshold of 1 is equivalent to a hard constraint.

A stochastic CSP consists of a number of *decision stages*. In a one-stage stochastic CSP, the decision variables are set before the stochastic variables. In an n-stage stochastic CSP, $\mathcal{X}$ and $\mathcal{S}$ are partitioned into n disjoint sets, $\mathcal{X}_1, \ldots, \mathcal{X}_n$ and $\mathcal{S}_1, \ldots, \mathcal{S}_n$. To solve an n-stage stochastic CSP an assignment to the variables in $\mathcal{X}_1$ must be found such that, given random values for $\mathcal{S}_1$, assignments can be found for $\mathcal{X}_2$ such that, given random values for $\mathcal{S}_2$, ..., assignments can be found for $\mathcal{X}_n$ so that, given random values for $\mathcal{S}_n$, the hard constraints are satisfied and the chance constraints are satisfied in the specified fraction of scenarios. As noted in the introduction, the *SCPwLR* is a 2-stage stochastic CSP in which the domains of $\mathcal{X}_1$ are discrete, but the domains of $\mathcal{X}_2$ are continuous. Furthermore, the constraints on $\mathcal{X}_2$ are all linear.

2.2 Benders Decomposition

Although Benders' decomposition algorithm dates back to the 1960s and there is now a sizeable OR literature in this area extending the original approach, it has only recently been used by the constraint programming community in developing hybrid models. The reader is directed to Benoist et al. [3], Xia et al. [17], Eremin and Wallace [4], Hooker and Ottosson [7], Thorsteinsson [16], Jain and Grossmann [9] for applications of BD in constraint programming.

Benders decomposition [2, 5] was presented for solving models of the type:

$$\max\{c^T x + f(y) | Ax + F(y) \leq b, x \in \mathbb{R}^p_+, y \in S\} \tag{1}$$

where $x \in \mathbb{R}^p_+$ (the p-dimensional non-negative Euclidean space), $y \in \mathbb{R}^q$, and S is an arbitrary subset of $\mathbb{R}^q$. Furthermore, A is an (m, p) matrix, $f(y)$ is a scalar function and $F(y)$ an m-component vector function both defined on S, and b and c are fixed vectors in $\mathbb{R}^m$ and $\mathbb{R}^p$, respectively.

A key concept in Benders' algorithm is that of partitioning the variables into two sets – x and y – and projecting the problem onto the complicating variables, y. Benders' method decomposes this model in such a way that it can be solved as an alternating sequence of linear programs and programs of "complicating" variables. In the case of Eq.(1), once y is fixed to $\bar{y}$, the initial linear program is:

$$f(\bar{y}) + \min\{(b - F(\bar{y}))\lambda | A^T \lambda \geq c, \lambda \in \mathbb{R}^m_+\}, \tag{2}$$

In other words, the algorithm partitions the given problem in Eq.(1) into two such subproblems: a programming problem (which may be linear, non-linear, discrete, etc.) defined on S, and a linear programming problem defined in $\mathbb{R}^p_+$. An example is the mixed-integer programming problem in which certain variables may assume any value on a given interval, whereas others are restricted to integral values only. Then, in order to avoid the laborious calculation of a complete set of constraints for the feasible region in the first problem, a multi-step procedure is designed leading, in a finite number of steps, to a set of constraints determining an optimum solution of the given problem.

The classic BD algorithm was proposed for mixed-integer linear programming problems, the cut generation of which is based on the duality theorem of linear programming. The algorithm functions as follows: It determines trial values for the addressed problem by solving a program called the master problem – the program of complicating variables. The cost of this trial plan is determined using the so-called slave problem, Eq.(2). The slave problem also calculates dual multipliers, λ, which measure the marginal change in the trial plan. These dual multipliers are used to form new constraints that are added to the master problem, which is then re-solved to determine a new trial plan. The process continues alternately solving the master and slave problems, until the algorithm has found an optimal plan or one that is within an acceptable tolerance of optimality.

3 Benders Decomposition Applied to *SCPwLR*

In this section, BD is proposed as a solution method for *SCPwLR*. We consider only the 2-stage *SCPwLR*, but the method can easily be extended to address multi-stage *SCPwLR* without loss of generality. The method described is a *hybrid* since it requires a collaboration of CP and LP methods.

As mentioned, BD partitions the decision variables into two sets, x and y. For *SCPwLR*, partitioning is made with respect to the two decision stages: the first stage decision variables, which constitute the set of complicating variables y, form a CP model, and, since the recourse action is assumed to be linear, the second stage decision variables form an LP model. Hence, the "master" problem is a CP, whereas the "slave" problem, corresponding to the scenarios and the recourse actions taken, is an LP. In this context, Benders decomposition achieves separability of the second stage decisions, solving a separate LP for each scenario.

Consider the following 2-stage *SCPwLR*: min $\{f(y)+\sum_{k=1}^{K} p_k Q_k(y) | y \in Y\}$. Here, k indexes the finitely-many scenarios, with p_k the probability of scenario k. The first-stage variables y are set before the scenario is observed. After the kth scenario is observed, the set of second-stage decision variables x_k are set. The cost (assumed to be linear) of the second stage in scenario k is $Q_k(y) = \min\{q_k x | W_k x = h_k - T_k y, x \geq 0\}$. That is, x is a recourse, which must be chosen so as to satisfy some linear constraints in the least costly way.

We assume that recourse is *complete*, i.e., for any choice of y and scenario, there is always a non-empty set of x, $\{x | W_k x = h_k - T_k y, x \geq 0\} \neq \emptyset$. The objective is to minimize the expected total costs of both stages.

The deterministic equivalent model is a large-scale problem, which simultaneously selects the first-stage variables y and the second-stage variables x_k for every scenario k.

SCPwLR Model:

$$z = \min \; \{f(y) + \sum_{k=1}^{K} p_k q_k x_k \;|\; T_k y + W_k x_k = h_k, \quad x_k \geq 0, \quad y \in Y\} \tag{3}$$

3.1 Independent Subproblems

Given an arbitrary first stage decision $\overline{y}$, define a function $Q_k(\overline{y})$ equal to the optimum of the second stage for each scenario $k = 1, ..., K$:

Slave (Primal) Model:

$$Q_k(\overline{y}) = \min \; \{q_k x_k \; | W_k x_k = h_k - T_k \overline{y}, \quad x_k \geq 0\} \tag{4}$$

Now, an upper bound on the optimal value of z, defined in (3), is:

$$f(\overline{y}) + \sum_{k=1}^{K} p_k Q_k(\overline{y}) \tag{5}$$

Under the assumption of complete recourse, the linear programming dual of the second-stage problem for scenario k, as given in (4), is the linear program:
Slave (Dual) Model:

$$Q_k(\overline{y}) = \max\ \{(h_k - T_k\overline{y})\lambda_k \mid W_k^T\lambda_k \leq q_k, \quad \lambda_k \text{ free}\} \tag{6}$$

Note that the constraints are now independent of y; in other words, the feasible region is not affected by the choice of y. Denote by $\Lambda_k = \{\lambda_k | W_k^T\lambda_k \leq q_k\}$ the polyhedral feasible region of the second-stage problem for scenario k. Denote by $\widehat{\lambda}_k^i$ the ith extreme point of Λ_k, $i = 1, ..., I_k$, where I_k is the total number of extreme points of the problem for scenario k. By enumerating the large, but finite, number of extreme points of Λ_k, we can write, $Q_k(y) = \max_{i=1,\ldots,I_k}\{\widehat{\lambda}_k^i(h_k - T_k y)\}$, which demonstrates that $Q_k(y)$ is a piecewise-linear convex function.

3.2 Complete and Partial Master Problems

Benders' "complete master problem" then uses this representation of $Q_k(y)$ to provide an alternative method for evaluating z,
Complete Master Model:

$$z = \min\ \{f(y) + \sum_{k=1}^{K} p_k \max_{i=1,\ldots,I_k} \{\widehat{\lambda}_k^i(h_k - T_k y)\} \mid y \in Y\} \tag{7}$$

While it is possible in principle to solve the problem using Benders' complete master problem, in practice the magnitude of the number of dual extreme points makes it prohibitively expensive. However, if a subset of the dual extreme points of Λ_k are available then we obtain an underestimate of $Q_k(y)$, which we denote:

$$Q_k^{'}(y) = \max_{i=1,\ldots,M_k} \{\widehat{\lambda}_k^i(h_k - T_k y)\} \tag{8}$$

where $M_k \leq I_k$.

Using dual information obtained after M evaluations of $Q_k(y)$, we obtain a "partial master problem", which provides a lower bound on the solution of z:
Partial Master Model:

$$\min\ \{f(y) + \sum_{k=1}^{K} p_k \max_{i=1,\ldots,M_k} \{\widehat{\lambda}_k^i(h_k - T_k y)\} \mid y \in Y\} \tag{9}$$

However, there is no guarantee that the partial master problem yields a bounded solution. If it produces an unbounded solution then the direction of

Algorithm 1. BD-SCPwLR

```
input  : Set of scenarios, S
         z = min{f(y) + Σ_{∀k∈S} p_k q_k x_k | T_k y + W_k x_k = h_k, x_k ≥ 0, y ∈ Y}
output: {z*, y*, x_k*}
begin
    ȳ ← an initial feasible y
    c ← f(ȳ)
    up ← ∞
    low ← −∞
    ∀k ∈ S,  Cut_k ← ∅
    while up − low > ε do
        for k ∈ S do
            Slave_k ← Q_k(ȳ) = max{(h_k − T_k ȳ)λ_k | W_k^T λ_k ≤ q_k, λ_k free}
            λ̂_k ← Solve(Slave_k)
            Cut_k ← Cut_k ∪ {λ̂_k(h_k − T_k y)}
        c ← f(ȳ) + Σ_{∀k∈S} p_k Q_k(ȳ)
        if c < up then up ← c
        Master ← min{f(y) + Σ_{∀k∈S} p_k max{Cut_k} | y ∈ Y}
        ȳ ← Solve(Master)
        c ← min{f(ȳ) + Σ_{∀k∈S} p_k max{Cut_k | y = ȳ}}
        if c > low then low ← c
    return z* ← low, y* ← ȳ, ∀k ∈ S   x_k* ← dual vars from Solve(Slave_k)
end
```

the *extreme ray* must be determined and the Benders cut, $0 \geq \widehat{\lambda}_k^r(h_k - T_k y)$, must be added accordingly to bound the unbounded polyhedral set.

Benders' algorithm solves the current "partial master problem", obtaining a new $\overline{y}$ (a new trial solution) and an underestimate $\sum_{k=1}^{K} p_k Q_k^{'}(\overline{y})$ of the associated expected second-stage cost.

3.3 Iterative Process

The actual expected second-stage cost, $\sum_{k=1}^{K} p_k Q_k(\overline{y})$, is then evaluated by solving the second-stage problem for each scenario. Additional terms, in the form of $\{\widehat{\lambda}_k(h_k - T_k y)\}$, are added to the partial master problem to complete the iteration. Each additional term is actually another cut added to the model.

At each iteration of Benders' algorithm, then, the slave problem solution provides an upper bound for z, and, the partial master solution provides a lower bound for z. It can be proved that the above iterative procedure terminates in a finite number of iterations. An attractive feature of this algorithm is the availability of upper and lower bounds on the optimal objective value, which both converge to this value as optimality is achieved. The upper bound is generated by a sequence of feasible solutions to the problem, so the best of these may be taken as a solution if the procedure is terminated short of optimality.

The complete BD algorithm for the *SCPwLR* is presented in Algorithm 1.

4 An Illustrative Example: News Vendor Problem

We now illustrate the *SCPwLR* solution method using a modified version of the well-known "news vendor problem", a stochastic inventory replenishment problem which can be described as follows. Given a stochastic distribution for the demand of a product, what is the optimal order quantity, y^*, if only one order can be placed before actual demand is observed. Assume we have no initial inventory. The decision maker has to order an amount $y \geq 0$ at unit price $c = 3$. Unsold goods can be returned to the supplier with a salvage value of $v = 1$. In case of high demand, the firm expedites to avert an impending stockout with a cost of $e = 8$ per unit of excess demand. The maximum amount of units that can be ordered is initially $R = 20$. However, the quota can be increased by $r = [11, 13, 15, 17]$ in a nested manner, following a fixed payment of $h = [10, 12, 14, 16]$ which is also nested. Therefore, the maximum quota of 76 units can be obtained with a cost of 52. Demand is a discrete random variable denoted by ξ. ξ takes the values of $\{15(0.1), 25(0.2), 35(0.3), 45(0.3), 55(0.1)\}$, in which the values in parentheses are the probabilities, p.

A stochastic constraint program for the above problem is as follows:

$$\begin{array}{l}
\min cy + \sum_{i=1}^{4} h_i k_i + \sum_{s=1}^{5} p_s(ex_{1s} - vx_{2s}) \\
\text{s.t.} \\
y + x_{1s} - x_{2s} = \xi_s, \quad s = 1, ..., 5 \\
\sum_{i=1}^{4} r_i k_i + 20 >= y \\
k_i = 0 \Rightarrow k_{i+1} = 0, \quad k_i \in \{0, 1\}, \quad i = 1, ..., 3
\end{array}$$

where x_{1s} and x_{2s} denote expedited order and salvage amounts, respectively.

In the above model, y and k_i denote the first-stage decision variables, x_{1s} and x_{2s} are the second-stage decision variables, where s denotes a scenario, and the cost term $\sum_{s=1}^{5} p_s(ex_{1s} - vx_{2s})$ corresponds to the expected recourse cost. This problem has linear recourse. This partitioning of decision variables yields the following master and slave problems:

Master Problem

$$\begin{array}{l}
\min \quad cy + \sum_{i=1}^{4} h_i k_i + \\
\sum_{s=1}^{5} p_s \max\{\widehat{\lambda}_s(\xi_s - y)\} \\
\text{subject to} \\
\sum_{i=1}^{4} r_i k_i + 20 >= y \\
k_i = 0 \Rightarrow k_{i+1} = 0 \quad i = 1, ..., 3 \\
k_i \in \{0, 1\}
\end{array}$$

Slave Problems $\quad s = 1, ..., 5$

$$\begin{array}{l}
\max \ (\xi_s - \overline{y})\lambda_s \\
\text{subject to} \\
\lambda_s \leq e \\
\lambda_s \geq v \\
\lambda_s \text{free}
\end{array}$$

Table 1 presents the step-by-step application of Benders' algorithm to our *SCPwLR* problem.

We start with a feasible solution of $y = 0$ and $k = [1, 1, 1, 1]$, which is actually the worst possible ordering policy. At the first iteration 5 independent trivial slave problems are solved. The optimal solutions are $\lambda_{1,...,5} = 8$. Next we calculate the upper bound that these solutions imply. Eq.(5) provides an upper bound on the optimal solution to the original problem, which is 340 here. At the second step of the first iteration the partial master problem is solved with the added Benders cuts, $\max\{8(\xi_s - y)\}$, giving a lower bound of -40. Subsequent

Table 1. Steps of Benders' Decomposition

Problem	Iteration	y^*	k^*	λ^*	obj value	Lower Bound	Upper Bound
Initial values	0	0	[1,1,1,1]	–	–	$-\infty$	$+\infty$
Slave	1	–	–	[8,8,8,8,8]	340	–	340
Master	1	76	[1,1,1,1]	–	-40	-40	–
Slave	2	–	–	[1,1,1,1,1]	240	–	240
Master	2	44	[1,1,0,0]	–	155.8	155.8	–
Slave	3	–	–	[1,1,1,8,8]	155.8	–	155.8

iterations of the algorithm can be followed from Table 1. In this instance the lower and upper bounds converge to the optimal solution of 155.8 in five steps.

5 Computational Experiments

This section presents computational results of using Benders' Decomposition in *SCPwLR* on the capacitated version of the Warehouse Location Problem (CWLP) (see [1], [6], [10], [11] and [13]), and stochastic version of the Template Design Problem [14].

5.1 Stochastic Capacitated Warehouse Location Problem

Let $I = \{1, ..., N\}$ be potential warehouse locations to supply a uniform product. A facility can be opened in any location $i \in I$. Opening a facility at location i has a non-negative fixed cost, f_i. Each open facility i can provide a limited amount C_i of commodity. Let $J = \{1, ..., M\}$ denote stores that are supplied by the open warehouses. For any pair (i, j) given, there is a unit production and transportation cost $g_{ij} \geq 0$. Each store can be supplied by exactly one warehouse. The probabilistic customer demands, ξ_j, are only known following stores' order placements to warehouses. Stores incur a fixed penalty cost for each unit they backlog, e_j, and fixed holding cost for each unit of excess inventory, h_j, they have. The goal is to determine a subset of the set of potential warehouse locations at which to operate warehouses, and an assignment of all clients to these facilities so as to minimize the expected total cost of operating the system. This problem is a generalisation of the well-known set covering problem and, therefore, an NP-hard problem in the strong sense.

A constraint model for the deterministic version of the above problem is given in [8]. This model is extended to comply with the stochastic demand assumption. The decision variables are:

- $k_i \in \{0, 1\}$ denoting whether warehouses i is in operation or not,
- $u_j \in I$ showing the supplier for store j,
- $y_{u_j,j} \geq 0$ is the amount warehouse u_j delivers to store j,
- $x^+_{j,s}$ and $x^-_{j,s}$ denote the excess inventory and shortage, respectively, at the end of the period at store j, if scenario $s \in S$ is realised.

The certainty equivalent CP model is

$$\min \sum_{j\in J} g_{u_j,j} y_{u_j,j} + \sum_{i\in I} f_i k_i + \sum_{j\in J}\sum_{s\in S} p_s(e_j x^-_{j,s} + h_j x^+_{j,s})$$

s.t.

$$k_{u_j} = 1 \qquad \forall j \in J$$

$$\sum_{j\in J} y_{u_j,j}(u_j = i) \leq C_i \qquad \forall i \in I$$

$$y_{u_j,j} - \xi_{j,s} = x^+_{j,s} - x^-_{j,s} \qquad \forall j \in J, \forall s \in S$$

In the above formulation, the first stage (k_i, u_j, $y_{u_j,j}$) and second stage ($x^+_{j,s}$, $x^-_{j,s}$) decision variables are employed to partition the given model. In this case, the master and slave problems for the stochastic CWLP are defined as

Master Problem

$\min\ \sum_{j\in J} g_{u_j,j} y_{u_j,j} + \sum_{i\in I} f_i k_i +$
$\sum_{s\in S} \max\{p_s \sum_{j\in J} \widehat{\lambda}_{j,s}(\xi_{j,s} - y_{u_j,j})\}$
s.t.
$k_{u_j} = 1,\ \ \forall j \in J$
$\sum_{j\in J} y_{u_j,j}(u_j = i) \leq C_i,\ \ \forall i \in I$

Slave Problems $\forall s \in S, \forall j \in J$

$\max\ (\xi_{j,s} - \overline{y}_{u_j,j})\lambda_{j,s}$
s.t.
$-h_j \leq \lambda_{j,s} \leq e_j$
$\lambda_{j,s}$ free

Although the slave problems are expressed in a linear program structure, in which $\lambda_{j,s}$ are dual decision variables, the simplicity of the resultant independent linear programs can be exploited to solve the problems to optimality without resorting to Linear Programming. The optimal solution to any sub-problem is in the form:

$$\lambda^*_{j,s} = \begin{cases} -h_j & \text{if } \ \xi_{j,s} - \overline{y}_{u_j,j} \leq 0 \\ e_j & \text{if } \ \xi_{j,s} - \overline{y}_{u_j,j} \geq 0 \end{cases}, \quad \forall s \in S, \forall j \in J \tag{10}$$

The objective function of the master problem represents a "multiple-cut" approach to the Benders' decomposition. In this version, each scenario contributes to the cut generation process with a single cut. This excessive number of cuts may increase the size of the master problem to the point at which finding a solution is prohibitively long. Alternative approach is to aggregate scenario cuts into one, so as to reduce the detrimental effect of size on the solution performance. This so-called "single-cut" version is then in the form of $\Phi \geq \max\{\sum_s \sum_j p_s(\xi_{j,s} - y_{u_j,j})\widehat{\lambda}_{j,s}\}$, which leads to the objective function:

$$\min \sum_{j\in J} g_{u_j,j} y_{u_j,j} + \sum_{i\in I} f_i k_i + \Phi. \tag{11}$$

Although the single-cut approach does not provide cuts as strong as the multiple-cut approach, it is still computationally less expensive.

Experiments were conducted on 50 SCWLP instances using a 1.2 GHz computer. These instances vary mainly in numbers of warehouses (between 2 to 10), stores (between 2 to 5) and scenarios (between 4 to 1331). The holding cost is taken as 1 throughout the experiments. Three different shortage cost values are used: 4, 6 and 8. The warehouse capacities are chosen in the range of [20,110]; fixed operating costs, [30,120]; random demands, [5,50]; transportation costs, [1,4]. We assume that the number of states random demand variables have in one instance is the same for all stores. Given n random variable states and j stores, the number of scenarios in an instance is n^j.

In the first step of the experiment, instances were modelled as a stochastic constraint program whose formulation is given above. The SCP models were solved using OPLStudio Solver6.0 with a time limit of 1 hour. The upper bounds for variables are chosen as follows: for y_j and x_j^-, maximum possible demand for store j; for x_j^+, the difference between the maximum and minimum demand values. The variable ordering heuristic employed assigns u_j, k_{u_j}, and $y_{u_j,j}$ in that order. The solution time (in seconds) and the number of nodes visited during search are given in Table 2 under the column heading "SCP".

Step two of the experiment repeated the first with an embedded linear relaxation. The linear relaxation enables the solver to produce lower/upper bounds by solving an LP at each node of the CP search tree. The constraint solver also uses the LP solution to guide its search. The results of using embedded linear relaxation are given in Table 2 in the next two columns with a heading "SCP with LR". We also tried using linear relaxation with the variable ordering used in the first step. However, the results show that in this case linear relaxation does not prune the search space further, but incurs overhead.

In the next step of the experiment, Benders decomposition was applied to the test suite. The algorithm was implemented using ILOG Cplex9.0 and Solver6.0. The initial feasible solution was defined by adopting a no-order policy for all stores. However, since each store must be assigned to a warehouse, the least costly warehouse is operated and its fixed cost is incurred to be able to serve all stores. In this step, the "multiple-cut" version of BD was used. The results are given under the heading "BD with Multiple-Cuts". The results displayed in column "step", show the number of steps (solving a master or a slave problem defines a single step) BD takes before obtaining and proving the optimality of a solution. The column headed "Gap" gives the optimality gap for the first feasible solution, which is in the 5% gap. This experiment was repeated with "single-cuts". The results are listed under the heading "BD with Single-Cuts".

We experimented with two heuristics to test the utility of starting with a more informed solution. In heuristic-I, an expected value problem is designed to find an initial solution by replacing random demands with their maximum possible values. In heuristic-II, half the value of the maximum demands are taken as deterministic demand values. The deterministic CP models were solved to generate initial solutions. Results are presented in Table 2.

From Eq.(10), it is clear that there are only two possible values – either $-h_j$ or e_j – for any dual variables λ_j of the subproblems. Therefore, it is possible to built the "complete master" model, which can be solved to optimality without

Table 2. Experimental Results – Stochastic Capacitated Warehouse Location Problem

No	# W	# S	# Scen	SCP		SCP with LR		BD with Multiple-Cuts					BD with Single-Cuts					Heuristic-I		Heuristic-II	
				Time	# Choice	Time	# Choice	Time	Step	Gap	Time	Step	Time	Step	Gap	Time	Step	Time	Step	Time	Step
1	2	2	4	0.07	361	0.22	634	0.07	5	2.7	0.07	4	0.03	5	2.7	0.03	4	0.04	8	0.02	6
2	2	2	9	0.22	1031	0.38	848	0.13	5	2.4	0.13	4	0.05	7	3.7	0.03	4	0.06	10	0.05	8
3	2	2	16	0.32	1687	0.56	1015	0.22	5	0	0.22	5	0.04	7	2.5	0.03	5	0.06	10	0.05	8
4	2	2	25	0.87	4464	0.74	1048	0.33	5	0	0.33	5	0.04	6	1.7	0.03	5	0.07	9	0.06	7
5	2	2	36	1.1	4913	1.2	1337	0.57	5	0	0.57	5	0.05	8	3.3	0.03	5	0.07	10	0.06	7
6	2	2	49	2.0	8068	2.3	1685	1.6	6	0.43	0.98	5	0.09	8	4.1	0.04	5	0.11	11	0.10	10
7	2	2	64	2.0	11190	2.5	2212	1.7	6	0.48	1.1	5	0.08	9	4.6	0.04	5	0.11	12	0.09	9
8	2	2	81	2.0	10724	3.3	2577	2.2	6	0.45	1.4	5	0.08	8	1.3	0.05	6	0.10	11	0.06	10
9	2	2	100	2.9	14669	4.3	3040	2.7	6	0.2	1.7	5	0.11	11	3.0	0.06	6	0.11	12	0.09	9
10	2	2	225	15	48301	39	15343	19	7	4.4	11	5	0.60	23	2.4	0.12	9	0.37	18	0.43	20
11	3	3	8	3.7	7598	11	36148	9.7	9	3.6	6.3	6	0.73	11	0.0	0.73	11	0.70	10	0.52	10
12	3	3	27	7.0	14798	24	37565	62	11	0.58	30	6	2.1	21	3.8	1.5	16	2.5	24	1.8	22
13	3	3	64	16	35607	52	36690	91	9	0.59	61	6	2.1	19	4.0	0.84	10	2.3	22	1.7	18
14	3	3	125	33	59942	128	42856	280	11	1.3	180	9	3.1	25	2.8	1.1	14	4.1	32	3.2	26
15	3	3	216	62	88078	250	51250	660	11	1.5	420	9	3.5	27	2.5	1.1	14	3.7	28	3.9	28
16	3	3	343	130	156102	390	54552	1000	11	1.3	640	8	3.8	28	3.9	1.1	14	3.5	28	3.1	32
17	3	3	512	450	363736	2200	250467	2600	11	0.82	1700	9	2.8	22	3.9	0.67	10	2.9	23	3.4	28
18	3	3	729	950	487978	3400	216757	–	–	0.33	3600	9	3.6	23	3.8	0.99	13	3.6	25	4.6	23
19	3	3	1000	1500	600508	–	–	–	–	–	–	–	4.8	25	3.1	1.3	12	4.4	25	4.6	21
20	3	3	1331	2300	797668	–	–	–	–	–	–	–	5.0	25	3.1	1.3	12	4.3	28	5.3	23
21	6	4	16	620	927903	800	1405123	1200	7	3.4	1200	6	13	9	3.1	13	8	4.6	3	4.2	4
22	6	4	81	2900	1040436	–	–	–	–	–	–	–	40	17	2.1	40	16	57	16	54	18
23	6	4	256	–	–	–	–	–	–	–	–	–	40	19	2.6	20	15	77	30	71	26
24	8	3	8	15	32817	29	70983	16	5	1.5	16	4	1.2	5	0.0	1.2	5	1.6	4	1.2	4
25	8	3	27	79	95022	64	81632	240	7	2.2	130	5	2.9	7	3.7	1.8	5	3.3	6	3.3	8
26	8	3	64	140	123451	110	80861	480	7	4.1	250	5	4.1	9	2.9	2.8	6	4.1	8	4.3	10
27	8	3	125	510	259604	370	152197	2600	7	0	2600	6	12	13	4.3	8.6	10	9.5	16	7.4	10
28	8	3	216	1600	713402	1300	341135	–	–	–	–	–	16	17	3.9	7.2	10	24	24	22	20
29	8	3	343	3100	1145120	1800	275315	–	–	–	–	–	14	19	4.8	5.6	11	29	26	16	16
30	8	3	512	–	–	3500	384398	–	–	–	–	–	31	24	4.4	9.9	13	32	26	39	26
31	8	4	16	610	698528	2000	3664085	850	5	0	850	5	9.0	5	0.0	9.1	5	16	4	8.1	4
32	8	4	81	–	–	–	–	–	–	–	–	–	21	6	2.9	13	5	27	5	16	5
33	8	4	256	–	–	–	–	–	–	–	–	–	110	15	4.5	58	11	200	18	140	14
34	8	5	32	–	–	–	–	–	–	–	–	–	41	5	0.0	41	5	67	3	54	4
35	8	5	243	–	–	–	–	–	–	–	–	–	480	8	3.7	160	5	530	5	460	7
36	9	3	8	13	28202	65	213637	40	6	0	40	6	2.1	9	4.1	2.1	9	1.1	4	0.65	4
37	9	3	27	60	79583	100	202190	350	8	1.7	200	7	4.1	10	4.1	2.8	9	3.1	7	2.8	7
38	9	3	64	140	114204	480	609580	960	9	4.8	440	6	8.1	17	1.1	6.4	14	9.6	20	8.7	16
39	9	3	125	340	189756	860	550976	–	–	4.8	1900	6	22	24	3.7	5.7	12	23	28	21	24
40	9	3	216	600	289801	1300	469528	–	–	–	–	–	18	24	3.4	5.1	12	22	30	19	26
41	9	4	16	710	1091206	1600	3387047	700	7	0	700	7	8.0	9	0.0	7.9	9	3.5	4	2.9	4
42	9	4	81	2700	972937	–	–	–	–	–	–	–	27	16	0.98	18	12	27	16	19	11
43	9	4	256	–	–	–	–	–	–	–	–	–	27	13	1.7	20	10	60	18	36	16
44	9	5	32	–	–	–	–	–	–	–	–	–	140	9	4.6	140	8	46	4	41	4
45	10	3	8	6.0	10025	21	51635	7.7	4	0	7.7	4	0.89	5	0.0	0.89	5	1.1	3	0.63	4
46	10	4	16	330	379947	790	1431662	240	4	0	240	4	5.1	5	0.0	5.1	5	9.4	4	4.2	4
47	10	4	81	2700	991063	–	–	–	–	–	–	–	23	15	4.7	18	12	31	16	18	12
48	10	4	256	–	–	–	–	–	–	–	–	–	44	19	5.0	32	14	65	18	47	19
49	10	5	32	–	–	–	–	–	–	–	–	–	97	7	0.0	97	7	37	4	28	4
50	10	5	243	–	–	–	–	–	–	–	–	–	310	11	4.4	310	10	170	5	220	8

any Benders iteration, for this test problem. The complete master model is tried on these 50 instances. However, the observed computational performance is very discouraging. The solution times are on the average 100 times more than "BD with Single-Cuts" solution times, and 2 times more than "SCP".

The results in Table 2 show that monolithic SCP – either with variable ordering or linear relaxation – could not prove optimality in 11 instances under 1 hour. At termination, in only 2 instances the best-so-far feasible solutions were optimal. The results also point out another strong side of BD approach. If an optimality gap which is less than 5% is considered satisfactory, then the solution time is halved on average for the addressed test suite. It should also be noted that we obtained the optimal solutions in 8 out of 50 cases.

A multiple regression at confidence level 0.95 with a constant coefficient 0 gives us an insight to the BD algorithms' exact behavior on SCWL problem. The dependent variable is defined as the ratio of the solution times $st(.)$, $st(CP)/st(BD_{single})$ and independent variables of # warehouses, # stores, # scenarios. The adjusted R^2 is 0.83, which demonstrates that the overall regression model is meaningful. The regression coefficients are 4.76 (warehouses), -3.00 (stores) and 0.33 (scenarios). The corresponding t-statistics are 1.72, -0.49, 14.01, hence only the "scenarios" coefficient is significant. The results indicate that as the number of scenarios increases the performance of BD is more significant.

The two initial-solution heuristics give mixed results. In some instances the overhead of solving an additional CP model to obtain a better starting solution is not worth the effort. However, cheaper heuristics that exploit the unique structure of the problem addressed can be designed and the total solution time performance can be improved.

5.2 Stochastic Template Design Problem

The deterministic **template design problem** (prob002 in CSPLib) is described as follows. Given is a set of variations of a design, with a common shape and size and such that the number of required "pressings" of each variation is known. The problem is to design a set of templates, with a common capacity to which each must be filled, by assigning one or more instances of a variation to each template. A design should be chosen that minimises the total number of "runs" of the templates required to satisfy the number of pressings required for each variation. As an example, the variations might be for cartons for different flavours of cat food, such as fish or chicken, where ten thousand fish cartons and twenty thousand chicken cartons need to be printed. The problem would then be to design a set of templates by assigning a number of fish and/or chicken designs to each template such that a minimal number of runs of the templates is required to print all thirty thousand cartons. In the stochastic version of the problem, the demand for each variation is uncertain.

Proll and Smith address this problem by fixing the number of templates and minimising the total number of pressings [14]. We adopt their model herein, extending it to comply with the stochastic demand assumption. We use the following notation: N, number of variations; T, number of templates (T=2, for all instances of the test suit); S, number of slots on each template; K, number of scenarios (demand for each variation is uncertain); c_h, scrap cost; c_p, shortage cost; $a_{i,j}$, number of slots designated to variation i, on template j; R_j, number of required "runs" of template j; x_i, an auxiliary variable; $d_{i,k}$, demand for variation i in scenario k; $e_{i,k}$, total scrap (variation i in scenario k); $b_{i,k}$, total shortage (variation i in scenario k); p_k, probability of observing scenario k.

The certainty equivalent CP model is:

$$\min \sum_{i=1}^{N} \sum_{k=1}^{K} p_k (c_p b_{ik} + c_h e_{ik})$$
subject to
$$\sum_{i=1}^{N} a_{ij} = S, \forall j \in \{1, ..., T\},$$
$$\sum_{j=1}^{T} a_{ij} R_j = x_i, \forall i \in \{1, ..., N\}, \text{ and}$$
$$x_i = d_{ik} + e_{ik} - b_{ik}, \forall i \in \{1, ..., N\}, \forall k \in \{1, ..., K\}.$$

In the above formulation, the first stage (a_{ij}, R_j) and second stage (x_i, e_{ik}, b_{ik}) decision variables are employed to partition the given model. In this case, the master and slave problems for the Stochastic Template Design Problem are defined as

Master Problem
$$\min \sum_{k=1}^{K} \max\{\sum_{i=1}^{N} p_k (d_{ik} - x_i)\widehat{\lambda}_{ik}\}$$
subject to
$$\sum_{i=1}^{N} a_{ij} = S, \quad \forall j \in \{1, ..., T\}$$
$$\sum_{j=1}^{T} a_{ij} R_j = x_i, \quad \forall i \in \{1, ..., N\}$$

Slave Problems,
$$\forall i \in \{1, ..., N\}, \forall k \in \{1, ..., K\}$$
$$\max \ (d_{ik} - \overline{x}_i)\lambda_{ik}$$
subject to
$$-c_h \leq \lambda_{ik} \leq c_p, \ \lambda_{ik} \text{ free}$$

Table 3. Experimental Results – Stochastic Template Design Problem

				SCP		Complete Benders		BD with Multiple-Cuts					BD with Single-Cuts				
No	N	S	Scen	Time	#choice	Time	#choice	Time	step	gap	Time	step	Time	step	gap	Time	step
1	3	6	10	340	846,584	190	845,660	4,400	13	0	4,400	13	9.5	33	4.1	7.9	29
2	3	9	10	1,400	3,401,506	780	3,400,897	–	–	–	–	–	8.1	31	4.8	7.4	26
3	4	2	10	230	703,957	140	694,949	3,100	27	4.0	2,100	25	62	43	3.7	42	36
4	4	3	10	470	1,153,468	270	1,145,436	5,500	23	0.6	3,100	21	41	39	4.7	26	32
5	4	4	10	1,900	4,165,262	1,100	4,159,062	–	–	–	–	–	190	49	4.3	130	40
6	4	5	10	690	1,630,615	380	1,627,743	–	–	–	–	–	380	41	3.4	380	36
7	4	6	10	–	–	5,700	20,909,785	–	–	–	–	–	670	52	3.5	510	44
8	4	7	10	–	–	–	–	–	–	–	–	–	820	53	4.8	600	40
9	4	8	10	–	–	–	–	–	–	–	–	–	1,800	50	4.4	1,000	37
10	4	9	10	–	–	–	–	–	–	–	–	–	5,900	49	3.3	4,900	43
11	4	6	11	–	–	6,800	21,302,918	–	–	–	–	–	480	51	4.1	410	44
12	4	6	12	–	–	–	–	–	–	–	–	–	1,100	52	4.6	640	41
13	4	6	13	–	–	–	–	–	–	–	–	–	190	58	4.9	160	43
14	4	6	14	–	–	–	–	–	–	–	–	–	1,300	57	3.3	760	42
15	4	6	15	–	–	–	–	–	–	–	–	–	790	53	3.5	780	42
16	4	6	16	–	–	–	–	–	–	–	–	–	1,800	55	4.4	1,500	40
17	4	6	17	–	–	–	–	–	–	–	–	–	540	54	4.8	370	38
18	4	6	18	–	–	–	–	–	–	–	–	–	290	53	3.7	230	40
19	4	6	19	–	–	–	–	–	–	–	–	–	590	61	3.9	500	49
20	4	6	20	–	–	–	–	–	–	–	–	–	400	59	4.2	360	40

Experiments, summarised in Table 3, were conducted on 20 stochastic template design instances using an Intel Centrino 2GHz computer with 1GB RAM. Allowed solution time was 2 hours. A dash in the table indicates this time was exceeded without finding the optimal solution.

We compared four different solution methods: stochastic constraint programming (solved using Ilog OPLStudio and Solver 6.0), and three versions of Benders Decomposition (solved using Ilog Cplex 9.0 and Solver 6.0). In the first, the complete master problem, which can be solved to optimality without any Benders iterations, was built and solved using Solver 6.0. In the second and third, the multiple cut and single cut versions of BD were used. For the stochastic constraint program and complete Benders formulation, the number of choice points explored to find and prove optimality are shown. For the latter two Benders variations, the "step" column indicates the number of steps (solving a master or a slave problem is counted as a step) BD takes before proving optimality. The "Gap" column gives the optimality gap for the first feasible solution found with an optimality gap of 5% or less.

The results show that monolithic SCP can solve only the smaller instances in the time allowed. The performance of the complete Benders formulation is comparable, giving better times and solving two more instances. The performance of the two BD approaches is at polar opposites. The multiple-cut variant performs relatively poorly, solving fewer instances than SCP and taking much more time. However, the single-cut variant is clearly the strongest approach that we tested, solving all 20 instances.

6 Conclusion

This paper has aimed to enhance the effectiveness of the stochastic constraint programming framework by extending the use of the well-known Benders' decomposition algorithm, which has proved to be useful in mathematical programming, to solve stochastic constraint programs with linear recourse, *SCPwLR*. First and second stage decision variables are used to decompose the stochastic constraint program into master and slave problems. The unique structure of stochastic constraint programs, which is based upon a scenario tree representation, yields independent slave sub-problems, one for each scenario considered in the scenario tree. This natural slave problem decomposition has the obvious benefit of solving a set of small problems, and hence to a degree relieving the difficulty of dealing with a large scenario tree.

In our test problems, it was shown that the slave problem decomposes into trivial scenario problems, each of which is a boundary value problem and can be solved simply by checking the objective function coefficient and deciding whether the single decision variable takes the lower or the upper limit of its domain. Computational experiments confirmed the potential of Benders' decomposition method as an efficient solution algorithm for these problems.

An attractive feature of this algorithm is the availability of upper bounds and lower bounds produced by the slave and master problem solutions, respectively. The upper bound is generated by a sequence of feasible solutions to the problem, so the best of these may be taken as a solution if the procedure is terminated short of optimality. Furthermore, the best-so-far lower bound can be used to produce a metric for the optimality gap.

Although at present we consider only 2-stage *SCPwLR*, the ideas presented here can be generalised to n-stage *SCPwLR* without loss of generality. In this case, Benders' algorithm is applied in a recursive manner. We expect the performance discrepancy between the monolithic model and the decomposed model to be magnified as the number of stages grows. A further extension of this work should consider the case in which the linear recourse assumption is relaxed and recourse actions with complex structures are allowed. Hooker and Ottosson [7] provide a method for generating Benders cuts in such situations by generalising the linear programming dual of a sub-problem to an "inference" dual. We will adopt this approach for general stochastic CSP.

Acknowledgements. S. Armagan Tarim is supported by Science Foundation Ireland under Grant No. 03/CE3/I405 as part of the Centre for Telecommunications Value-Chain-Driven Research (CTVR) and Grant No. 00/PI.1/C075. Ian Miguel is supported by a UK-Royal Academy of Engineering/EPSRC Research Fellowship.

References

1. Beasley, J.E.: An algorithm for solving large capacitated warehouse location problems. European Journal of Operational Research, **33** (1988) 314–325
2. Benders, J. F.: Partitioning Procedures for Solving Mixed-Variables Programming Problems. Numerische Mathematik, **4** (1962) 238–252
3. Benoist, T., Gaudin, E., Rottembourg, B.: Constraint Programming Contribution to Benders Decomposition: A Case Study. Proceedings of the 8th International Conference on Principles and Practice of Constraint Programming, LNCS **2470** (2002) 603–617
4. Eremin, A., Wallace, M.: Hybrid Benders Decomposition Algorithms in Constraint Logic Programming. Principles and Practice of Constraint Programming, Proceedings of the 7th International Conference, CP 2001, Paphos, Cyprus, LNCS **2239** (2001) 1–15
5. Geoffrion, A. M.: Generalized Benders decomposition. Journal of Optimization Theory and Applications, **10** (1972) 237-260
6. Holmberg, K., Ronnqvist, M., Yuan, D.: An exact algorithm for the capacitated facility location problem with single sourcing. European Journal of Operational Research, **113** (1999) 544–559
7. Hooker, J. N., Ottosson, G.: Logic-based Benders decomposition. Mathematical Programming, **96** (2003) 33–60
8. ILOG Inc.: OPL Studio 3.7, Studio Users Manual, (2003)
9. Jain, V., Grossmann, I. E.: Algorithms for Hybrid MILP/CP Models for a Class of Optimization Problems. INFORMS Journal on Computing, **13** (2001) 258–276
10. Khumawala, B. M.: An Efficient Branch-Bound Algorithm for the Warehouse Location Problem. Management Science. **18** (1972) 718–731
11. Krarup, J., Pruzan, P. M.: The simple plant location problem: Survey and synthesis. European Journal of Operational Research. **12** (1983) 36–81
12. Manandhar, S., Tarim, S. A., Walsh. T.: Scenario-Based Stochastic Constraint Programming. Proceedings of IJCAI-2003, Acapulco, Mexico. (2003) 257–262

13. Mirchandani, P. B., Francis, R. L.: Discrete Location Theory. John Wiley and Sons, (1990)
14. Proll, L., Smith, B.M. Integer linear programming and constraint programming approaches to a template design problem. INFORMS Journal on Computing 10(3):265–275, 1998.
15. Tarim, S. A., Manandhar, S., Walsh. T.: Stochastic Constraint Programming: A Scenario-Based Approach, Constraints 11(1), 2006.
16. Thorsteinsson, E. S.: Branch-and-Check: A Hybrid Framework Integrating Mixed Integer Programming and Constraint Logic Programming. Principles and Practice of Constraint Programming, Proceedings of the 7th International Conference, CP 2001, LNCS **2239** (2001) 16–30
17. Xia, Q., Eremin, A., Wallace. M.: Problem Decomposition for Traffic Diversions. Proceedings of the 1st International Conference, Integration of AI and OR Techniques in Constraint Programming for Combinatorial Optimization Problems, CPAIOR 2004, LNCS **3011** (2004) 348–363

The Challenge of Exploiting Weak Symmetries

Roland Martin

Darmstadt University of Technology,
Algorithmics Group,
64289 Darmstadt, Germany
martin@algo.informatik.tu-darmstadt.de

Abstract. In contrast to a proper symmetry, a weak symmetry acts only on a subset of the variables and the weakly symmetric equivalent solutions preserve the feasibility state only with respect to a subset of the constraints. Therefore, breaking weak symmetries on the whole problem with standard techniques would lead to a loss of solutions. Weak symmetries occur in different application fields like planning, scheduling and manufacturing as well as in the fields of soft constraints. We introduce a technique that enables us to exploit weak symmetries and state experimental results on a real world problem to show the gain in using this technique.

1 Introduction

Weak symmetries act only on a subset of the variables and the weakly symmetric solutions satisfy only a subset of the constraints of the problem. Therefore, weak symmetric solutions preserve the state of feasibility only with respect to the subset of variables the weak symmetry acts on and only for the constraints these variables satisfy. If two solutions s_1 and s_2 are weakly symmetric there is in general no symmetry function that maps s_1 to s_2 or vice versa. The solutions s_1 and s_2 are only symmetric with respect to the variables the weak symmetry acts on. Weak symmetries occur in many fields of applications and have already been discovered and identified in planning, scheduling and model checking (see [1] - [5]). In particular real world optimisation problems contain weak symmetries. Often the objective function makes a symmetry weak. We will see an example of such a problem in Section 5. A whole research area where weak symmetries arise is soft constraints. Since weak symmetries are very common but not yet tackled, symmetry breaking methods for weak symmetries are needed.

Symmetry breaking is crucial for the success of constraint programming to achieve a better performance of the search process. Various techniques have been proposed for symmetry handling. In general it is done by reformulating the model [6] excluding the symmetry up-front via additional constraints [7], breaking it during the search [8, 9, 10] or by a combination thereof. A considerable amount of work has already been done in the fields of symmetry breaking (e.g. [6, 7, 8, 9, 10, 11, 12, 13]).

In contrast to a proper symmetry, a weak symmetry cannot be simply broken. This is due to the modus operandi of symmetry breaking techniques. Symmetry breaking techniques exclude all but one representative of each equivalence class of solutions from the search tree. Therefore breaking a weak symmetry with standard techniques leads to a loss of solutions. Nonetheless, we introduce a technique that enables us to break

B. Hnich et al. (Eds.): CSCLP 2005, LNAI 3978, pp. 149–163, 2006.

weak symmetries without losing solutions. We decompose a problem P in a subproblem P_1 and P_2, where P_1 contains all the variables the weak symmetry acts on and all constraints that are respected by symmetric solutions of these variables. Our technique transforms the weak symmetry of P into a proper symmetry on P_1. On this subproblem the symmetry can be broken using all kinds of symmetry breaking mentioned above. Therefore only one solution for each equivalence class is found in P_1. An additional variable (further on called *SymVar*) is used to model the symmetric equivalents of this solution. The symmetric equivalents (determined by the solution of P_1 and the SymVar) are then passed successively to the rest of the problem encapsulated in P_2. If a symmetric equivalent satisfies the constraints of P_2, the variables in P_2 (that are not part of P_1) are assigned to search for a feasible solution to P. If it does not, a different symmetric solution is passed to P_2 until one satisfies P_2. If none satisfies P_2 a different solution to P_1 is sought.

Weak symmetry breaking does not conflict with proper symmetry breaking. It is possible to break the weak symmetry on a subproblem and break other existing symmetries on the whole problem concurrently, making the symmetry breaking effort more powerful. Still, weak symmetries have to be detected by the modeller to apply our technique. To our best knowledge up to now there is no approach that tackles the problem by modelling. However, in [4] the problem is considered from a group theoretical background.

In Section 2 the formal background and basic definitions are given. Throughout the paper we will consider the magic square problem as a running example to explain our ideas. The problem description and a basic model of this problem is also given here. Section 3 comprise the definition and theoretical ideas of weak symmetries while Section 4 introduces our technique to handle weak symmetries with SymVars. Section 5 comprises a short introduction to a real world problem and the results on applying SymVars to handle weak symmetries in this problem. Section 6 concludes the results and gives an outlook to future work.

2 Formal Background and Prerequisites

First of all we fix our terminology.

Definition 1 (Constraint Satisfaction Problem – CSP)
A CSP is characterised by $P = (X, D, C)$, *where*

- $X = \{x_1, \ldots, x_n\}$ *is the set of variables;*
- $D = \{d_1, \ldots, d_n\}$ *is the set of the domains for the variables in* X*;*
- $C = \{c_1, \ldots, c_m\}$ *is the set of constraints, where each constraint states a relation over a subset of variables.*

For an optimisation problem we just extend this formulation to $P = (X, D, C, h)$, where X, D and C are defined as above and h is the objective function. [1]

[1] Note that in standard CP techniques the objective function h can be represented by a constraint that tightens with the search. The objective value is then represented by a variable. Therefore, it is sufficient to regard only satisfaction problems.

Definition 2 ((Partial) Variable Assignment)
Consider a CSP $P = (X, D, C)$.

In a **variable assignment** *each variable* $x_i \in X$ *of* P *is assigned a value* $v_i \in d_i$. *In a* **partial variable assignment** *only a subset of the variables* $x_i \in X$ *of* P *is assigned a value* $v_i \in d_i$.

Definition 3 ((Partial) Solution)
Consider a CSP $P = (X, D, C)$.

If a variable assignment is consistent with all the constraints in C *it is* **feasible** *and called a* **solution** *to* P.
If the assigned variables of a partial variable assignment are consistent with all the constraints in C *the partial variable assignment is* **feasible** *and called a* **partial solution** *to* P.

Definition 4 (Solution Symmetry) *[13]*
Consider a CSP $P = (X, D, C)$.

A **solution symmetry** *of* P *is a permutation of the set* $X \times D$ *that preserves the set of solutions to* P.

From now on we will speak of symmetries instead of solution symmetries. A symmetry partitions the search space into classes of equivalent variable assignments. All variable assignments in each class are either feasible or infeasible [8].

To illustrate weak symmetries we use a small well-known running example the magic square problem. Here we state the problem description and a basic modelling approach. Based on this model we introduce weak symmetries in the following sections.

Running Example: Magic Square Problem. In the magic square problem, the numbers $1, \ldots, n^2$ have to be assigned to a $n \times n$ square such that the sum of the numbers in each row, in each column and in both main diagonals are equal. The value m for this sum necessarily satisfies $m = \frac{n^3+n}{2}$. A standard model is presented in the following:
Variables X:

- $\text{square}_{ij}, i, j \in N, N = \{1, \ldots n\}$ (the magic square)

Domains D:

- $\forall i, j \in N : \text{square}_{ij} \in \{1, \ldots, n^2\}$ (all possible numbers)

Constraints C:

- $\forall i \in N : \sum_{j \in N} \text{square}_{ij} = m$ (each row sums up to m)
- $\forall j \in N : \sum_{i \in N} \text{square}_{ij} = m$ (each column sums up to m)
- $\sum_{i \in N} \text{square}_{ii} = m$ (diagonal sums up to m)
- $\sum_{i \in N} \text{square}_{i,n+1-i} = m$ (anti diagonal sums up to m)
- alldifferent(square) (all numbers are assigned)

The magic square problem has the same symmetries as the n-queens problem, the rotations and reflection of the matrix and the combination thereof – eight symmetries in total (including the identity) [8]. We refer to these kinds of symmetries as the chessboard symmetries in the following. In addition certain combinations of row and column permutations lead to symmetric solutions.

For example permuting the first with the second row and the last with the last but one row and analogue the columns transforms a feasible magic square in a new feasible magic square.

In the following we will neglect symmetry breaking constraints in the model and state the constraints that break the weak symmetry only. However, symmetry breaking constraints can be stated together with the weak symmetry breaking constraints.

3 Weak Symmetry

3.1 Weak Symmetry Definition

Weak symmetries act on problems with special properties. To characterize weak symmetries we first define weakly decomposable problems. In a weak decomposition of a problem all variables and constraints that are respected by the weak symmetry are gathered in one subproblem.

Definition 5 (Weakly Decomposable Problem)
A problem $P = (X, D, C)$ is **weakly decomposable** *if it decomposes into two subproblems $P_1 = (X_1, D_1, C_1)$ and $P_2 = (X_2, D_2, C_2)$ with the following properties:*

$$X_1 \cap X_2 \neq \emptyset \tag{1}$$
$$X_1 \cup X_2 = X \tag{2}$$
$$C_1 \cup C_2 = C \tag{3}$$
$$C_1 \cap C_2 = \emptyset \tag{4}$$
$$C_2 \neq \emptyset \tag{5}$$
$$D_1 = pr_1(D) \tag{6}$$
$$D_2 = pr_2(D) \tag{7}$$

where pr_i denotes the projection to the subspace defined by the subset X_i of the variables in P.

The first condition states that P_1 and P_2 contain a subset of shared variables (namely $X_1 \cap X_2$). These variables have to assume the same values in both subproblems to deliver a feasible solution to P. Therefore they link both problems. Without that restriction the problem would be properly decomposable. The second and third condition states that none of the variables and constraints of the original problem P are lost. Furthermore the third and fourth condition state that C_1 and C_2 is a partition of C. Basically this is not necessary for feasibility. A constraint could be in both subsets (if defined on $X_1 \cap X_2$ only) but would be redundant for one of the problems because the solution to the other subproblem would already satisfy this constraint. Therefore, this is just a question of efficiency. The fifth condition states that P_2 is not allowed to be unconstrained. However, note that this restriction does not hold for P_1. This is since we want to group the symmetric data in P_1 and a problem without constraints is perfectly symmetric. Every CSP is weakly decomposable, and usually there will be multiple weak decompositions. However, we concentrate on weak decompositions where the weak symmetry acts as a proper symmetry on P_1.

Definition 6 (Weak Symmetry)
Consider a weakly decomposable problem P with a decomposition (P_1, P_2).
A symmetry $f : X_1 \to X_1$ *on* P_1 *is called a* **weak symmetry on** P *with respect to the decomposition* (P_1,P_2) *if it cannot be extended from* X_1 *to a symmetry on* X.

The intention of the decomposition of the problem is that X_1 contains all symmetric variables (and only those) and X_2 contains the rest of the variables. The gain is that we get a subproblem where the weak symmetry affects all variables and all constraints (P_1) and therefore acts as a proper symmetry on it and one subproblem that is not affected by the weak symmetry (P_2).

3.2 An Example: Magic Square Problem

The idea for the weak decomposition of the magic square problem is that P_1 consists of the problem to find a distribution of the numbers such that the row and column constraints are satisfied but not necessarily the diagonal constraints. These constraints are part of P_2. This decomposition introduces the symmetries of row and column permutation on P_1. These symmetries are the weak symmetries of P. For the purpose of simplicity we will concentrate on the weak symmetry of column permutations only. This is no violation of the idea. In fact, this corresponds to partial symmetry breaking.

The weak decomposition of the magic square problem:

P_1 (assigning the numbers with respect to the row and column constraints):

- $X_1 : \text{square}_{ij}, i, j \in N, N = \{1, \dots n\}$ (the magic square)
- $D_1 : \forall i, j \in N : \text{square}_{ij} \in \{1, \dots, n^2\}$
- C_1:
  - $\forall i \in N : \sum_{j \in N} \text{square}_{ij} = m$ (each row sums up to m)
  - $\forall j \in N : \sum_{i \in N} \text{square}_{ij} = m$ (each column sums up to m)
  - alldifferent(square) (all numbers are assigned)

P_2 (check whether the solution of P_1 also respects the diagonal constraints):

- X_2 :
  - $\text{square}_{ii}, i \in N$ (variables of the diagonal)
  - $\text{square}_{i,n+1-i}, i \in N$ (variables of the anti diagonal)
- D_2 :
  - $\forall i \in N : \text{square}_{ii} \in N$
  - $\forall i \in N : \text{square}_{i,n+1-i} \in N$
- C_2:
  - $\sum_{i \in N} \text{square}_{ii} = m$ (diagonal sums up to m)
  - $\sum_{i \in N} \text{square}_{i,n+1-i} = m$ (anti diagonal sums up to m)

Note that the variables in P_2 already have values assigned by P_1 and none have to be reconsidered in P_2. Therefore the only task in P_2 is to check whether the solution of P_1 also satisfies P_2. A (feasible) solution of P_1 may now be infeasible with P_2 since the diagonal constraints are violated. However, a permutation of the solution of P_1 (which is still feasible for P_1) may be also feasible for P_2.

Example for a magic square of size 4 with the magic number $m = 34$:

4	5	11	14
7	16	2	9
10	1	15	8
13	12	6	3

4	5	14	11
7	16	9	2
10	1	8	15
13	12	3	6

The magic square on the left satisfies P_1 but does not satisfy the diagonal constraints. However, if the third and fourth column are permuted the resulting magic square satisfies also the diagonal constraints and therefore P_2

3.3 Problems Containing Weak Symmetries

There are well known problems like the magic square problem that comprise weak symmetries under specific weak decompositions. However, weak symmetries do not only occur in academical problems. More often they can be found in real world optimisation problems. An example of such a problem is investigated in Section 5. Introducing an objective function to a problem often yields weak symmetries, since different variable assignments achieve different objective values. For example the asymmetric TSP is weakly symmetric since reversing a tour leads to a different length of the tour. A whole research area where weak symmetries arise are soft constraints. In soft constraints basically a solution is evaluated and the best solution found is returned. Thus, it is very similar to optimisation. As a short example consider map colouring with different weights for the colours used. Permutation of the colours in a solution may yield a different value and therefore the solutions are weakly symmetric and not properly symmetric. Symmetry breaking in soft constraints is often not possible (since the symmetry is actually a weak symmetry). Therefore, soft constraints problems where the hard version of the problem comprises symmetries have weak symmetries that can be handled by the technique introduced in the next section.

4 Breaking Weak Symmetries

As seen in the last section, weak symmetries occur in a great variety of problems, and standard symmetry breaking methods cannot be applied to handle weak symmetries successfully. Therefore new methods are needed to handle weak symmetries. Here we introduce a new method that breaks weak symmetries without losing solutions.

4.1 Theoretical Idea

The challenge in weak symmetry breaking is actually not the symmetry breaking part but not to lose solutions by breaking the weak symmetry. As mentioned earlier the weak symmetry is a proper symmetry on P_1, and any method of symmetry breaking can be used. However, by breaking the symmetry on P_1, any solution s_{P_1} of P_1 will represent its equivalence class of solutions. All these solutions have to be considered when determining a solution to P. Even if s_{P_1} does not satisfy P_2 a different solution $\pi(s_{P_1})$ in the same equivalence class may satisfy P_2, where $\pi(s_{P_1})$ is a permutation of s_{P_1}.

Therefore we need a way to represent all these solutions in the search process. We introduce a new variable that identifies which element of the equivalence class is represented in the further search process. This variable is the SymVar.

Definition 7 (Symmetry Variable)
Consider a CSP $P = (X, D, C)$ *with a weak decomposition* (P_1, P_2) *and a weak symmetry* f *on* P.

A **symmetry variable (SymVar)** $\pi \in S[X_1]$ *represents the group of symmetric solutions of* f *in* P_1. *Its domain is the symmetric group on* X_1, *denoted by* $S[X_1]$.

If the SymVar is the identity then the solution passed to P_2 is the one found in P_1. In any other case the permuted solution of P_1 (which is equivalent with respect to the weak symmetry) is passed to P_2. The solution of P_1 together with the assignment of the SymVar represents a partial variable assignment to P_2 and P. It is checked whether it also satisfies the constraints of P_2 and if so all variables in $X_2 \backslash X_1$ are assigned for finding a solution to P_2. If the partial assignment does not satisfy P_2 a different element of the equivalence class is considered by a different value for the SymVar. If none of the elements satisfy P_2 a new solution to P_1 is sought. This way the whole problem is investigated and no solution is lost. Note that only for solutions of P_1 the SymVar is instantiated.

Theorem 1 (Solution Preservation).
The solution space of P *is totally reflected by the decomposition* (P_1, P_2) *and a SymVar* π *such that every solution of* P *can be uniquely represented by a solution to* P_1, *an assignment to the SymVar and a solution to* P_2.

Proof. A solution of P yields a solution to P_1 and P_2 directly. π can be chosen as the identity. A solution to P_1, a SymVar assignment $\pi \in S[X_1]$ and a solution to P_2 can be transformed into a solution of P by assigning the permutation under π of the solution to P_1. P_2 commits all variables $x_i \in \{X_2 \backslash X_1\}$ to P. Since π restores all solutions of P_1 that are excluded by the weak symmetry breaking no solution is lost and the solution space of P is totally reflected by the decomposition (P_1, P_2) and π.

4.2 Modelling Approach

In practice this concept of a single SymVar as a representative is not supported in constraint programming solvers on the level of modelling. Therefore instead of one variable we use a set of variables. A feasible variable assignment to these variables then represents a specific element of the equivalence class.

Definition 8 **(P_{sym})**
Consider a CSP $P = (X, D, C)$ *with a weak decomposition* (P_1, P_2) *and a weak symmetry* f *on* P.
$P_{sym} = (X_{sym}, D_{sym}, C_{sym})$ *is a subproblem of* P *that models the weak symmetry* f. X_{sym} *is the set of SymVars representing the variables of* P_1. D_{sym} *is the domain for all SymVars and* C_{sym} *is the set of constraints that model the symmetric group induced by* f. *A solution of* P_{sym} *represents an element of the symmetric group induced by* f.

If the weak symmetry is a permutation of n elements there would be n SymVars with a domain of $\{1, \ldots, n\}$ and an alldifferent constraint ensuring that every feasible assignment to X_{sym} is a permutation.

In the Magic Square Problem
Consider the column permutation to be weak. For each column of the matrix a SymVar is introduced that represents all variables in this column. An assignment $\text{symCol}_i = j$ means that the column i is permuted to the position of column j.

P_{sym}:

- X_{sym}:
  - $\text{symCol}_i, i \in N$
- D_{sym}:
  - $\forall i \in N : \text{symCol}_i \in N$
- C_{sym}:
  - $\text{alldifferent}(\text{symCol})$

For the search process this means that the set of SymVars has to be assigned before the specific element of the equivalence class is determined. Although more variables have to be assigned when using a set of SymVars instead of a single SymVar this allows some more flexibility in the approach. Firstly, it allows to steer the search for the elements of the equivalence class by posting variable and value ordering constraints on the set of SymVars. This way promising elements can be evaluated earlier which can be crucial for constraint satisfaction where just one solution is needed. Secondly, a partial assignment of the SymVars can be evaluated as infeasible with the constraints of P_2. Thereby the whole subgroup of elements represented by this partial SymVar assignment can be pruned by simple backtracking. Note that weak symmetries may occur in combination with proper symmetries in a problem formulation. That is not a problem. The proper symmetry can be dealt with as usual while the weak symmetry is handled as described in this article. Thus, it is possible to break all symmetries of a problem – proper and weak – concurrently (as long as SymVars are introduced for the weak symmetries), making the symmetry breaking effort more powerful. Since weak symmetry breaking does not exclude solutions of P no solution is lost. Proper symmetry breaking does only exclude solutions that are symmetric on P. We just have to show that proper symmetry breaking does not exclude a weakly symmetric solution. But since weakly symmetric solutions cannot be mapped on each other (only with respect to the variables in X_1) they are not excluded by proper symmetry breaking by definition.

To solve P we consider the partial solution $s_{P_{sym}}$. When a solution is found, the search backtracks and reconsiders values for the SymVars to determine a new solution.

All these solutions are symmetric equivalents to the solution s_{P_1}. Only when the search backtracks and variables in X_1 are reconsidered, a solution for a different equivalence class can be found.

By using SymVars we can break the symmetry in P_1 but do not lose any symmetric solution in an equivalence class.

The Complete Magic Square Problem Using SymVars
P:

- X:
  - $\text{square}_{ij}, i, j \in N$ (the magic square)
  - $\text{symCol}_i, i \in N$ (the SymVars for the columns)
- D:
  - $\forall i, j \in N : \text{square}_{ij} \in \{1, \ldots, n^2\}$
  - $\forall i \in N : \text{symCol}_i \in N$
- C:
  - $\forall i \in N : \sum_{j \in N} \text{square}_{ij} = m$ (each row sums up to m)
  - $\forall j \in N : \sum_{i \in N} \text{square}_{ij} = m$ (each column sums up to m)
  - alldifferent(square) (all numbers are assigned)
  - $\forall i \in \{2, \ldots, n\} : \text{square}_{1,i-1} < \text{square}_{1,i}$ (orders the columns in increasing order to break the column permutation)
  - $\sum_{i \in N} \text{square}_{i,\text{symCol}_i} = m$ (diagonal sums up to m)
  - $\sum_{i \in N} \text{square}_{i,n+1-\text{symCol}_i} = m$ (anti diagonal sums up to m)
  - alldifferent(symCol) (a permutation of the columns)

In the computational study we will only consider optimisation problems where P_1 is the basic problem, that is $X_2 \backslash X_1$ is just the optimisation variable and C_2 just contains the optimisation constraint (i.e. the optimisation function) and P_2 imposes additional constraints for optimisation.

4.3 Related Work

There is an approach by W. Harvey [4] that regards the problem of weak symmetries from a group theoretical point of view. Basically the problem is regarded as a symmetric relaxation. The idea is to relax some constraints on the problem which makes the problem more symmetric. The symmetry is broken on the symmetric relaxation and symmetric solutions are then derived by using the software package GAP [14].

The theory behind both approaches (the one considered in this article and that of W. Harvey) is basically the same. The symmetric relaxation approach is somewhat more generic, allowing more freedom in the realisation and implementation of the techniques used to solve the problem. Therefore it seems very promising. The difference to our approach is that the symmetric equivalents are computed via group theory instead of using variables and constraints.

As mentioned in the introduction the strength in our approach is that it is based on plain modelling. That means that it can be used for every constraint programming solver and does not require software or self-written routines to adapt a problem suitably.

At the moment a comparison between the two approaches is not possible. However, this is subject to future joint work for the author and W. Harvey.

5 Experimental Results

In this section we present some experimental results of a relaxed real world problem from the field of automated manufacturing. Due to space restrictions we only state an informal problem description here. For a formal problem description of the original problem see [15].

5.1 Problem Description

In the problem certain components must be mounted on PC boards by a mounting machine consisting of several mounting devices. The task is to maximise the workload of the whole machine. We concentrate only on a subproblem of the whole solving process. That is to find a setup of component types for the individual mounting devices to maximise the potential workload.[2]

The machine consists of several mounting devices. Each mounting device has access to a set of component types (called setup) that are to be mounted on the PC boards. In addition each mounting machine has only access to a part of the PC board layout and can therefore only mount components inside this visibility area (see Figure 1). The PC board layout is specified by a list of mounting tasks. A mounting task is specified by a component type and a position where to mount this component type.

The problem is modelled as follows: The machine is represented by an $m \times n$ variable matrix $A^{m \times n}$ where m is the number of different component types that can be assigned to a mounting device and n is the number of mounting devices on the machine. The domain of variables $a_{ij} \in A$ is the set of component types. An assignment $a_{ij} = k$ means that a component of type k is placed on the mounting device j in the ith slot.

The constraints:

- No component type may be assigned more than once to a column
- Certain component types may not be assigned together in a column
- Each component type achieves a certain workload when assigned to a column. The workload differs from column to column. This represents the visibility of the mounting device.

5.2 Weak Symmetry Modelling of the Problem

The weak symmetry of the problem is that the mounting devices are symmetric in terms of assigning a setup. So a feasible setup is feasible independent from the mounting device it is assigned to. But each mounting device has a different visibility of the board. So certain mounting tasks cannot be seen (and therefore not performed) by certain mounting devices. That means a setup achieves different workloads depending to which mounting device it is assigned. Therefore the permutation of the setups on the machine is the weak symmetry.

[2] The actual workload assigned to the devices is a subset of the workload determined in this subproblem. But the higher the possible workload the higher the degree of freedom for the concrete assigning problem not considered here.

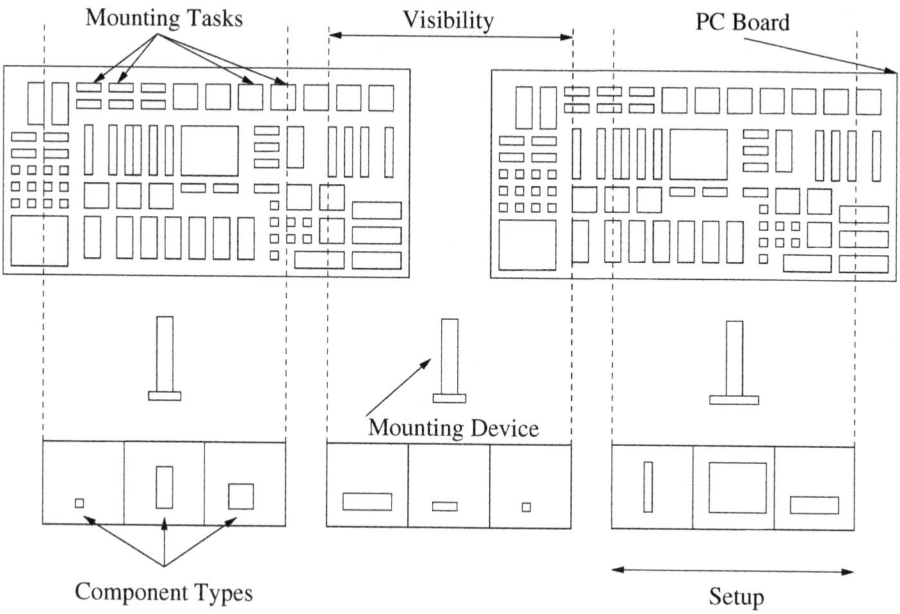

Fig. 1. A machine consisting of three mounting devices each with a setup of three components

This is modelled by introducing a SymVar $place_i$ for each setup i. An assignment $place_i = j$ means that the ith setup is assigned to the jth mounting device on the machine. In the model that means that the column i is permuted to the column j in the matrix A representing the machine setup. To ensure that the assignment of the SymVars is a permutation an alldifferent constraint is stated on them. The weak symmetry is broken by stating column ordering constraints in P_1.

5.3 Experimental Results

Instance Data. We tested about 100 randomly generated instances of the machine size $A^{8\times 20}$ (twenty mounting devices and eight component types in a setup). These are the dimensions of real world instances. All instances use the same visibility (which yields the workload) but different numbers of components per type and there are 80 different component types.

The Approaches. The two competing approaches are the standard approach (a standard model of the problem) and the weak symmetry approach (altering the standard approach by introducing SymVars). In both approaches values of the columns (i.e. the assigned component types to the mounting device represented by this column) are ordered increasingly to disallow its elements to move along the rows. In the weak symmetry approach in addition the column permutation symmetry (which is the weak symmetry of the problem) is broken by ordering the columns lexicographically increasing [10]. Both symmetries are broken by stating a set of constraints.

Search Heuristics. We tried several heuristics for both approaches but we will only consider a best-to-best comparison here to achieve reasonable results. The search heuristic for the standard approach is a greedy approach. For each column the component types achieving the highest workload are chosen. The component types are chosen by increasing type number to avoid conflicts with the symmetry breaking constraints.

The search heuristic for the weak symmetry approach is to find a feasible matrix assignment for the machine matrix (P_1). Then a permutation of the setups (columns) is determined greedily. This is done by determining for each setup the permutation where it achieves the best value for the objective function.

Results. We used ILOG OPL to model the problem and solve it using ILOG OPL Studio 3.5. We chose a time limit of ten minutes for the search process. This is the time that can be spent in a real world scenario for finding a solution. Note that this is just a fraction of the time it takes to solve the problem exhaustively.

In the table 1 the first column describes the number of the instance followed by the technique used. The third and fourth column give the value and the time in seconds for the first solution that is found. The fifth and sixth column give the same information for the best found solution. We compared in in the seventh column after which time in seconds the weak symmetry approach outperforms the standard approach in terms of the quality of the solution. In the eighth column the total quality increase by using the weak symmetry approach is given. In the last column the saving in runtime using the weak symmetry approach for the best solution is given.

We compare how long it takes the two approaches to find the first solution and what is the best solution they found within the time limit. Also we state the time when the weak symmetry approach outperforms the standard approach. Also we state the percentage increase for the quality of the best solution using the weak symmetry approach compared to the standard approach and the percentage decrease in runtime for the best solution using the weak symmetry approach compared to the standard approach.

All instances yield comparable results so we present here only a subset of the results due to space limitations. Nonetheless, this subset reflects the results of the instance set.

5.4 Conclusions of the Results

Quality of the Solutions. The first solution found by the standard approach is always better than that of the weak symmetry approach. This is due to the fact that the standard approach assigns the matrix greedily to the matrix. In the weak symmetry approach the matrix is assigned without respect of the workload this assignment achieves. Only the permutation is determined greedily. The matrix assignment cannot be done greedily in the weak symmetry approach, since such an assignment inflicts with the weak symmetry breaking constraints.

The best solution is always found by the weak symmetry approach. The relative improvement ranges between 1 and 3 %.

Runtime. The first solution is mostly found earlier by the standard approach. However, the weak symmetry approach has more variables and constraints such that the time in

Table 1. The results for twenty instances of the test case

Instance	Strategy	First Sol	Solv Time	Best Sol	Solv Time	Weak outperforms	Quality Increase %	Runtime Decrease %
1	Standard	836	0.7	855	557	–	–	–
	Weak	777	1.5	876	58	27.4 s	2.5	89.6
2	Standard	842	0.6	858	574	–	–	–
	Weak	785	1.5	880	115	12.0 s	2.6	80.0
3	Standard	837	1.0	860	385	–	–	–
	Weak	821	1,4	878	129	3.4 s	2.1	66.5
4	Standard	845	0.6	858	467	–	–	–
	Weak	760	1.4	871	308	33.0 s	1.5	34.0
5	Standard	843	0.7	857	133	–	–	–
	Weak	818	1.4	881	71	24.0 s	2.8	46.6
6	Standard	835	0.8	857	154	–	–	–
	Weak	796	1.4	883	51	11.4 s	3.0	66.9
7	Standard	839	0.7	854	214	–	–	–
	Weak	794	1.4	881	48	11.4 s	3.2	77.6
8	Standard	837	0.7	850	230	–	–	–
	Weak	785	1.4	879	45	8.2 s	3.4	80.4
9	Standard	839	0.7	853	263	–	–	–
	Weak	788	1.5	875	52	8.3 s	2.6	80.2
10	Standard	840	0.7	856	551	–	–	–
	Weak	772	1.4	882	55	11.6 s	3.0	90
11	Standard	842	0.7	863	404	–	–	–
	Weak	770	1.4	878	177	30.5 s	1.7	56.2
12	Standard	839	27.0	861	551	–	–	–
	Weak	769	1.5	873	197	1.5 s	1.4	64.2
13	Standard	841	14.6	857	217	–	–	–
	Weak	764	1.4	872	60	1.4 s	1.8	72.4
14	Standard	839	0.6	855	484	–	–	–
	Weak	757	1.5	865	57	41.4 s	1.2	88.2
15	Standard	837	0.7	857	430	–	–	–
	Weak	750	1.4	867	57	13 s	1.2	86.7
16	Standard	837	14,7	855	412	–	–	–
	Weak	768	1.5	866	61	41.7 s	1.3	85.2
17	Standard	835	26.7	857	347	–	–	–
	Weak	773	1.4	869	195	1.5 s	1.4	43.8
18	Standard	835	0.7	851	518	–	–	–
	Weak	761	1.5	859	66	49.1 s	0.9	87.3
19	Standard	835	0.7	851	145	–	–	–
	Weak	790	1.5	869	59	7.5 s	2.1	59.3
20	Standard	832	0.7	853	537	–	–	–
	Weak	770	1.5	872	63	9.3 s	2.2	88.3

each decision node in the search tree takes more time. In some of the instances the standard approach found the first solution very late. These instances were harder to solve. However, the weak symmetry approach had no problem with these instances.

The time to find a first solution was in all instances about 1.5 seconds. Therefore this approach seems very robust.

The weak symmetry approach achieves very good performance for finding the best solutions. The saving in runtime reaches from 30 to 90 % and on average over 70 %. Therefore this approach finds a local optimum in a relatively short time. And the quality of this local optimum is always better than that of the standard approach.

Also the weak symmetry approach outperforms the standard approach very fast. Within the first minute all the solutions found by the weak symmetry approach achieve a better objective value. In many cases this is achieved within ten seconds and for the instances where the standard approach finds the first solution very late the weak symmetry approach dominates from the beginning.

5.5 Concluding the Results

The weak symmetry approach outperforms the standard approach clearly in this scenario in terms of the quality of the best solution and more impressively in terms of runtime and domination.

Although the first solution is found later and is worse than the solution of the standard approach, the weak symmetry approach dominates very fast and until the end of the run.

6 Conclusions and Outlook

We introduced the theory and definitions of weak symmetries and presented a remodelling technique that enables us to break weak symmetries without losing solutions. Also we showed a real world application from the field of automated manufacturing that comprises weak symmetries. We presented results on a relaxed version of this problem. These results yield that using our technique to handle weak symmetries is promising.

There are several research directions on weak symmetries. It would be interesting to investigate weak symmetries on soft constraint problems or other problems. Also automatic detection of weak symmetries seems to be a very interesting task.

Also investigate the search with different filtering algorithms would be interesting. Also achieving back propagation from P_2 to P_1 is desirable and not investigated yet.

A computational study on combining weak symmetry breaking with dynamic symmetry breaking techniques like SBDx [8, 9] or symmetry breaking constraints [10] is interesting, since in this approach the symmetry breaking was done statically by stating constraints up-front.

Acknowledgments

The author would like to thank the following people for discussing my ideas and giving valuable hints and suggestions to this paper: Michela Milano, Zeynep Kiziltan, Meinolf Sellmann, Rico Gaudlitz, Stephan Kolassa and Marco Gaertler.

References

1. Peter Gregory *Almost–Symmetry in Planning* SymNet Workshop on Almost-Symmetry in Search, New Lanark, 2005
2. Alastair Donaldson *Partial Symmetry in Model Checking* SymNet Workshop on Almost-Symmetry in Search, New Lanark, 2005
3. Roland Martin *Approaches to Symmetry Breaking for Weak Symmetries* SymNet Workshop on Almost-Symmetry in Search, New Lanark, 2005
4. Warwick Harvey *Symmetric Relaxation Techniques for Constraint Programming* SymNet Workshop on Almost-Symmetry in Search, New Lanark, 2005
5. Warwick Harvey *The Fully Social Golfer Problem* SymCon'03: Third International Workshop in Constraint Satisfaction Problems, Kinsale, Ireland, 2003
6. Barbara M Smith *Reducing Symmetry in a Combinatorial Design Problem* School of Computing Research Report 2001.01, University of Leeds, January 2001. Presented at the CP-AI-OR Workshop, April 2001.
7. J.F. Puget *On the satisfiability of symmetrical constrained satisfaction problems* Proceedings of the 7th International Symposium on Methodologies for Intelligent Systems (ISMIS-93), Springer, 1993
8. I. Gent, B. Smith *Symmetry Breaking in Constraint Programming* In Horn, W., ed.: Proceedings of the 14th European Conference on Artificial Intelligence, pp. 599-603, 2000
9. T. Fahle, S. Schamberger, M. Sellmann *Symmetry Breaking* Proceedings of the 7th International Conference on Principles and Practice of Constraint Programming (CP-01),Springer,2001
10. Zeynep Kiziltan *Symmetry Breaking Ordering Constraints* Dissertation Thesis, Uppsala University, 2004
11. R. Backofen and S. Will *Excluding Symmetries in Constraint-Based Search* In: Principles and Practice of Constraint Programming, pp. 73-87,1999
12. J.-F. Puget *Symmetry Breaking Using Stabilizers* In Rossi, F., ed.: Proceedings of 9th International Conference on Principles and Practice of Constraint Programming (CP2003), Springer, 2003
13. D. Cohen, P. Jeavons, C. Jefferson, K.E. Petrie, B.M. Smith *Symmetry Definitions for Constraint Satisfaction Problems* In van Beek, P., ed.: Proceedings of 11th International Conference on Principles and Practice of Constraint Programming (CP2005), Springer, 2005
14. The GAP Group *GAP - Groups, Algorithms, and Programming, Version 4.3, 2002* http://www.gap-system.org
15. Rico Gaudlitz *Optimization Algorithms for Complex Mounting Machines in PC Board Manufacturing* Diploma Thesis, Darmstadt University of Technology, 2004

On Generators of Random Quasigroup Problems

Roman Barták*

Charles University, Faculty of Mathematics and Physics,
Malostranské nám. 2/25, Prague, Czech Republic
roman.bartak@mff.cuni.cz

Abstract. Problems that can be sampled randomly are a good source of test suites for comparing quality of constraint satisfaction techniques. Quasigroup problems are representatives of structured random problems that are closer to real-life problems and hence more suitable for benchmarking. In this paper, we describe in detail generators for Quasigroup Completion Problem (QCP) and Quasigroups with Holes (QWH). In particular, we study an improvement of the generator for QCP that produces a larger number of satisfiable problems by using propagation through the all-different constraint. We also re-formulate the algorithm for generating QWH that is much faster than the original generator. Finally, we provide an experimental comparison of all presented generators.

1 Introduction

Generators of random samples for problems are a useful source of problem instances for testing constraint satisfaction algorithms. Writing generators for some types of problems, like a Random CSP [11], is not a complicated task but it could be more complicated for other types of problems, typically for structured problems like quasigroup problems. This paper gives all necessary information for researchers that would like to use quasigroup problems as benchmarks.

The quasigroup problems have been first proposed as a benchmark domain for constraint satisfaction algorithms in [6]. The basic idea is to find a completion of a partial Latin square representing the multiplication table of a quasigroup. Hence, the problem is called a *Quasigroup Completion Problem* (QCP). The generator for a QCP should produce a partial Latin square that can be completed to a full Latin square. However, the generator proposed in [6], which fills random values in randomly selected cells of the table, falls short on this task especially when more values should be filled in. Gomez and Selman [6] observed a behavior of the generator similar to phase transition with satisfiable instances on one side, unsatisfiable instances on the other side, and hard instances in between. Shaw et al. [14] proposed an improvement of this generator based on propagation through the all-different constraint [13]. Their algorithm generates a larger number of satisfiable instances that can be used for testing solvers. It preserves the phase transition behavior but it generates satisfiable instances on both sides and it makes the phase transition crispier.

* Supported by projects 1M0021620808 and MSM0021620838 of the MŠMT.

B. Hnich et al. (Eds.): CSCLP 2005, LNAI 3978, pp. 164 – 178, 2006.

The difficulty of QCP generators is that they do not guarantee production of satisfiable instances only. This complicates usage of such generators for testing incomplete solving algorithms because when the solving algorithm did not find a solution, it is not clear whether no solution exists or the algorithm is not able to find it. Therefore another benchmark domain based on quasigroups has been proposed in [1] that guarantees generation of satisfiable instances. This benchmark domain uses the same idea as a QCP, that is completing a partially filled Latin square, but it differs in how the incomplete Latin square is obtained. The idea is to punch holes into a randomly generated complete Latin square so the obtained partial Latin square can surely be completed. Hence, this benchmark domain is called *Quasigroups With Holes* (QWH). Unfortunately, the authors of QWH did not provide all the details on generating QWH problems. It is a pity because generating randomly distributed QWH problems is a non-trivial task based on strong theoretical results presented in [9].

The contribution of this paper is threefold. First, we will give all the details on algorithms for generating random instances of QCP and QWH problems so interested readers will be able to write their own generators based on the presented algorithms. Second, we will propose a reformulated algorithm for generating QWH problems that is significantly faster then the original algorithm from [9]. Last but not least, we will present an empirical comparison of all presented generators so readers can select one that best suits their needs.

The paper is structured as follows. In the next section, we will introduce the terminology on quasigroups and Latin squares. In Section 3, we will describe the Quasigroup Completion Problem and its relevance to real-world problems and we will discuss two generators of QCP. In Section 4, the ideas behind Quasigroups With Holes will be explained, the original QWH generator will be presented in detail, and the reformulated generator will be introduced. The paper is concluded by an experimental evaluation of the quality and time efficiency of the generators.

2 Quasigroups and Latin Squares

A *quasigroup* is an ordered pair (Q, •), where Q is a set and • is a binary operation on Q such that the equations $a \bullet x = b$ and $y \bullet a = b$ are uniquely solvable for every pair of elements a, b in Q. The cardinality of the set Q is called an *order* of the quasigroup. Let N be the order of the quasigroup Q then the multiplication table of Q is a table of size N×N such that the cell at the coordinates (x,y) contains the result of the operation $x \bullet y$ (for simplicity we expect Q to be a totally ordered discrete set and so the rows and columns of the multiplication table can be indexed by the elements of Q). The multiplication table of the quasigroup must satisfy a property that in each row of the table, each element of the set Q occurs exactly once, and similarly in each column of the table, each element of Q occurs exactly once (see Figure 1A). Thus, the multiplication table defines a *Latin square*.

We say that a Latin square of order N is *partial* or *incomplete* if the table of size N×N is partially filled in such a way that no symbol occurs twice in a row or in a column (see Figure 1B). If the table is filled completely then we are speaking about a *complete Latin square*. Note that it is easy to generate a complete Latin square of any order. We take some permutation of the elements in Q. We put it in the first row of the table, and, in each subsequent row, we shift the permutation one element to the right and the superfluous element on the right is filled in the first cell of the row (see Figure 1C). However, this method does not produce every Latin square. In fact, generating any Latin square of a given order with a uniform probability is a non-trivial task [9].

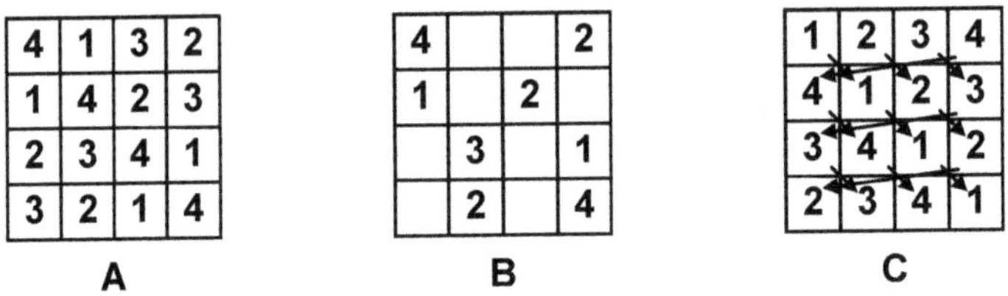

Fig. 1. A Latin square (A), a partial Latin square (B), and a simple process of generating a complete Latin square (C)

The problem of finding a complete Latin square can be stated as a constraint satisfaction problem in the following way. Assume, that the cells of a Latin square of order N are denoted by the variables with the domain {1,…,N}. Then the property of the Latin square can be described by a set of binary inequality constraints posted between every pair of variables that are either in the same row or in the same column. The constraint network for this CSP has N^2 nodes representing the variables and $N^2(N-1)$ edges representing the binary constraints. The network is highly structured – there are 2N interconnected clusters of size N (each cluster connects the variables from a single row or a single column). Moreover, there exists a path of maximal length two between any two nodes so the constraint network has a so-called *small world topology*. Nowadays the binary inequality constraints in each row and column can be encapsulated into an all-different constraint which achieves stronger pruning and makes the problem easier to solve (but still cannot solve the problem of any order [5,8]).

3 Quasigroup Completion Problem

As we showed in the previous section, a Latin square can be modeled as a CSP so it can serve as a benchmark domain for constraint satisfaction algorithms. We also sketched a simple algorithm to find a complete Latin square so such a benchmark is not very challenging. Assume now, that some cells in the Latin square are pre-filled, we have a partial Latin square, and the task is to determine whether the empty cells can be filled in such a way that we obtain a complete Latin square. Gomez and Selman [6] proposed this new benchmark based on completing partial Latin squares and they called it a *Quasigroup Completion Problem* (QCP). The problem is parameterized by the order of a Latin square and by the number of filled cells. Formally, the Quasigroup Completion Problem is described by a pair $\langle N, p \rangle$, where N is an order of the Latin square to be completed and p is a *filling ratio*, that is the ratio between the number of pre-filled cells and the total number of cells (N^2).

Pre-assigning some values to variables modeling the Latin square introduces perturbations in the structure of the constraint network which makes the structure similar to that found in real-world domains like scheduling and experimental design [8]. A particular real-life problem that maps directly to the above mentioned problem of completing a partially filled Latin square is the problem of assigning wavelengths to routes in fiber-optic networks [10]. Note also that the Quasigroup Completion Problem is known to be an NP-complete problem [4]. Not surprisingly, the straightforward constraint model with the all-different constraints cannot be used alone to solve instances of higher order (34 and more) [8] and more sophisticated techniques like hybrid algorithms [8] or dual models with special value selection heuristics [5] are necessary. This makes the problem non-trivial and hence interesting as a benchmark for comparing constraint satisfaction techniques. This benchmark bridges the gap between purely random problems like a Random CSP and highly structured problems.

The question now is how to generate random instances of QCP, in particular how to select the cells to be pre-filled for a given QCP $\langle N,p \rangle$. One possible model could be selecting the cell to be filled with the probability p. Let us call it a *model A* similarly to the classification used for Random CSPs [11]. Another possibility is to select exactly $\lfloor pN^2 \rfloor$ cells to be filled, where $\lfloor X \rfloor$ means the closest (to X) integer between X and 0. Let us call it a *model B*. In this paper we will study the model B, where the cells to be filled are selected randomly and uniformly. We use a random generator that selects uniformly and randomly $\lfloor pN^2 \rfloor$ different elements from the set $\{0,\ldots,N^2-1\}$. Each such element z represents a position in the Latin square of order N that can be described by the coordinates $\langle 1+\lfloor z/N \rfloor, 1+(z \bmod N)\rangle$ (Figure 2).

0	1	2	3
4	5	6	7
8	9	10	11
12	13	14	15

Fig. 2. A linear encoding of the positions of cells in a Latin square of order 4

The second open question is how to select a value to be assigned to a given cell. The basic requirement is that the values in cells in each row and in each column must be different. So, when selecting a value for the cell in the position $\langle x,y \rangle$, this value must be different from the values already assigned to the cells of the row x and to the cells of the column y. We propose the following simple technique based on constraint propagation through binary inequalities. Latin square is modeled as a CSP as described in the previous section using binary inequalities between the variables of the same row and of the same column. For a cell to be assigned (the cell selection process is described in the previous paragraph), we select randomly a value from the current domain of respective variable. Then the problem is made arc consistent which means that the value is removed from the variables of the same row and of the same column. Consequently, when selecting a value for the next cell, the domain contains only the values that are different from already assigned values in the same row and in the same column. This technique mimics the behavior of the original generator from [6]. It ensures that only valid Latin squares are generated, that is no symbol occurs twice in a row or in a column. However, because of incompleteness of constraint propagation we cannot guarantee that a "completable" Latin square is found. Figure 3 shows a situation where a bad initial value selection makes filling of another cell impossible. Note that any generator attempting to generate values one by one suffers from this problem.

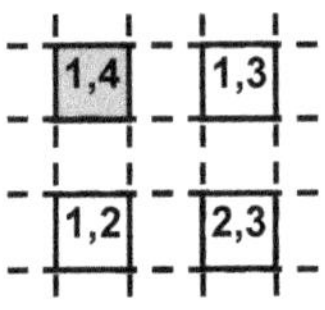

Fig. 3. The problem of simple QCP generators. If value 1 is selected for the top left cell then no complete Latin square exists.

When looking at Figure 3 we can see that if value 4 is selected for the top left cell then the above problem does not occur. Therefore, it might be useful to enhance the generator by allowing a *shallow backtracking* that can try another (randomly selected) value after an immediate failure. This process is repeated until a value is found or all values were tried. It is still possible that no value for the variable is found so this technique does not guarantee finding a valid Latin square but the hope is that it increases chances to find one. Unfortunately, our preliminary experiments showed that this technique does not increase the number of generated valid instances (on average). Note that the generator should produce the random problems fast so its complexity should not be exponential. Therefore, we cannot use full backtracking (probably incomplete search might be used but we did not try it yet).

Another option how to improve chances of finding a value for the variable is strengthening constraint propagation to remove more inconsistent values from the domains. As we already mentioned, there is a natural way how to strengthen propagation in the constraint model for Latin squares – using the all-different constraint by Régin. This approach has already been proposed in [14] – we will present a detail experimental comparison of both generators later in the paper. It will show that the generator based on all-different constraints produces a higher number of satisfiable instances.

4 Quasigroups with Holes

As we already mentioned, the main problem of a QCP is that the generators cannot guarantee production of satisfiable benchmark instances which could cause problems when evaluating incomplete solving techniques. In the previous section we described a method that increases the number of satisfiable instances via strengthening constraint propagation, but this method still does not guarantee satisfiability (see the next section for experimental justification of these claims). It would be possible to accompany the proposed generator by an algorithm that filters the unsatisfiable instances. Still, the problem is that for some parameters the generator does not produce a valid instance and hence no satisfiable instance is available for evaluation. This happens typically in the area where the hardest problems settle (see the section on experiments) so it would be beneficial if the generator produces satisfiable instances directly. Surprisingly, it is often difficult to develop a direct generator of satisfiable instances. The problem with such generators is that they should not be biased in the sense that the generator should produce any satisfiable instance with a uniform distribution. Therefore, the simple generator of complete Latin squares described in Section 2 is not appropriate because it produces Latin squares with a specific structure only (and hence, completing such Latin squares is not a difficult task).

The paper [1] proposes a direct generator for satisfiable quasigroup problems. The idea is to generate a complete Latin square to which a fraction of holes is punched. The resulting incomplete Latin square is then guaranteed to be satisfiable. This problem is called *Quasigroups With Holes* (QWH). However, the problem of generating uniformly distributed Latin squares is non-trivial. Actually, the generator is not described in [1] and the reader is referred to the paper [9] which describes the method and gives a theoretical justification. In the next paragraphs, we will survey the method from [9], we will present the QWH generator based directly on this method, and then we will reformulate the generator to work directly with the Latin squares.

4.1 Original Generator

Jacobson and Matthews [9] proposed a method for generating uniformly distributed random Latin squares by randomly traversing a graph, where nodes correspond to Latin squares and edges describe transformations between the Latin squares. They proved that the diameter of the graph is $4(N-1)^2$, where N is the order of the Latin square. It means that the minimal distance between two Latin squares is no greater than $4(N-1)^2$ so it is possible to obtain any Latin square from a given Latin square in $4(N-1)^2$ moves. The QWH generator can be conceived as follows. We start with a Latin square generated by the method described in Figure 1C. After performing $4(N-1)^2$ random moves we obtain any Latin square with uniform probability [9]. The open question is how to perform a move, that is, how to transform one Latin square into another Latin square. We will answer this question in the following paragraphs.

To simplify description of moves, Jacobson and Matthews proposed to extend the graph by nodes describing so-called improper Latin squares where the condition of a Latin square is violated a "little" (see below). Then the diameter of the new graph and hence the minimal distance between any two (proper or improper) nodes is bounded by $2(N-1)^3$ (for a formal proof see [9]). They represent the Latin square of order N by a contingency table f of size N×N×N that contains {0,1} values only. The condition on a Latin square (in each row and in each column, each element appears exactly once) is then equivalent to the formulas:

$$\forall x, y \in \{1,\ldots,N\} \sum_{z \in \{1,\ldots,N\}} f(x,y,z) = 1 \qquad (a)$$

$$\forall x, z \in \{1,\ldots,N\} \sum_{y \in \{1,\ldots,N\}} f(x,y,z) = 1 \qquad (b)$$

$$\forall y, z \in \{1,\ldots,N\} \sum_{x \in \{1,\ldots,N\}} f(x,y,z) = 1 \qquad (c)$$

Basically, x and y describe the coordinates of the cell and z describes the element in the cell (x,y) if $f(x,y,z)=1$. Formula (a) says that exactly one element is assigned to the cell (x,y), formula (b) says that the element z appears exactly once in the row x, and formula (c) says that the element z appears exactly once in the column y. We call a Latin square with the above (proper) contingency table a *proper Latin square*. An *improper Latin square* is defined by the (improper) contingency table satisfying the conditions (a)-(c) but allowing exactly one element of the contingency table to contain value -1.

Now, it is easier to formulate the moves as operations over (proper and improper) contingency tables. Assume that we start with a proper contingency table. We select randomly a cell of f such that $f(x,y,z) = 0$ and we will try to increase this value by one which is equivalent to assigning the value z to the cell (x,y). Each line in f containing the cell (x,y,z) must hold a cell filled by one according to (a)-(c). Let x', y', and z' be the indexes of these lines. These coordinates define a sub-cube in the contingency table with nodes at (x,y,z), (x,y,z'), (x,y',z), (x',y,z), (x',y,z'), (x',y',z), (x,y',z'), and (x',y',z') (see Figure 4). If we increase the value in $f(x,y,z)$ by one then we need to decrease the values in $f(x,y,z')$, $f(x,y',z)$, $f(x',y,z)$ by one to keep the conditions (a)-(c) valid. Next, the values in $f(x',y',z)$, $f(x,y',z')$, $f(x',y,z')$ must be increased by one and finally the value in $f(x',y',z')$ must be decreased by one. If all these operations are performed then visibly the conditions (a)-(c) hold again. However, it may happen that the value in $f(x',y',z')$ will become -1, in the case that $f(x',y',z')=0$, but this will be the only cell with a negative value (see Figure 4).

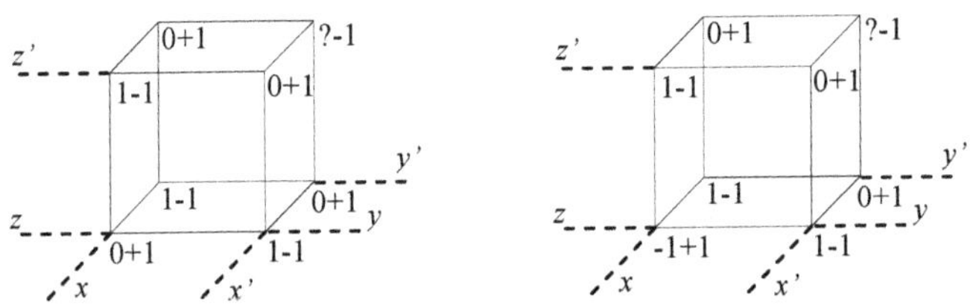

Fig. 4. A plus/minus one move in the proper (left) and improper (right) contingency table

Notice that if we start with a cell such that $f(x,y,z) = -1$ (the contingency table is improper) then we can perform the same set of operations as above and again we will obtain either a proper or improper contingency table (Figure 4 right). Hence the above described mechanism specifies moves between proper and improper contingency tables. Notice that the cell (x,y,z) is chosen randomly for a proper contingency table, while this cell is unique in the improper contingency table. Conversely, points x', y', and z' are unique in the proper table, while these points are chosen randomly in the improper table. This randomness is crucial to obtain random moves. Jacobson and Matthews showed that on average after N such random moves we will obtain a proper contingency table describing a Latin square of order N. Figure 5 shows the algorithm for a single move. By using information about the diameter of graph with nodes marked by Latin squares (see above) we propose to do at least $2(N-1)^3$ such moves and then stop when a proper contingency table is obtained.

```
move
   find x,y,z s.t.
     if f is improper then f(x,y,z)=-1
     if f is proper then f(x,y,z)=0
   find x',y',z' s.t. f(x',y,z)=f(x,y',z)=f(x,y,z')=1
   // if f is proper then these points are unique
   // if f is improper then there are two choices
   //   for each point, select one point randomly
   increase f(x,y,z),f(x,y',z'),f(x',y,z'),f(x',y',z)
   decrease f(x,y,z'),f(x,y',z),f(x',y,z),f(x',y',z')
end move
```

Fig. 5. The algorithm for move between contingency tables

4.2 Reformulated Generator

In the previous section we presented the algorithm for moves between proper and improper contingency tables. Notice that if the contingency table is improper, which happens when $f(x',y',z')$ becomes -1, then the next move starts with $f(x',y',z')$ that will be increased by one. Moreover, one of the cells $f(x',y',v)$ or $f(x',y',z)$ will be decreased by one, where v is the original value at position (x',y'). This is because the improper contingency table describes the situation when two values, z and the original value v in (x',y'), are assigned to the cell (x',y') at the same time (recall, that $f(x',y',z)$ has been increased by one in the step preceding this situation). To prevent appearance of two elements in a single cell we propose to postpone assignment of z to the cell (x',y') to the next move. Before assigning the value we check whether the value in (x',y') is z'. If this is true then we put z there so we get a proper Latin square and we can stop the sequence of improper moves. Otherwise, we also assign the value z to the cell (x',y'), but we take the original value in this cell and "propagate" it further. Figure 6 describes how the values are moved between the cells.

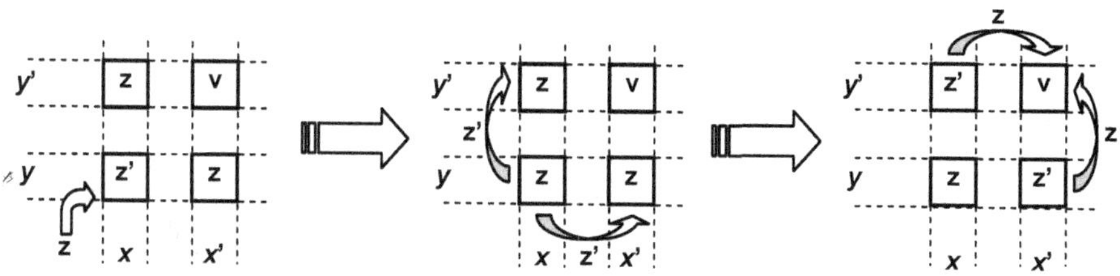

Fig. 6. Shifting values in a Latin square when the value z should be placed in position (x,y)

The above idea can be encoded using data structures describing directly a Latin square instead of its contingency table. Figure 7 shows the algorithm for moving between proper Latin squares directly. The move is started with a random position (x,y) and a random value z to be placed there: `proper_move(x,y,z,z)`. When the procedure stops, a proper Latin square is obtained and another random move can be started. Notice that if the Latin square is improper then there are two positions in the row x and two positions in the column y where the value v is located. In such a case, one position in the column and one position in the row are selected randomly. If the position is selected deterministically, for example the first found position, then the algorithm starts cycling! As in the original generator we propose to call the procedure `proper_move` at least $2(N-1)^3$ times (including the recursive calls inside `proper_move`) so every Latin square can be obtained with uniform probability.

```
proper_move(x,y,z,v)
  z' ← table(x,y)
  if z'=v then table(x,y) ← z, return
  y' ← a position (column) of cell with v in the row x
  x' ← a position (row) of cell with v in the column y
   // if z=v then x' and y' are unique
   //  otherwise there are two such positions,
   //   one position is selected randomly
  table(x,y) ← z
  table(x,y') ← z'
  table(x',y) ← z'
  proper_move(x',y',v,z')
end proper_move
```

Fig. 7. The algorithm for move between proper Latin squares

5 Experimental Results

We have implemented the presented generators using the clpfd library [3] of SICStus Prolog version 3.11.2. All presented results were accomplished under Windows XP Professional on 1.8 GHz Pentium 4 with 512 MB RAM. The running time was measured in milliseconds via the `statistics` predicate with the `walltime` parameter. The results of a hundred runs are presented. QCP-orig is the original QCP generator [6], QCP-alldiff is the generator using all-different constraints [14], QWH-orig is the QWH generator using contingency tables (Section 4.1), and QWH-new is the reformulated QWH generator (Section 4.2).

5.1 Generator Quality

Generators of random problems are expected to produce problems in the whole spectrum of their parameters. In our first experiment, we measured the number of generated partial Latin squares relative to the number of attempts to generate a problem. Recall, that the generator should produce a partial Latin square, namely no symbol occurs twice in a row or in a column, with a given filling. Figure 8 shows the result for Latin squares of order 30 and different filling ratios. Notice that the original QCP generator falls short on the task of generating problems where more pre-filled cells are requested. Actually, the generator is not able to produce any instance when the filling ratio is greater than 72%. This is not surprising because the more cells should be pre-filled the higher probability is that no value can be found for some cell (see Figure 3). A similar behavior can be observed for the QCP-alldiff generator but thanks to stronger propagation via all-different constraints the chances to select a consistent value increases and hence the generator is still able to produce some instances. It is a pity that the papers [6,14] proposing these generators did not mention this feature, probably because the authors used Latin squares of small orders (below 20) where this behavior cannot be observed. For the sake of completeness, let us highlight that the QWH generators always produce a problem instance.

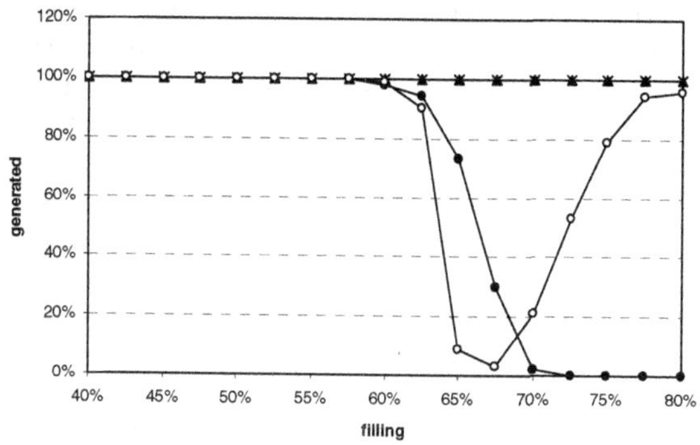

Fig. 8. The relative number of generated problems for the quasigroup problems of order 30 (●: QCP-orig, ○: QCP-alldiff, ▲: QWH-orig, ×: QWH-new)

The second feature that we focused on is the "hardness" of the generated problems. We used the presented generators to produce partial Latin squares of order 30 which is the border where the quasigroup problems are non-trivial but still solvable by standard constraint satisfaction techniques [8]. To solve the problem we used a standard MAC algorithm with the constraint model using all-different constraints, "smallest domain first" variable selection, and "minimal value first" value selection. We used a time limit of 2 minutes to solve each problem (there are some very hard instances that would prevent finishing experiments in a reasonable time if timeout is not used).

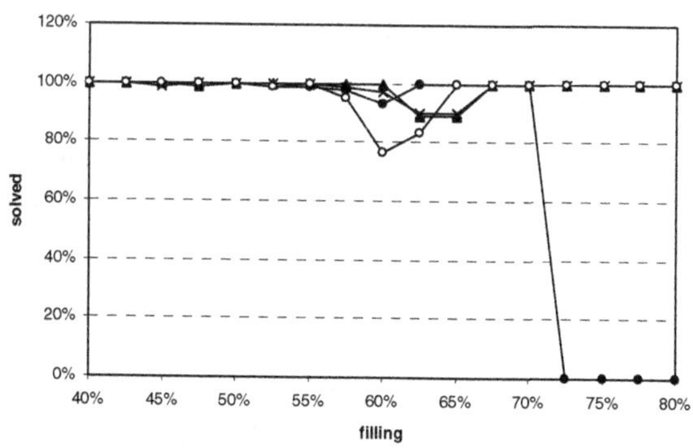

Fig. 9. The relative number of solved problems for the quasigroup problems of order 30 (●: QCP-orig, ○: QCP-alldiff, ▲: QWH-orig, ×: QWH-new)

Figure 9 shows a relative number of solved instances as a function of filling ratio. As we can see most of the generated problems are solvable within the 2 minutes timeout but there are some instances around 62% that were not solved. This is a first indication where the hard problems might settle but it does not show yet how hard the problems are. No problem is generated by QCP-orig for filling rations above 72% and hence no problem is solved there.

We compare hardness of the generated problems by measuring runtime of the above described straightforward solver when solving the problems generated by the studied generators. Figure 10 shows median runtime to solve the generated problems. By solving the problem we understand finding a completion of the partial Latin square or proving that no completion exists. This experiment brought some surprising results. First, the phase transition area is shifted for the QWH generators towards the area with a higher filling ratio (in comparison with the QCP generators). Second, the QCP-alldiff generator produces the hardest to solve instances. This could be caused by using the all-different constraints both inside the QCP-alldiff generator and inside the solver, but we have no evidence of this (probably trying another solving approach might show whether the generated instances are hard in general). Finally, notice that the QCP-orig generator produced quite easy problems. We have observed the above mentioned features for Latin squares of other orders too.

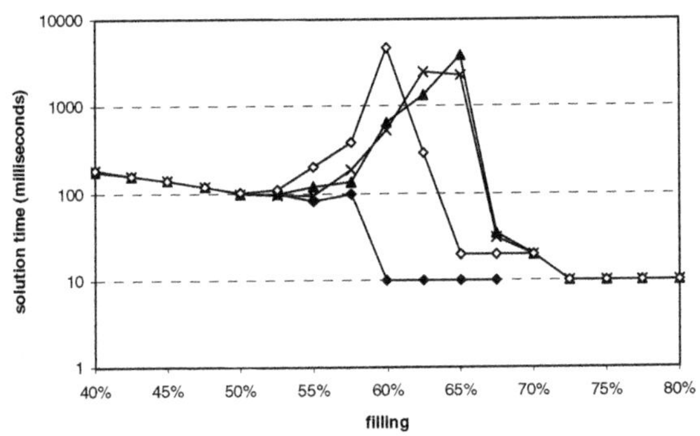

Fig. 10. Median solution time in milliseconds (logarithmic scale) for the quasigroup problems of order 30 (●: QCP-orig, ○: QCP-alldiff, ▲: QWH-orig, ×: QWH-new)

As we already mentioned, it should be clear whether the generator produces satisfiable instances or not. Production of satisfiable instances is especially important when the problems are used to compare incomplete algorithms like local search techniques or incomplete depth-first search techniques [2]. In the next experiment we measured the number of satisfiable instances among the solved problems. Figure 11 shows the relative number of satisfiable instances for Latin squares of order 30 and different filling ratios. QWH generators are guaranteed to produce satisfiable instances; the experiment just confirmed this feature. Hence these generators are appropriate for providing instances to compare incomplete algorithms. The behavior of QCP-orig generator with satisfiable instances on one side and unsatisfiable instances on the other side has already been presented at [6]. However, taking in account Figure 9, we can deduce that no satisfiable instance is generated for larger filling ratios simply because no instance is generated there. Hence the conclusions in [6] are a bit misleading because the readers might expect that QCP-orig produces unsatisfiable instances for larger filling ratios which is not true in general (especially for higher order of

Latin squares). The number of satisfiable instances produced by QCP-alldiff is also decreasing around the phase transition area but it increases again for large filling ratios. Our other experiments (not presented here) showed that the area with a smaller number of satisfiable instances enlarges with increasing order of the Latin square. Nevertheless, QCP-alldiff might still be appropriate for generating problems used to compare complete algorithms.

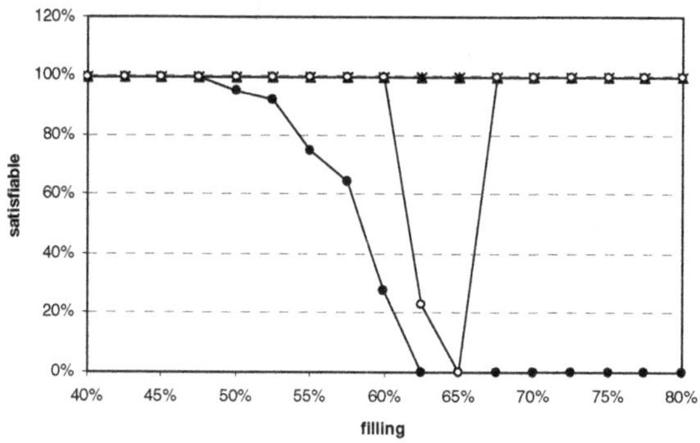

Fig. 11. The relative number of satisfiable instance for the quasigroup problems of order 30 (●: QCP-orig, ○: QCP-alldiff, ▲: QWH-orig, ×: QWH-new)

In our last experiment, we tried to estimate how complicated the generated problems are if the constraint model with all-different constraints is used. In particular, we measured the number of cells that have a value after the all-different constraints are posted and propagated but before search is started. Mean values among the consistent problems are presented in Figure 12. The dashed line indicates the initial filling produced by generators so the curves above this line indicate that additional values are deduced by the initial constraint propagation using the all-different constraints. Notice that for the filling ratio smaller than 60%, no values for additional cells were deduced while for the filling ratio greater than 70%, the values of all the variables were set using constraint propagation (so no search is necessary to solve the problem). We can see that the initial constraint propagation deduced more values for the problems produced by the QCP-all generator in comparison to the QWH generators. This is probably caused by using the all-different constraints during generation. Hence the QCP-alldiff produces instances with a larger number of pre-filled cells than requested. As proposed in [14] the intended filling can be achieved by measuring the total number of instantiated variables (including those instantiated through propagation) and stopping the generation process when this number is equal to the required filling. However, this technique makes the generator "less random" because some cells are filled by propagation rather than randomly. Moreover, this technique is not applicable to QWH generators that do not use propagation. If we use an assumption that stronger initial pruning means that the problems are easier for solving using the CP technology then the QWH generator produces harder problems in the phase transition area. This fits our observation from Figure 10, but recall that the phase transition area is shifted to smaller filling ratios for QCP-alldiff.

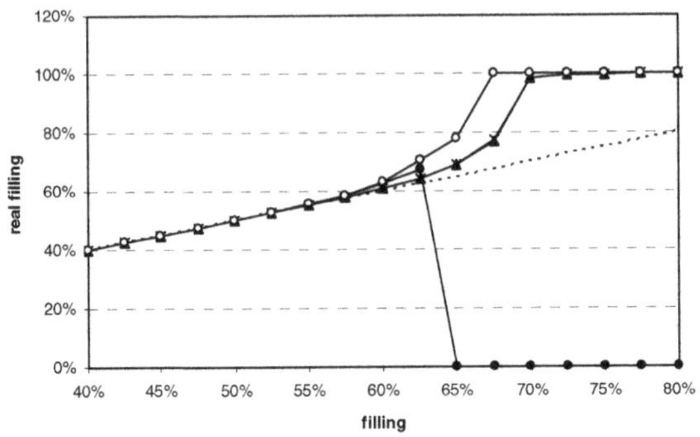

Fig. 12. The relative number of pre-filled cells using all-different constraints for the quasigroup problems of order 30 (●: QCP-orig, ○: QCP-alldiff, ▲: QWH-orig, ×: QWH-new)

5.2 Generator Efficiency

Sometimes the generators of benchmark problems run off-line so they produce problems that are put into benchmark libraries. Nevertheless, in case of random samples of problems, the generators are frequently used on-line to generate problems that are used immediately to test the solvers. In this second case, it is desirable for the generator to be fast (the users do not want to waste time by generating the problems).

We measured the runtime of studied generators to show how appropriate the generators are for on-line experiments. Figure 13 shows the runtime as a function of the filling ratio and Figure 14 shows the runtime as a function of the order of a Latin square. Visibly the better quality of the QCP-alldiff generator is paid-off by longer runtime. Moreover, the runtime of the QCP-alldiff generator increases faster than the runtime for the new QWH generator and from the order 50, it is actually slower. Consequently, the QCP-alldiff generator pays-off only for smaller order of the Latin square which also takes in account our discussion from the previous section. Recall that QCP-alldiff seems to produce the hardest to solve instances (Figure 10) so we believe that this generator is still appropriate for comparing complete solving techniques.

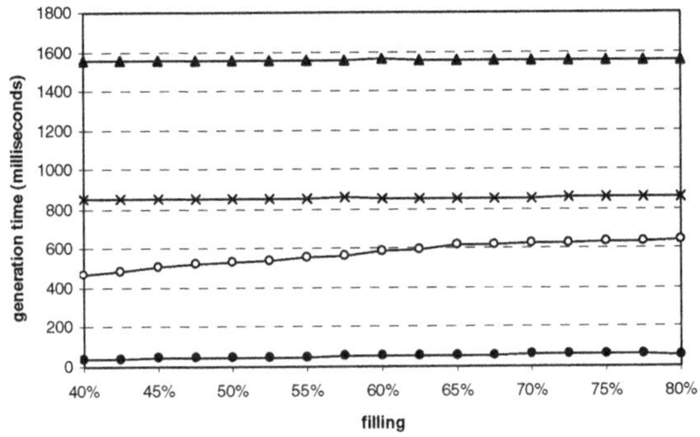

Fig. 13. The time (in milliseconds) to generate a quasigroup problem of order 30 and variable filling (●: QCP-orig, ○: QCP-alldiff, ▲: QWH-orig, ×: QWH-new)

Despite the fact that the original QCP generator is very fast, we do not recommend its usage simply because it produces less problem instances and the generated problem instances are order of magnitude easier to solve (Figure 10) in comparison to other presented generators. The runtime of QWH generators is slower than the original QCP generator, but recall that all instances produced by the QWH generators are satisfiable, which makes the QWH generators the only choice for testing incomplete solving techniques. Notice also that the reformulated QWH generator is about two times faster than the original QWH generator.

Figure 14 compares the runtimes of the generators on problems with a fixed filling ratio 0.6 and with changing order of a Latin square. We have selected the filing ratio 0.6 because it is within the phase transition region, however, we performed experiments with other filling ratios and the results were similar.

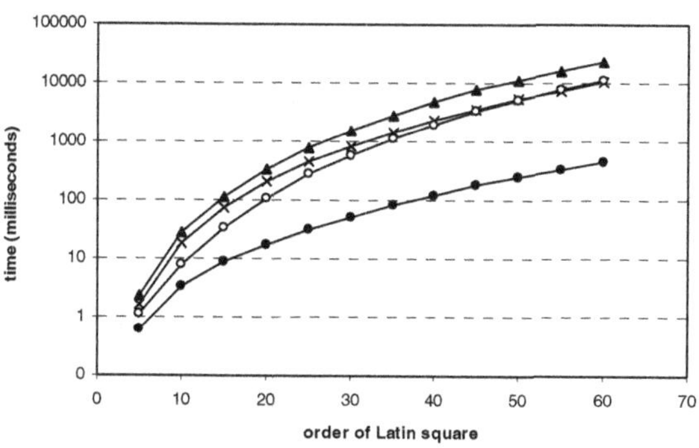

Fig. 14. The time (in milliseconds, a logarithmic scale) to generate a quasigroup problem with the filling ratio 0.6 (●: QCP-orig, ○: QCP-alldiff, ▲: QWH-orig, ×: QWH-new)

6 Conclusions

Completion of a partial Latin square is an interesting problem whose structure is close to real-life problems [7,10]. It is also a non-trivial problem [4] whose solving requires sophisticated techniques [5,8]. Finally, it is a problem whose instances can be generated randomly as a Quasigroup Completion Problem (QCP) [6] or Quasigroups With Holes (QWH) [1]. These features make the completion of partial Latin squares an ideal candidate for benchmarking constraint satisfaction techniques. In this paper, we studied the generators for both QCP and QWH and we provided detailed guidelines how to construct such generators. This alone is an important contribution because writing the generator for QWH is a non-trivial problem. Moreover, as far as we know this is the first paper in the CSP literature giving the exact description of the generator for QWH. We experimentally compared the existing generators and we proposed a reformulated version of the QWH generator that is much faster than the original generator. Even if the QWH generators are slower than the original QCP generator, their quality measured as a number of produced satisfiable instances is much higher. Hence, the QWH generators are appropriate to prepare problem instances for testing incomplete algorithms like in [2] while the QCP generators may still be useful for testing complete algorithms like in [12].

References

1. Achlioptas, D., Gomes, C., Kautz, H., Selman, B.: Generating Satisfiable Problem Instances. In Proceedings of the Seventeenth National Conference on Artificial Intelligence. AAAI Press (2000) 256–261
2. Barták, R., Rudová, H.: Limited Assignments: A New Cutoff Strategy for Incomplete Depth-First Search. In Proceedings of the 2005 ACM Symposium on Applied Computing. ACM (2005) 388–392
3. Carlsson, M., Ottosson, G., Carlson, B.: An Open-ended Finite Domain Constraint Solver. In Programming Languages: Implementations, Logics, and Programming. LNCS 1292. Springer-Verlag (1997)
4. Colbourn, C.: The Complexity of Completing Partial Latin Squares. Discrete Applied Mathematics 8 (1984) 25–30
5. Dotú, I., del Val, A., Cebrián, M.: Channeling Constraints and Value Ordering in the Quasigroup Completion Problem. In Proceedings of Eighteenth International Joint Conference on Artificial Inteligence. Morgan Kaufmann Publishers (2003) 1372–1373
6. Gomez, C., Selman, B.: Problem Structure in the Presence of Perturbations. In Proceedings of Fourteenth National Conference on Artificial Intelligence. AAAI Press (1997) 221–226
7. Gomez, C., Shmoys, D.: Completing Quasigroups or Latin Squares: A Structured Graph Coloring Problem. In Proceedings Computational Symposium on Graph Coloring and Generalizations (2002)
8. Gomez, C., Shmoys, D.: The Promise of LP to Boost CSP Techniques for Combinatorial Problems. In Proceedings CPAIOR'02 (2002) 291–305
9. Jacobson, M.T., Matthews, P.: Generating Uniformly Distributed Random Latin Squares. Journal of Combinatorial Designs 4 (1996) 405–437
10. Kumar, S.K., Russell, A., Sundaram, R.: Approximating Latin Square Extensions. Algorithmica 24 (1999) 128–138
11. MacIntyre, E., Prosser, P., Smith, B., Walsh, T.: Random Constraint Satisfaction: theory meets practice. In Principles and Practice of Constraint Programming - CP98. LNCS 1520. Springer-Verlag (1998) 325–339
12. Meseguer, P., Walsh, T.: Interleaved and Discrepancy Based Search. In Proceedings of 13th European Conference on Artificial Intelligence. Wiley (1998) 239–243
13. Régin, J.-Ch.: A filtering algorithm for constraints of difference in CSPs. In Proceedings of Twelfth National Conference on Artificial Intelligence. AAAI Press (1994) 362–367
14. Shaw, P., Stergiou, K., Walsh, T.: Arc Consistency and Quasigroup Completion. In Proceedings of the ECAI-98 workshop on non-binary constraints (1998)

Author Index

Lecture Notes in Artificial Intelligence (LNAI)

Vol. 3735: A. Hoffmann, H. Motoda, T. Scheffer (Eds.), Discovery Science. XVI, 400 pages. 2005.

Vol. 3734: S. Jain, H.U. Simon, E. Tomita (Eds.), Algorithmic Learning Theory. XII, 490 pages. 2005.

Vol. 3721: A.M. Jorge, L. Torgo, P.B. Brazdil, R. Camacho, J. Gama (Eds.), Knowledge Discovery in Databases: PKDD 2005. XXIII, 719 pages. 2005.

Vol. 3720: J. Gama, R. Camacho, P.B. Brazdil, A.M. Jorge, L. Torgo (Eds.), Machine Learning: ECML 2005. XXIII, 769 pages. 2005.

Vol. 3717: B. Gramlich (Ed.), Frontiers of Combining Systems. X, 321 pages. 2005.

Vol. 3702: B. Beckert (Ed.), Automated Reasoning with Analytic Tableaux and Related Methods. XIII, 343 pages. 2005.

Vol. 3698: U. Furbach (Ed.), KI 2005: Advances in Artificial Intelligence. XIII, 409 pages. 2005.

Vol. 3690: M. Pěchouček, P. Petta, L.Z. Varga (Eds.), Multi-Agent Systems and Applications IV. XVII, 667 pages. 2005.

Vol. 3684: R. Khosla, R.J. Howlett, L.C. Jain (Eds.), Knowledge-Based Intelligent Information and Engineering Systems, Part IV. LXXIX, 933 pages. 2005.

Vol. 3683: R. Khosla, R.J. Howlett, L.C. Jain (Eds.), Knowledge-Based Intelligent Information and Engineering Systems, Part III. LXXX, 1397 pages. 2005.

Vol. 3682: R. Khosla, R.J. Howlett, L.C. Jain (Eds.), Knowledge-Based Intelligent Information and Engineering Systems, Part II. LXXIX, 1371 pages. 2005.

Vol. 3681: R. Khosla, R.J. Howlett, L.C. Jain (Eds.), Knowledge-Based Intelligent Information and Engineering Systems, Part I. LXXX, 1319 pages. 2005.

Vol. 3673: S. Bandini, S. Manzoni (Eds.), AI*IA 2005: Advances in Artificial Intelligence. XIV, 614 pages. 2005.

Vol. 3662: C. Baral, G. Greco, N. Leone, G. Terracina (Eds.), Logic Programming and Nonmonotonic Reasoning. XIII, 454 pages. 2005.

Vol. 3661: T. Panayiotopoulos, J. Gratch, R. Aylett, D. Ballin, P. Olivier, T. Rist (Eds.), Intelligent Virtual Agents. XIII, 506 pages. 2005.

Vol. 3658: V. Matoušek, P. Mautner, T. Pavelka (Eds.), Text, Speech and Dialogue. XV, 460 pages. 2005.

Vol. 3651: R. Dale, K.-F. Wong, J. Su, O.Y. Kwong (Eds.), Natural Language Processing – IJCNLP 2005. XXI, 1031 pages. 2005.

Vol. 3642: D. Ślęzak, J. Yao, J.F. Peters, W. Ziarko, X. Hu (Eds.), Rough Sets, Fuzzy Sets, Data Mining, and Granular Computing, Part II. XXIII, 738 pages. 2005.

Vol. 3641: D. Ślęzak, G. Wang, M. Szczuka, I. Düntsch, Y. Yao (Eds.), Rough Sets, Fuzzy Sets, Data Mining, and Granular Computing, Part I. XXIV, 742 pages. 2005.

Vol. 3635: J.R. Winkler, M. Niranjan, N.D. Lawrence (Eds.), Deterministic and Statistical Methods in Machine Learning. VIII, 341 pages. 2005.

Vol. 3632: R. Nieuwenhuis (Ed.), Automated Deduction – CADE-20. XIII, 459 pages. 2005.

Vol. 3630: M.S. Capcarrère, A.A. Freitas, P.J. Bentley, C.G. Johnson, J. Timmis (Eds.), Advances in Artificial Life. XIX, 949 pages. 2005.

Vol. 3626: B. Ganter, G. Stumme, R. Wille (Eds.), Formal Concept Analysis. X, 349 pages. 2005.

Vol. 3625: S. Kramer, B. Pfahringer (Eds.), Inductive Logic Programming. XIII, 427 pages. 2005.

Vol. 3620: H. Muñoz-Ávila, F. Ricci (Eds.), Case-Based Reasoning Research and Development. XV, 654 pages. 2005.

Vol. 3614: L. Wang, Y. Jin (Eds.), Fuzzy Systems and Knowledge Discovery, Part II. XLI, 1314 pages. 2005.

Vol. 3613: L. Wang, Y. Jin (Eds.), Fuzzy Systems and Knowledge Discovery, Part I. XLI, 1334 pages. 2005.

Vol. 3607: J.-D. Zucker, L. Saitta (Eds.), Abstraction, Reformulation and Approximation. XII, 376 pages. 2005.

Vol. 3601: G. Moro, S. Bergamaschi, K. Aberer (Eds.), Agents and Peer-to-Peer Computing. XII, 245 pages. 2005.

Vol. 3600: F. Wiedijk (Ed.), The Seventeen Provers of the World. XVI, 159 pages. 2006.

Vol. 3596: F. Dau, M.-L. Mugnier, G. Stumme (Eds.), Conceptual Structures: Common Semantics for Sharing Knowledge. XI, 467 pages. 2005.

Vol. 3593: V. Mařík, R. W. Brennan, M. Pěchouček (Eds.), Holonic and Multi-Agent Systems for Manufacturing. XI, 269 pages. 2005.

Vol. 3587: P. Perner, A. Imiya (Eds.), Machine Learning and Data Mining in Pattern Recognition. XVII, 695 pages. 2005.

Vol. 3584: X. Li, S. Wang, Z.Y. Dong (Eds.), Advanced Data Mining and Applications. XIX, 835 pages. 2005.

Vol. 3581: S. Miksch, J. Hunter, E.T. Keravnou (Eds.), Artificial Intelligence in Medicine. XVII, 547 pages. 2005.

Vol. 3577: R. Falcone, S. Barber, J. Sabater-Mir, M.P. Singh (Eds.), Trusting Agents for Trusting Electronic Societies. VIII, 235 pages. 2005.

Vol. 3575: S. Wermter, G. Palm, M. Elshaw (Eds.), Biomimetic Neural Learning for Intelligent Robots. IX, 383 pages. 2005.

Vol. 3571: L. Godo (Ed.), Symbolic and Quantitative Approaches to Reasoning with Uncertainty. XVI, 1028 pages. 2005.

Vol. 3559: P. Auer, R. Meir (Eds.), Learning Theory. XI, 692 pages. 2005.

Vol. 3558: V. Torra, Y. Narukawa, S. Miyamoto (Eds.), Modeling Decisions for Artificial Intelligence. XII, 470 pages. 2005.

Vol. 3554: A.K. Dey, B. Kokinov, D.B. Leake, R. Turner (Eds.), Modeling and Using Context. XIV, 572 pages. 2005.

Vol. 3550: T. Eymann, F. Klügl, W. Lamersdorf, M. Klusch, M.N. Huhns (Eds.), Multiagent System Technologies. XI, 246 pages. 2005.

Vol. 3539: K. Morik, J.-F. Boulicaut, A. Siebes (Eds.), Local Pattern Detection. XI, 233 pages. 2005.

Vol. 3538: L. Ardissono, P. Brna, A. Mitrović (Eds.), User Modeling 2005. XVI, 533 pages. 2005.

Vol. 3533: M. Ali, F. Esposito (Eds.), Innovations in Applied Artificial Intelligence. XX, 858 pages. 2005.